Mormons and Mormonism

Mormons and Mormonism

An Introduction to an American World Religion

Edited by Eric A. Eliason

University of Illinois Press
Urbana and Chicago

Library of Congress Cataloging-in-Publication Data
Mormons and Mormonism : an introduction to an
American world religion / edited by Eric A. Eliason.
p.   cm.
Includes bibliographical references and index.
ISBN 0-252-02609-8 (alk. paper)
ISBN 0-252-06912-9 (pbk. : alk. paper)
1. Mormon Church. I. Eliason, Eric A. (Eric Alden), 1967–
BX8637.M67   2001
289.3—dc21   00-008707

1 2 3 4 5 C P 5 4 3 2 1

Contents

Acknowledgments

For the suggestions, encouragement, and inspiration they have provided, I wish to thank the following individuals: Jan Shipps, Tad Tuleja, Ron Esplin, Doris Dant, Richard Cracroft, Ron Walker, Howard Miller, Richard Ouellette, William A. Wilson, Gary Bergera, Dean May, Steven Olsen, Robert Abzug, William H. Goetzmann, the other contributors to this book, and my family, especially my wife, Stephanie Smith Eliason.

Special thanks are due Sharon Boyle, RoseAnn Ramos, Kaleo Valerga, Jennifer Griffith, and Marcy Thayne for their many hours spent scanning articles for this collection. As is perhaps appropriate for a book intended in part for undergraduates, many students assisted in the preparation of the manuscript. Linda Hunter Adams, director of the BYU Humanities Publications Center, volunteered the students in her 1999 editing class at Brigham Young University for the job: Rozalyn Bird, Erick Carlson, Peter Carr, Christina Cloward, Elizabeth Easton, Kristine Fielding, Katie Greener, Carolynne Hall, Krista Halverson, Ted Hartman, Hilary Hendricks, Kimberly Hicken, Coral Hicks, Jennifer Hodge, Loralee Ingles, Peter Jasinski, Rachael Lauritzen, Richard McClellan, Cynthia Munk, Ann Sheldon, Susan Sims, Daniel Smith, Jennifer Smith, Rebecca Vernon, Melinda Waite, Melody McGrath Warnick, Emily Wegener, and Megan Wilding. Without their help this project may have never been completed. David Allred helped coordinate final correspondence with contributors.

I also wish to thank my editor at the University of Illinois Press, Liz Dulany, whose faith, persistence, and good advice drove this project to its completion. This project's reviewers, Grant Wacker and Randall Balmer, helped shape it into its final form and provided valuable insights.

Appreciation is extended to the contributors and their publishers for permission to reprint the essays appearing here. Three essays have been revised by their authors. The other essays appear in their entirety and have been edited for style.

Terryl L. Givens, "'This Great Modern Abomination': Orthodoxy and Heresy in American Religion," is reprinted from *The Viper on the Hearth: Mormons, Myths, and the Construction of Heresy* (New York: Oxford University Press, 1997), 76–93. Copyright © 1997 by Terryl Givens. Used by permission of Oxford University Press, Inc.

Nathan O. Hatch, "The Populist Vision of Joseph Smith," is reprinted from *The Democratization of American Christianity* (New Haven, Conn.: Yale University Press, 1992), 113–22. Copyright © 1989 by Yale University.

Michael Hicks, "Noble Savages," is reprinted from *Mormonism and Music: A History* (Urbana: University of Illinois Press, 1989), 209–27.

Richard T. Hughes, "Soaring with the Gods: Early Mormons and the Eclipse of Religious Pluralism," is a revised version of his essay that appeared in *The Lively Experiment Continued*, ed. Jerald C. Brauer (Macon, Ga.: Mercer University Press, 1987), 135–59.

Colleen McDannell and Bernhard Lang, "Modern Heaven . . . a Theology," is reprinted from *Heaven: A History* (New Haven: Yale University Press, 1988), 313–22. Copyright © 1988 by Colleen McDannell and Bernhard Lang.

Dean L. May, "Mormons," is a slightly revised version of the essay printed in *Harvard Encyclopedia of American Ethnic Groups*, ed. Stephen Thernstrom (Cambridge, Mass.: Harvard University Press, 1980), 720–31. © 1980 by the President and Fellows of Harvard College. Reprinted by permission of Harvard University Press.

Richard D. Poll, "Utah and the Mormons: A Symbiotic Relationship," is reprinted from *New Views of Mormon History: A Collection of Essays in Honor of Leonard J. Arrington*, ed. Davis Bitton and Maureen Ursenbach Beecher (Salt Lake City: University of Utah Press, 1987), 323–41.

Jan Shipps, "'Is Mormonism Christian?' Reflections on a Complicated Question," first appeared in this form in *Sojourner in the Promised Land: Forty Years among the Mormons* (Urbana: University of Illinois Press, 2000). "Beyond the Stereotypes: Mormon and Non-Mormon Communities in Twentieth-Century Mormondom" is reprinted from *New Views of Mormon History: A Collection of Essays in Honor of Leonard J. Arrington*, ed. Davis Bitton and Maureen Ursenbach Beecher (Salt Lake City: University of Utah Press, 1987), 343–60.

Rodney Stark, "The Basis of Mormon Success: A Theoretical Application," is an updated version of his essay that appeared in *Latter-day Saint Social Life:*

Social Research on the LDS Church and Its Members, ed. James T. Duke (Provo: Brigham Young University Religious Studies Center, 1998), 29–70.

Grant Underwood, "Mormonism, Millenarianism, and Modernity," is a revised version of his essay that appeared in *The Millenarian World of Early Mormonism* (Urbana: University of Illinois Press, 1993), 139–42.

Mormons and Mormonism

Introduction

Eric A. Eliason

The crux of Mormonism's religious claims and most of the revolutionary implications of its theology are encapsulated in Latter-day Saints' literal acceptance of the narrative reality of one event. Any treatment of the Mormon experience from a historical or theological point of view rightly begins here. In the spring of 1820, a spiritually troubled boy in rural western New York read in James 1:5 (KJV): "If any of you lack wisdom, let him ask of God, that giveth to all men liberally, and upbraideth not; and it shall be given him." Following this admonition, the boy went into the woods to pray for religious guidance. To his astonishment, the result of his personal appeal was for him to be thrust into the center stage of world religious history. God the Father and Jesus Christ appeared to him in the flesh as two distinct physical persons. They appointed the boy as the prophet through whom religion by revelation would be restored to the earth for the first time since the death of Jesus' original apostles. Through him the world would be prepared for the Second Coming of Christ and the biblically promised "restoration of all things."[1]

This boy, Joseph Smith, had many subsequent extraordinary religious experiences. In 1830, he published the Book of Mormon as a companion book of Scripture to the Bible. By young Joseph's own account, he received this book in the form of golden plates from an angel named Moroni. During his life as a mortal man, Moroni had compiled the volume with his father, Mormon. Their book contained a sacred history of extinct Christian peoples in pre-Columbian America to which Mormon and Moroni belonged. The young prophet explained that he translated the inscriptions on the golden plates, not through any special scholarly training, but by the "gift and power of God." This book that bears the prophet Mormon's name was for many years much more well known than the First Vision and earned Joseph Smith's followers their nickname. During the translation process, the young prophet experienced further visitations by an angelic John the Baptist and the apostles Peter, James, and John, who gave Joseph Smith and his associates the priesthood authority they needed to implement the promised restoration and to establish the Church of Jesus Christ of Latter-day Saints.

These accounts have come to be remembered by Mormons as the foundational sacred episodes of their religious tradition. They also established the Mormon doctrinal ideas that most clearly set them apart from traditional Christianity—namely that humans, angels, and gods are of essentially the same species of physical beings but are in different stages of development. Whether one regards this explosion of other-worldly contact as concrete factual occurrences (as believing Latter-day Saints do), as delusions or fabrications (as some of Mormonism's detractors do), or as complex subjective psychological experiences (as some middle-of-the-road scholars do), it remains that these accounts and Joseph Smith's further revelations form the doctrinal and organizational nucleus of what many historians consider the most innovative and successful religion to emerge during the spiritual ferment of antebellum America. Driven by intolerant neighbors, Mormons rode on and sometimes pushed ahead of the cresting wave of American westward expansion. Finally staying put in what is now Utah—despite interference that endured until the turn of the twentieth century—Mormons emerged as the dominant religious culture of the Intermountain West. With explosive growth that has pushed its worldwide membership past eleven million, the Church of Jesus Christ of Latter-day Saints is increasingly regarded by scholars as the first American-born world religion.[2]

In this collection of essays scholars examine the emergence, growth, and cultural character of Mormonism from a variety of perspectives. The essays were chosen with the general interested reader in mind but also with the goal of assembling from disparate sources an anthology suitable for use as a supplementary textbook in courses on American religious history, religious studies, and the emerging interdisciplinary field of Mormon studies. This volume is not intended to be a comprehensive reader but rather an affordable sampler providing a few examples of the wide variety of topics within this field's scope.[3] In choosing essays for inclusion, I have made an effort to gather significant pieces that are difficult to obtain or are hidden in books that address a broader topic and thus might not attract the attention of someone interested specifically in Mormonism. Only three of these pieces have been revised for this publication, and thus most reflect the thinking and knowledge of the time they were written.

The eleven essays here address Mormonism in terms of the issues that define it as an emergent world religion. The writers focus on the dynamics of group identity formation and the nature of the "cultural footprint" Mormonism has made on the American West and continues to make worldwide. Another common denominator is the special attention each author pays to broader historical, geographic, social, cultural, literary, and theological contexts. Some of the scholars review the whole of Mormondom from a particular angle, such as ethnicity or American identity. Others take a more penetrating look at one significant aspect of the religion, such as the Book of Mormon, music, intercultural contact, or millenarianism.

This collection focuses on the last thirty years of Mormon studies scholarship—widely regarded as the most productive and professional period of Mormon historiography. This era merits some explanation so that the essays here can be placed in the context of the intellectual and institutional history to which they belong. Some observers have felt "the New Mormon History" is an appropriate moniker for the movement that created this era. However, few of the mostly LDS scholars who have professionalized Mormon history would call themselves "New Mormon Historians." Many feel that the label is an empty signifier referring more to the perceptions and simplifying needs of nonspecialists outside the field than to any movement, time period, or scholarly approach within Mormon studies. "The New Mormon History" is a problematic term at best, but it often comes up in discussions of late twentieth-century Mormon historiography.

With few exceptions, before the latter half of the twentieth century very little Mormon history was written for any purpose other than to defend or disprove the theological claims of Mormonism—and a vast chasm separated these two camps. Echoes from this chasm still reverberate today. However, with some antecedents in the 1940s and 1950s, a "third way" emerged in the late 1960s as the dominant mode for writing Mormon history.[4] This "New Mormon History" under the vigorous leadership of the prolific Leonard J. Arrington ushered in the professionalization of Mormon historical writing and the formation of the Mormon History Association.[5] Most of these practitioners were Latter-day Saints who saw themselves not so much as "neutral" on the issue of the divinity of Mormon origins as intent on setting the Mormon story within the broader sweep of American history and employing the rigorous research and documentation standards of academia. Their efforts won the respect of both secular academics and many presiding leaders in the LDS Church.[6] From 1972 to 1982, Arrington held the position of LDS Church Historian, which had traditionally been retained by a religious leader of high office rather than a professional scholar.[7]

While some Church authorities approved of this move, others grew concerned that members might assume that scholarship produced by History

Division personnel bore a suggestion of imprimatur. They did not want to be beholden to reviewing everything Arrington and his colleagues produced. Some saw the New Mormon History not as an effort toward accuracy, objectivity, and professionalism but as a desacralization of what must be regarded with reverence as sacred history by believing Latter-day Saints.

Some Latter-day Saints worried that the New Mormon Historians were too eager to focus on sensational topics with the potential to erode the faith of Latter-day Saints—such as Joseph Smith's apparent familiarity with nineteenth-century folk magic and the beginning and end of Church-sanctioned plural marriage.[8] Scholars responded that while such work did not represent their main interests, fuller understandings of the past would only bolster well-founded faith. They suggested that scholars could better address difficult issues than could those who might misrepresent or even aggressively exploit them.

Between 1980 and 1982, the professional historians at the Church Office Building in Salt Lake City were transferred to Brigham Young University. The time that some in the Mormon historical community have come to call "Camelot" was over.[9] Some interpreted this move as a retreat by the LDS Church from professional approaches to scholarship; others saw it as an opportunity for Mormon studies to flourish in the kind of environment only a university can provide. At BYU, some colleagues continued to question the work of those they called New Mormon Historians. Criticism came from those untrained in the methods of professional historical scholarship as well as from the philosophically sophisticated, who employed postmodernist theory to undercut what they regarded as the naturalistic assumptions and the naive fetishization of an impossible notion of objectivity that undergirded the New Mormon History.[10] Others wondered if the movement had become ossified and insular in failing to embrace interdisciplinary methods beyond the historical techniques that established Mormon studies.

Some important new scholarship, such as Terryl Givens's work excerpted in this volume, may have been influenced by the critics of New Mormon History. However, even the most constructive remarks continue to ring hollow for many scholars since critics have often seemed to rely on ad hominem arguments and by and large did not try (and were usually not trained) to produce the kind of scholarship for which they themselves yearned.[11] The shaping influence of these debates on contemporary Mormon scholarship is not yet clear, but a vigorous tradition of serious, sensitive, and professional Mormon studies scholarship has established itself. This tradition has attracted the attention of so many non-LDS scholars that over half the chapters in this volume were authored by "Gentiles."

The acknowledgment of the Mormon experience as a significant religious studies topic is recent. Although Mormon ideas and knowledge of Brigham Young's Rocky Mountain theocracy quickly became well known to educated people in Europe and America through the popular press in the first decades following their emergence, they were almost universally ridiculed as beneath serious scholarly discussion. Philip Schaff—the founder of American church history scholarship and its most prominent nineteenth-century practitioner—discounted Mormonism as having "not the slightest influence on the general character and religious life of the American people."[12] Robert Baird—another leading nineteenth-century church historian—called Mormons "ignorant dupes" and the Book of Mormon "the absurdest of all pretended revelation," predicting that Mormonism would soon collapse under the weight of its own preposterousness.[13]

While shadows of such thinking still lurk in some corners of academia today, by force of its longevity, impressive membership growth, and the proponents in all scholarly disciplines, the Mormon religion is making its way into serious discussions about American and worldwide religiosity. Indeed, Mormondom has emerged as one of religious scholarship's most pressing topics. (Ironically, academic interest in Mormons has grown while popular knowledge about Mormons has decreased in the United States. With the disappearance of both violent persecution and the controversial practice of plural marriage, Mormons have been deemed less newsworthy. While in the nineteenth century Brigham Young and his bodyguard Porter Rockwell were household names in the United States and much of Europe, few besides Mormons today are likely to know that Gordon B. Hinckley is the current president of the LDS Church and no one knows who his bodyguards are.)

A major exception to Baird's and Schaff's evaluations was that of Sir Richard Francis Burton, the British adventurer and pioneering ethnographer. In 1861, Burton pursued his long-unfulfilled desire to visit the new Mormon "holy land." He was intrigued by this emergent religious civilization built up in less than fifteen years after the Latter-day Saint flight from abuse in the East. On the first page of his travel account *City of the Saints,* Burton stated that his primary motivation for this journey was to add Salt Lake City—a "young rival" to Memphis, Benares, Jerusalem, Rome, and Mecca—to the list of exotic holy cities he had visited.[14] During his tour of Mormon country, Burton extended the same respectful deference to Mormon beliefs and society that he did to the major world religious cultures in which he had immersed himself in Africa, the Near East, and India. Burton's anachronistic cultural relativism, that is now almost commonplace, puzzled his ethnocentric Victorian readers when applied to the great religious cultures of the world, but the esteem he afforded to Mormons was simply baffling. Latter-day Saint religion was barely thirty years old at the time, and the prevailing opinion among the educated of Burton's day was that Mormonism was more a form of social dementia—an excuse for polygamous licentiousness—than a genuine religion.

Although balanced accounts of Utah society were written before Burton by sojourners passing through Mormon territory on other business, he was the first outside scholarly observer to take Mormonism seriously as a viable lifestyle and legitimate social presence worthy of serious inquiry.[15] He was also the first to personally interview plural wives about their family arrangements and to suggest that Mormons' healthy, rich, and complex culture qualified it as an emergent religious civilization on the world stage. While Burton's voice remained the exception for many years, more recent scholarship has become increasingly resonant with his critical but penetrating and empathetic approach. The fact that most of the essays in this collection were written by non-Mormons and published by presses outside of Utah underscores the increasingly broad influence of Mormon studies.

This shift in scholarly opinion resulted from several factors illustrated by the chapters in this collection. One was the professionalization of Mormon scholarship; another was the ethnographic turn in historical scholarship that Burton presaged. In recent decades, the accurate and in-depth portrayal of the complex ways in which cultures view themselves became at least as important, if not more important, to useful analytic explanation than the presuppositions, models, and theories of trained academic outsiders.[16] The implications of this thinking for religious history is that while scholars need not share the beliefs of those they write about, religious convictions should be portrayed as reasonable to the people who hold them as well as a legitimate and serious part of human experience that informs how people interact with each other and their environment.[17]

This principle has not been evenly applied to all groups, however. Ethnic and tribal cultures have benefited more from this approach than have religious communities. And among religions, mainstream, fashionable, and politically popular religions have perhaps benefited more than the unpopular. Popularity, of course, can be affected by distinctive practices, size, recent emergence, style, taste, association with immigrants, social or geographic isolation, and unusual beliefs.[18] In using Mormonism as their subject matter, the authors in this collection demonstrate that sensitivity to the insider perspective and the possibility that both inside and outside observers can contribute to serious scholarly understanding of religious movements are two principles that work for a wide range of religious groups.

Along these lines, the essays in this volume also address a peculiar aspect of the Latter-day Saint faith at this point in its history that makes it particularly well positioned to illustrate many social, cultural, and historical issues. Even while some scholars claim Mormonism has achieved world religion status, a few vociferous detractors still insist Mormonism is a dangerous cult. These claims represent two extremes in the sociological system of terms used to describe religions with regards to their size, sophistication, and respectability. In his germinal *Religious History of the American People* (1975), Sydney E. Ahlstrom points out the difficulty of sociologically classifying Mormonism: "One cannot even be sure if the object of our consideration is a sect, a mystery cult, a new religion, a church, a people, a nation, or an American subculture; indeed, at different times and places it is all of these."[19]

This condition is a testament not only to Mormonism's potential for all-encompassing social and religious power to those who believe it but also to its explosion of familiar sociological and theological patterns. For Mormons, this taxonomic shattering is evidence of the God-inspired uniqueness of its claims; for scholars, it provides an opportunity to look at the strengths and weaknesses of the terms and methods used to describe a variety of social phenomena. One challenge the contributors to this volume have faced is how to use the vocabularies of history, sociology, and theology to describe the ways in which the Mormon experience exposes the insufficiency of these very vocabularies. The contributors attempt to take apart and rebuild notions of how Latter-day Saint religion might be described in a way that compares Mormonism to other streams of human experience while at the same time acknowledges its uniqueness. Since so many key issues are present at once in Mormonism, the contributors help chart ways in which scholars studying other religions, peoples, or movements might profitably proceed.

While the contributors all illuminate these underlying core issues—and many show a firm command of interdisciplinary approaches—each author brings his or her own voice and specific training to the matter at hand. Dean L. May's essay is comprehensive, as is appropriate for a work that was originally an encyclopedia entry. Terryl L. Givens is a literary scholar who infuses his examination of anti-Mormon literature with an attention to the intricacy and power of words not always appreciated by historians. Rodney Stark's sociological model for the growth of new religious movements provides food for thought for historians and sociologists. It also has deeply informed his own examination of the dynamics of early Christian growth.[20] These many ways of looking at Mormonism offer useful commentary and underscore the multifaceted nature of the Latter-day Saint experience. However, they do not address the crucial issue of how to understand what Mormons conceive *themselves* to be.

The first chapter of this book directly tackles this question. It is a sensitive piece of ethnographic reconstruction that illuminates how the earliest Mormons themselves viewed their religion. Or, in more technical terms, it elucidates the foundational epistemological principles by which Mormonism would develop and the metaphysical and millennial landscape this epistemology revealed. It is perhaps not surprising that such a lively portrayal of the early Mormon mind comes from Richard T. Hughes, a modern scholar with roots in the Christian restorationist tradition. Restorationism's emergence preceded Mormonism by a few years and was in some ways similar—but in other aspects crucially dissimilar—to the early Latter-day Saint movement. Hughes's essay describing Mormonism in this historical context is a good place for the Mormon studies novice to start.

The second chapter suggests ethnicity as another useful way of thinking about the Mormon experience. Dean L. May provides an introductory sketch of Mormon history and culture, focusing on Joseph Smith's foundational religious experiences, the dynamics of identity formation, Mormon aesthetic principles, as well as worship and social practices in LDS communities. Since the article first appeared in 1980 twenty years of Church growth and changing attitudes toward "Gentiles" have made some of May's comments about Mormon social insularity and the predominantly western American character of worldwide Church leadership somewhat dated. Also, his assertion that Mormons exhibit many features of ethnicity has been challenged by those who stress that since many Latter-day Saints gain group identity through conversion as well as cultural inheritance, they cannot properly be considered ethnic.[21] Nevertheless, the "ethnic Mormon" concept is still a central issue of debate in Mormon studies, and May's essay is a classic that remains an unsurpassed and underread thumbnail sketch.

Even more controversial than Mormon ethnicity—a debate largely confined to academics—is the question of whether Mormonism is a Christian religion. This point of dispute between Mormons, who vehemently affirm their Christianity, and some theologically conservative evangelical Protestants, who just as vehemently deny it, is taken up by Jan Shipps, an avowed Methodist, the past president of the Mormon History Association, and one of the most respected scholars of Mormonism today.[22] It would be a mistake to view this issue as a quibblesome point relevant only to the LDS and evangelical Protestant parties involved. This topic was a chief source of American interreligious strife in the nineteenth century, and it continues, at a muted level, to be the major area of disagreement between two of the fastest-growing religious movements in the world. This question is also a key to determining whether the Latter-day Saint religion is a new world religion or a substream within the multifaceted Christian religion.

Shipps suggests that Mormonism's Christianity is perhaps not best answered by treating it as a zero-sum game with a winner and a loser. Historical and cultural matters are usually much too complex to allow such simple explanations. Though Shipps does not propose this explicitly, one possible response is to categorize the Latter-day Saint faith as a new fourth division of Christianity along with Orthodoxy, Roman Catholicism, and Protestantism.[23] However, it can be reasonably argued that Mormonism differs more historically, doctrinally, and canonically from the other great divisions of Christianity than these divisions differ from each other. One advantage to this position is that most Mormons would give it their endorsement, seeing themselves as neither Catholic, Protestant, Orthodox, nor even traditional Christians, but Christian nonetheless because of their belief in the prophetic restoration of the original church. Laying aside all groups' claims of Christian authenticity and merely comparing religious content, Mormonism might be said to fall somewhere between being a new Christian tradition and a new world religion. It is Christian in the same way that Christianity is Jewish: it has historical roots in, shares some canonical texts with, and displays doctrinal contiguities with an older religious tradition it seeks to revitalize. But it is a distinctly new religion based on new revelations.

Despite differences with other streams of the Christian tradition, Mormonism, like each of the other divisions, claims to be the most authentic contemporary expression of the ancient message of Jesus Christ. In an essay in *Trinity Journal,* the theologians Carl Mosser and Paul Owen took evangelical anti-Mormons to task for intellectual inattention and lack of scholarly rigor in responding to the emergence of a vigorous, well-trained, and increasingly sophisticated community of LDS scholars working on early Christian as well as Book of Mormon studies.[24] However, despite evidence that some early Christian beliefs correlate with distinctive LDS doctrines, but not with those of traditional Christians, most traditional Christian theologians continue to insist that LDS beliefs about the bodily nature of God and the physical separateness of God the Father and Jesus Christ constitute a denial of orthodox conceptions of the Trinity.[25] Also, Latter-day Saints' erasure of unassailable walls of separation between matter and spirit and humans and gods may be doctrinal differences serious enough to make Mormonism ultimately irreconcilable with traditional Christianity.[26] For Latter-day Saints, the validity and thoroughly Christian nature of their beliefs is not in question. But to what degree Mormons will want to engage in doctrinal dialogue to be considered "Christian" (by those who have narrowly defined and laid exclusive claims to the term) if this dialogue means downplaying what they regard as revealed doctrines *is* a question for coming generations of Latter-day Saints. Shipps's essay provides an overview of this matter and charts possibilities for future developments that may help reformulate the arguments.

In chapter 4, Terryl L. Givens provides a new view not only of the Christianity of Mormons but also more specifically of the religious motivations and methods for persecuting LDS people in nineteenth-century America. Givens's chapter is especially important as an examination of one of the worst examples of systematic religious intolerance in American history. According to Givens, for Americans' self-conception as a religiously tolerant nation to remain intact, a hegemonic rhetoric needed to emerge in the public sphere that denied the religious nature of Mormonism and instead described it as a political threat or social evil. Under the cover of this rhetorical shift, American culture, spurred in large part by evangelical ministers, mobilized its institutions against the rights, freedoms, and welfare of the Latter-day Saint people in the name of protecting the very American values they set about to subvert.[27] This strategy, well honed in its use against Mormons, is still used against small unpopular religious groups today.

In the contemporary United States, apart from the occasional anti-Mormon pamphlet, snide remark, media misrepresentation, or community opposition to temple construction, Latter-day Saints experience relative tolerance. Mormons around the world, however, still encounter prejudices and persecution first articulated by nineteenth-century anti-Mormons. If Mormonism turns out to indeed be America's contribution to the great religious traditions of the world, it seems also likely that anti-Mormonism may be America's contribution to the great prejudices of the world.

When it comes to Mormonism's contributions to world culture, nothing outstrips the subject of Nathan O. Hatch's essay—the central messages of the Book of Mormon. While this work may well be the Western Hemisphere's most significant indigenous sacred text, until recently, scholarly essays on Mormonism from outside the tradition have contributed little understanding to the social and religious significance of this book of Scripture. Instead, the authors usually did little more than repeat Mark Twain's quip that the book is "chloroform in print."[28] The dismissive assessment by Disciples of Christ founding father Alexander Campbell—whose movement lost many members to the Book of Mormon—was another favorite. Campbell claimed that the book was obviously a nineteenth-century fabrication since it merely rehearsed "every error and almost every truth discussed in New York for the last ten years."[29] Variations on Campbell's claim continue to be a main theme in Book of Mormon origin theories put forth by such scholars.[30] Latter-day Saint scholars, in contrast, have compared elements in the book to the cultural milieu of ancient Palestine and pre-Columbian America and have found many indications of the Book of Mormon's ancient origins.[31]

Instead of perpetuating clichéd aesthetic attacks on the Book of Mormon's style or speculating about the feasibility of Mormon and non-Mormon explanations for its emergence, Hatch argues for placing the content of the book itself, and its effect on those who read it, at center stage in the scholarly effort toward understanding the beginnings and continuing appeal of Mormonism. His essay offers a provocative early step in this endeavor by suggesting that the book's first believing readers regarded it as an exciting and impassioned document of social protest against the greed and socioeconomic inequality they saw around them. Hatch's work is part of a growing trend in scholarship that requires close empathetic readings of the Book of Mormon as a prerequisite to conducting social history on early Mormonism.[32] This scholarly interest parallels adherents' own rediscovery of this book of Scripture. Despite a long period of relative neglect in the late nineteenth and early twentieth centuries, most converts still cite the appeal of the Book of Mormon as a major part of their attraction to Mormonism.[33]

The Book of Mormon and Joseph Smith's subsequent revelations offered a startling new vision of humankind's nature and eternal destiny. Colleen McDannell and Bernhard Lang's contribution is a rendering of Mormons' view of the purpose of life, the conditions of salvation, and the nature and organization of the afterlife as it had developed by the beginning of the twentieth century. This chapter provides a short overview of the LDS heaven, or celestial kingdom, as a counterexample to the long trend among both liberal and conservative Christians alike toward an almost complete abandonment of detailed descriptions of what life in heaven will be like. For Latter-day Saint Christians, heaven remains a lively, fruitful, relatively well fleshed out place where families live together in similitude of the relationship between their Heavenly Father and Mother. The ordered rules of the Latter-day Saints' heavenly cosmos offer explanations for the belief in vicarious baptism for the dead, the emphasis on the holiness of parenthood, and the importance of family life on earth.

But Mormons do not just dwell on their particularly optimistic vision of the afterlife; they also have this-worldly utopian aspirations that have been worked out in the environmental conditions of specific geographic locales. Chapters 7 and 8 address Mormons in Utah and the significance of this state to the worldwide Church. In the history of the American West, Utah's theocratic government and strongly communitarian attempts to build a just social order—often through central planning, community ownership of business enterprises, and cooperative labor and financing—can be viewed as a particularly striking counterexample to Frederick Jackson Turner's hypothesis that the frontier experience brought into being American individualism, capitalism, and democracy.[34] Since less than 50 percent of the world's Latter-day Saints live in the United States, about 20 percent live in the Rocky Mountain West, and only about 15 percent live in Utah,[35] it might seem extravagant to devote two chapters of this collection to "Deseret." However, it should be remembered that Utah—which is over 70 percent LDS—is unique in having by far the largest denominational majority of any state and in being one of only two states with a simple majority of any religion.[36] Also, Utah continues to exert a powerful influence on the imaginations of Mormons throughout the world. A geographically contiguous "Mormon civilization" approaching two million people that encompasses not only Utah but also most of southeastern Idaho and significant portions of Wyoming, Arizona, New Mexico, Nevada, and Colorado is a spiritual comfort to marginalized Mormon minorities elsewhere in the world. The Mormon cultural "homeland"—like Punjab for the Sikhs—helps qualify Mormonism as a world faith.[37]

In describing this homeland in her second essay in this collection, Jan Shipps provides a subtle description of the often oversimplified Mormon/Gentile division that has long been the most significant social distinction in Utah. While she may overemphasize belief over practice in describing how Latter-day Saints categorize themselves, she rightly dispels the notion that the LDS community is uniformitarian and monolithic. In chapter 8, Richard D. Poll illuminates the relationship between the Church and Utah and explains how the two have evolved from existing as nearly synonymous concepts to being two distinct yet deeply intertwined entities as the Church has grown beyond the boundaries of the Great Basin.

Chapters 9 through 11 look to the future of Mormonism: culture clashes in ongoing missionary efforts, the developing nature of millennial expectations, and the broader sociological implications of worldwide variations in the growth rate. In chapter 9, Michael Hicks, a musicologist, looks at the acceptance of the LDS faith among Native Americans, Polynesians, and West Africans. He examines the challenges Mormon culture faces as it confronts, and seeks to make sense of, unfamiliar musical traditions with different views about what constitutes sacred and profane music. Through the lens of music history, he explores cultural retention versus assimilation in the process of convert acculturation. Just as early Christianity became inseparable from some aspects of the Roman Empire, Mormonism, as it spreads around the world, extends and transplants American sports, church architecture, organizational principles, styles of dress, and a religious historical consciousness grounded in events that happened along the American frontier.[38] To what degree this is an indispensable part of maintaining the social unity of a worldwide religion and to what degree it represents an unnecessary cultural exportation is an issue Mormons will likely continue to address with ever greater urgency for some time to come.

Not only in proselytizing but also in eschatology, Latter-day Saints have always had a strong orientation toward the future. Since the beginning of the restoration, Mormons have anticipated a literal Second Coming of Christ even as many Christians under the influence of the Enlightenment and modernism have given up this idea. Grant Underwood investigates the curious intersection of contemporary Mormon millenarianism and modernism. Underwood suggests that the LDS Church's financial and proselytizing success can be partially attributed to its selective embrace of modernism. Modernist organizational and communication principles are eagerly employed. However, unlike many Christian groups whose memberships are in decline, Mormons have eschewed modernism's relativistic morals and metaphysics.

Underwood's observations lead into the last chapter of this collection, in which Rodney Stark attempts to provide a theoretical framework for understanding Mormon proselytizing and community-building accomplishments. Using the Mormon example, he distills ten general principles by which new religious movements succeed or fail. Mormon recruitment success casts serious doubt on the predictions by luminaries such as Karl Marx, Emile Durkheim, and Sigmund Freud that "mystical" worldviews will soon wither before the irresistibility of secular substitutes. Stark also reviews his own previous forecasts for Mormon growth and finds them to have been overly cautious. Remaining somewhat cautious nonetheless, he revises his prognosis to predict continued phenomenal growth for the LDS Church and calls scholars to the attention of demographic evidence for the birth of a new world religion.

Even though Mormonism is establishing an international character, its growth has occurred mostly in the Western Hemisphere, and the United States has still by far the most Latter-day Saints.[39] The emergence of Mormonism as a new world (New World) religion begs the questions Why did America serve as its cradle? and What is the relationship between Mormonism and the American experience? A common LDS answer is that the relatively free and tolerant climate of the nineteenth-century American frontier provided the earliest possible time and place in history where the fullness of God's restored truth had any chance of long-term survival. Even in this environment, the tumult of the faith's early years reads like a series of narrow escapes from seemingly certain destruction.

Following the lead of Leo Tolstoy, who may have been the first to call Mormonism "the American religion," Gordon Wood, a leading historian of the early republic, suggests that despite the tension Mormonism's emergence caused early on, the new religion fulfills a need so crucial to the American experience that if it did not exist Americans would have to invent it.[40] In Wood's view, nineteenth-century Americans needed a religion to match their self-perceived originality, vitality, optimism, and divinely sanctioned position on the center stage of God's unfolding drama on earth. As the new nation sought to define itself after independence, Americans searched for ways to downplay or forget their European intellectual and cultural heritage. American romantics sought religious themes in their natural landscape and their own imagined spiritual images of "noble savages." While little hint of nature worship exists in Mormon theology and Richard L. Bushman has persuasively shown that the Book of Mormon is scarcely a romantic or American republican document, Joseph Smith did have his formative religious experiences in what came to be known as the Sacred Grove in the woods near his home and on the hillside from which he took the golden plates.[41] These experiences gave America and its indigenous inhabitants a Christian history in which Europeans took no part.

In an eccentric but creative reading of the meaning of religion in America, the literary critic Harold Bloom makes the LDS Church's link with the American experience even more fundamental than Wood does. Bloom suggests that the LDS doctrine's combination of radical insistence on every individual's responsibility, perfectibility, and immediate accessibility to divine revelation coupled with its this-worldly communitarian imperatives make it uniquely "The American Religion."[42] Even for nonadherents, the native-soil story of Mormonism is emblematic of Americans' self-perceived uniqueness, and its whirlwind of cleansing new revelations provides a break from troubling historical continuity with European religious corruption and strife. Because of this and Mormonism's ongoing vitality, Bloom predicts that Latter-day Saints will come to play a defining role in America's religious future and will influence all aspects of American culture.

Wood, Bloom, and the scholars in this volume have rediscovered what Richard Burton noticed long ago: Mormonism is an American religion; it may also be America's fledgling contribution to the great world faiths. Since Islam started in the seventh century, perhaps only two movements besides Mormonism— Sikhism and Bahá'í—can lay reasonable claim to the status of a new world religion based on their longevity, population, worldwide distribution, and doctrinal uniqueness. Of these three, the origin and development of the LDS faith is the best documented and most easily accessible to Western scholars. In the last few decades, there has been an explosion of interest in Mormon studies, but even this increase does not yet do justice to the significance of what is happening. I hope the essays in this book are harbingers of even greater things to come.

Notes

1. Joseph Smith's account of his First Vision experience can be found on the official Web site of the Church of Jesus Christ of Latter-day Saints: <http://www.lds.org/library/the%5Fpro%5Fjos/the%5Fpro%5Fjos.html> For an overview of known first-hand accounts of the First Vision, see Milton V. Backman Jr., *Joesph Smith's First Vision* (Salt Lake City: Bookcraft, 1971).

2. The Church of Jesus Christ of Latter-day Saints claimed 10,300,000 members at the end of 1997. See *Deseret News 1999–2000 Church Almanac* (Salt Lake City: Deseret News, 1998). Church membership does not include all the people who profess to be the authentic followers of Joseph Smith's restoration. In the ranks of "greater Mormonism" can be included 230,000 members of the Reorganized Church of Jesus Christ of Latter Day Saints, 30,000 to 80,000 members of mostly polygamist schismatic sects, 20,000 or so members of churches using the Book of Mormon, and thousands of independent practitioners of idiosyncratic varieties of Mormonism. See Steven L. Shields, *Divergent Paths of the Restoration* (Los Angeles: Restoration Research, 1990).

The College of St. Hild and St. Bede at the University of Durham in England held a conference 19–23 April 1999 devoted to whether Mormonism constituted a world religion. Amid much discussion about the viability of the concept of "world religion" itself by scholars such as Bryan Wilson, Ninian Smart, Douglas Davies, Malise Ruthven, and John Hinnells, a consensus emerged that the LDS faith makes as good a case, if not a better one, for being a world religion as any other faith does.

3. For further reading on Mormon studies scholarship, the following reference works are particularly useful: *Encyclopedia of Mormonism,* ed. Daniel H. Ludlow, 5 vols. (New York: Macmillan, 1992); *Mormon Americana: A Guide to Sources and Collections in the*

United States, ed. David J. Whittaker (Provo: Brigham Young University Studies, 1995); and *Utah History Encyclopedia,* ed. Allan Kent Powell (Salt Lake City: University of Utah Press, 1994).

4. For some examples of these antecedents, see Charles S. Peterson, "Speaking for the Past," in *The Oxford History of the American West,* ed. Clyde A. Milner II, Carol A. O'Connor, and Martha Sandweiss (New York: Oxford University Press, 1994), 743–69. See especially the discussion of Dale Morgan, Juanita Brooks, Nels Anderson, Lowrey Nelson, Thomas O'Dea, and Wallace Stegner on 758–60.

5. For an insightful overview of Leonard Arrington's career and the New Mormon History, see Ronald W. Walker, "Mormonism's 'Happy Warrior': Appreciating Leonard J. Arrington," *Journal of Mormon History* 25 (Spring 1999): 113–30. For a personal account, see Leonard Arrington, *Adventures of a Church Historian* (Urbana: University of Illinois Press, 1998).

6. Walker, "Mormonism's 'Happy Warrior,'" 123.

7. Ibid., 120.

8. The issue of folk magic and Mormonism warrants a brief mention of the most tragic episode in the history of Mormon studies. The burgeoning interest in Mormon scholarship in the 1970s and 1980s proved tempting territory for an individual eager to exploit for personal gain the enthusiasm of history professionals and document collectors.

Joseph Smith and his associates' participation in divining practices such as dowsing for water and searching for buried treasure on the frontier was known to historians, as was the common, but not uncontroversial, nature of such practices in this time and region. Later in life, Joseph Smith recorded giving up such things as youthful folly unrelated to his religious calling. In the 1980s, newly discovered documents suggested a strong link between these practices and the foundational religious events of Mormon theology. The most famous of these documents is the "salamander letter" ostensibly written by Joseph Smith's associate Martin Harris to William W. Phelps. This letter provided a very different account of Joseph Smith's receipt of the Golden Plates from the angel Moroni. The letter included this passage: "I take Joseph aside and he says it is true . . . the next morning the spirit transfigured himself from a white salamander in the bottom of the hole & struck me 3 times & held the treasure and would not let me have it . . . the spirit says I tricked you again." This letter gave a convincing piece of evidence to those who claimed that the origins of Mormonism had more to do with the worldview of folk magic and treasure hunting than Joseph Smith let on and than the contemporary LDS leadership was willing to admit.

But this letter and many other documents that emerged at the time—documents that challenged traditional historical understandings—proved to be forgeries. As the deception started to become clear, the forger attempted to murder people he feared would expose him. His letter bombs killed one person suspicious of him and the wife of another. In a third explosion, he injured himself and was incapacitated long enough for the police to connect him to the other bombings and arrest him for murder. The accused was Mark Hofmann, a document dealer who had become legendary in the LDS history community for his uncanny "discoveries" of provocative historical documents. In his plea-bargained testimony, he described himself as a practicing Mormon but longtime closet atheist who set out to undermine traditional understandings of Church history and to profit by doing so.

Mark Hofmann is serving a life sentence in the Utah State Penitentiary and has gained a reputation as one of the most masterful and prolific forgers of all time. Any historical document relating to Mormonism without a verifiable record of its where-abouts before the 1970s is still suspect as a possible forgery, as are other American historical documents. Thanks mostly to sensationalistic reporting about these events, the idea that folk magic is in some scandalous way closely related to the origins of Mormonism and the notion that the LDS Church tried to hide damning documents about its history still persist even though Hofmann's documents were proven forgeries and even though the Church held press conferences to release information about documents it had purchased from Hofmann.

The most balanced and comprehensive books to date on the Hofmann affair are Linda Sillitoe and Allen Roberts, *Salamander: The Story of the Mormon Forgery Murders* (Salt Lake City: Signature Books, 1989), and Richard E. Turley, *Victims: The LDS Church and the Mark Hofmann Case* (Urbana: University of Illinois Press, 1992).

D. Michael Quinn's *Early Mormonism and the Magic World View* (Salt Lake City: Signature Books, 1985) addressed the connections between folk magic and Mormonism from a Mormon and historical perspective. Except for two book reviews of this work—William A. Wilson's in *Brigham Young University Studies* (27 [1987]: 96–104), and one in *Western Historical Quarterly* (20 [1989]: 342–43), the issue of Mormonism and folk magic has not been addressed by scholars in the field most obviously suited to examine it—folklore. Without folklore-informed commentary on this issue, misconceptions remain uncorrected and serious questions are left unaddressed. Folklorists have helped demystify distinctions people commonly make between magic and religion by showing them to be functionally and structurally similar concepts whose differences have more to do with culturally constructed notions emerging from relationships of class and power than from intrinsic qualities of either phenomenon. For Mormons who understand this, the idea that the restoration of all truth might draw on folk magic is no more shocking than that Protestant hymns would find their way into LDS hymnbooks.

Perhaps the most creative contribution to American culture that owes its genesis to the question of Joseph Smith and folk magic is Orson Scott Card's "Alvin Maker" series of novels. Loosely based on Joseph Smith's life and set in an alternate 1800s America where folk magic is quite vibrant, the series has established itself as one of the most popular fantasy series of the 1980s and 1990s. See Orson Scott Card, *Seventh Son, Red Prophet, Prentice Alvin, Alvin Journeyman,* and *Heartfire* (New York: Tom Doherty Associates, 1987, 1988, 1989, 1995, and 1998).

9. Davis Bitton, "Ten Years in Camelot: A Personal Memoir," *Dialogue: A Journal of Mormon Thought* 16 (Autumn 1983): 9–33.

10. See, for example, David E. Bohn, "Our Own Agenda: A Critique of the Methodology of the New Mormon History," *Sunstone* 14 (June 1990): 45–49, and "Unfounded Claims and Impossible Expectations: A Critique of New Mormon History," in *Faithful History: Essays on Writing Mormon History,* ed. George D. Smith (Salt Lake City: Signature Books, 1992), 227–61; Neal W. Kramer, "Looking for God in History," *Sunstone* 8 (Jan.–Mar. 1983): 15–17; Louis C. Midgley, "The Challenge of Historical Consciousness: Mormon History and the Encounter with Secular Modernity," in *By Study and Also by Faith,* ed. John M. Lundquist and Stephen D. Ricks (Salt Lake City: Deseret Book and Foundation for Ancient Research and Mormon Studies, 1990), 2:502–51.

11. Walker, "Mormonism's 'Happy Warrior,'" 127.

12. Philip Schaff, *America: A Sketch of the Political, Social, and Religious Character of the United States of North America,* ed. Perry Miller (Cambridge, Mass.: Harvard University Press, 1961), 198, as quoted in Stephen R. Graham, *Cosmos in the Chaos: Philip Schaff's Interpretation of Nineteenth-Century American Religion* (Grand Rapids, Mich.: William B. Eerdmans, 1995), 225.

13. Robert Baird, *Religion in the United States of America* (Glasgow: Blackie and Son, 1844; reprint, New York: Arno Press, 1969), 647–49.

14. Richard F. Burton, *The City of the Saints and Across the Rocky Mountains to California* (New York: Longman, Green, Longman, and Roberts, 1861), 1.

15. See, for example, Howard Stansbury, *An Expedition to the Valley of the Great Salt Lake of Utah; Including Description of Its Geography, Natural History, and Minerals, and an Analysis of Its Waters, with an Authentic Account of the Mormon Settlement* (Philadelphia: Lippincott Grambo, 1852); and John W. Gunnison, *The Mormons or Latter-day Saints in the Valley of the Great Salt Lake: A History of Their Rise and Progress, Peculiar Doctrines, Present Condition, and Prospects, Derived from Personal Observation during a Residence among Them* (Philadelphia: Lippincott Grambo, 1852; reprint, Brookline: Paradigm Publications, 1993).

16. Clifford Geertz, *The Interpretation of Cultures* (New York: Basic Books, 1973).

17. This anthropologically informed shift in history has been paralleled by similar shifts in other fields. In sociology, rational choice theory is eclipsing theories of irrationality and psychosis in explaining the conversion and martyrdom of religious believers. See, for example, Laurence R. Iannaccone, "Sacrifice and Stigma: Reducing Free-Riding in Cults, Communes, and Other Collectives," *Journal of Political Economy* 100.2 (1992): 271–92; Laurence R. Iannaccone, "Why Strict Churches Are Strong," *American Journal of Sociology* 99 (1994): 1180–211; Rodney Stark and Laurence R. Iannaccone, "Rational Choice Propositions and Religious Movements," in *Religion and the Social Order: Handbook on Cults and Sects in America,* ed. David G. Bromley and Jeffrey K. Hadden (Greenwich, Conn.: JAI Press, 1993), 109–25; and Rodney Stark and Laurence R. Iannaccone, "A Supply-Side Reinterpretation of the 'Secularization' of Europe," *Journal for the Scientific Study of Religion* 33.3 (1994): 230–52.

In folklore studies, the experience-centered approach is the dominant methodology in analyzing personal narratives about religious and supernatural events. See, for example, Barbara Walker, ed., *Out of the Ordinary: Folklore and the Supernatural* (Logan: Utah State University Press, 1995); and David J. Hufford, *The Terror That Comes in the Night: An Experience-Centered Study of Supernatural Assault Traditions* (Philadelphia: University of Pennsylvania Press, 1982).

18. See Will Herberg, *Protestant-Catholic-Jew: An Essay in American Religious Sociology* (Chicago: University of Chicago Press, 1983). In this book Herberg demonstrates the process by which Protestant marginalization of all other religions gave way to a tripartite consensus of a new American mainstream religiosity that included Catholics and Jews but still excluded others.

19. Sydney E. Ahlstrom, *A Religious History of the American People* (Garden City, N.Y.: Image Books, 1975), 1:613.

20. Rodney Stark, *The Rise of Christianity: A Sociologist Reconsiders History* (Princeton: Princeton University Press, 1996), reprinted as *The Rise of Christianity: How the Obscure, Marginal Jesus Movement Became the Dominant Religious Force in the Western World in a Few Centuries* (New York: HarperCollins, 1997).

21. A well-reasoned argument against Mormon ethnicity can be found in Armand L. Mauss's *The Angel and the Beehive: The Mormon Struggle with Assimilation* (Urbana: University of Illinois Press, 1994), 60–74.

22. Jan Shipps has published numerous articles on the Latter-day Saints but her best-known work is also the most respected single-volume contemporary scholarly treatment of Mormonism: *Mormonism: The Story of a New Religious Tradition* (Urbana: University of Illinois Press, 1985).

23. In his book *Fire from Heaven: The Rise of Pentecostal Spirituality and the Reshaping of Religion in the Twenty-First Century* (Reading, Mass.: Addison-Wesley, 1995) Harvey Cox suggests that Pentecostalism is also a new division within Christianity, which would make it fifth in historical sequence and Mormonism still fourth.

24. Carl Mosser and Paul Owen, "Mormon Scholarship, Apologetics, and Evangelical Neglect: Losing the Battle and Not Knowing It?" *Trinity Journal* 19 (Fall 1998): 179–205.

25. For a detailed dialogue between a Mormon and an evangelical scholar, see Craig L. Blomberg and Stephen E. Robinson, *How Wide the Divide?: A Mormon and an Evangelical in Conversation* (Downers Grove, Ill.: Intervarsity Press, 1997). See also B. H. Roberts, *The Mormon Doctrine of Deity: The Roberts–van der Donkt Discussion, to Which Is Added a Discourse, Jesus Christ: The Revelation of God* (Salt Lake City: Deseret News, 1903). For an LDS response to traditional Christian arguments against the Christianity of Mormons, see Stephen E. Robinson, *Are Mormons Christian?* (Salt Lake City: Bookcraft, 1991). As Mosser and Owen contend, vitriolic, misleading, and amateurish attacks are common while serious scholarship providing an evangelical response to Mormon claims is virtually nonexistent. One possible exception is Francis J. Beckwith and Stephen E. Parrish's *The Mormon Concept of God: A Philosophical Analysis* (Lewiston, N.Y.: Edwin Mellen, 1991). But it too is flawed by serious misinterpretations of LDS beliefs.

26. Mosser and Owen, "Mormon Scholarship," 179.

27. For a more complete treatment of Mormon civil rights history, see Eric A. Eliason, "Mormons," in *The Encyclopedia of Civil Rights in America,* ed. Shelley Fisher Fishkin and David Bradley (New York: Salem Press, 1997), 612–16.

28. Mark Twain, *Roughing It* (New York: American Publishing Company, 1872; reprint, New York: Penguin, 1980), 102.

29. Alexander Campbell, *Delusions: An Analysis of the Book of Mormon* (Boston: Benjamin H. Greene, 1832), 13.

30. Brent Lee Metcalfe, ed., *New Approaches to the Book of Mormon* (Salt Lake City: Signature Books, 1993).

31. The best and most comprehensive introduction to Book of Mormon contextual studies is Noel B. Reynolds, ed., *Book of Mormon Authorship Revisited: The Evidence for Ancient Origins* (Provo: Foundation for Ancient Research and Mormon Studies, 1997).

32. For another example of the benefits of closely reading the Book of Mormon, see Royal Skousen, "How Joseph Smith Translated the Book of Mormon: Evidence from the Original Manuscript," *Journal of Book of Mormon Studies* 7, no. 1 (1998): 24–31, which shows how the corrections and revisions of the original manuscript and subsequent editions suggest that Joseph Smith apparently received the translation word for word and in some instances letter for letter. This finding overturns a previous theory that Joseph Smith dictated a loose translation from general impressions he received in his mind.

33. Noel B. Reynolds, "The Coming Forth of the Book of Mormon in the Twentieth Century," *Brigham Young University Studies* 38, no. 2 (1999): 7, 38–40.

34. The Turner hypothesis is articulated in Frederick Jackson Turner's "Social Forces in American History," *American Historical Review* 16 (Jan. 1911): 217–33. For a commentary on his legacy in the American historical profession, see Gerald D. Nash, *Creating the West: Historical Interpretations, 1890–1990* (Albuquerque: University of New Mexico Press, 1991). On nineteenth-century Mormon economic practices, see Leonard J. Arrington, *Great Basin Kingdom: An Economic History of the Latter-day Saints, 1830–1900* (Cambridge, Mass.: Harvard University Press, 1958); and Leonard J. Arrington, Feramorz Y. Fox, and Dean L. May, *Building the City of God: Community and Cooperation among the Mormons* (Salt Lake City: Deseret Book, 1976).

35. The best guide to current church membership statistics worldwide is the biennial *Deseret News Church Almanac* (Salt Lake City: Deseret News).

36. Only Rhode Island, which is 60 percent Roman Catholic, comes even close to Utah's denominational dominance. A comprehensive treatment of American religious demographics can be found in Barry A. Kosmin and Seymour P. Lachman's *One Nation under God: Religion in Contemporary American Society* (New York: Crown Trade Paperbacks, 1993).

37. The National Geographic Society recognizes this by depicting on its map of world religion a Mormon region distinct from Catholic, Protestant, and Eastern Orthodox

counterparts. See *National Geographic Atlas of the World,* 6th ed. (Washington, D.C.: National Geographic Society, 1990), 8. The primary work in defining the Mormon culture region is D. W. Meinig, "The Mormon Culture Region: Strategies and Patterns in the Geography of the American West, 1847–1964," *Annals of the Association of American Geographers* 55 (June 1965): 191–220. More up-to-date information on Mormon geography can be found in *Historical Atlas of Mormonism,* ed. S. Kent Brown, Donald Q. Cannon, and Richard H. Jackson (New York: Simon and Schuster, 1994).

38. Sports and architecture are intertwined in the long practice of building LDS meetinghouses with basketball courts as a standard feature. This is true not only in the United States but all over the world—even in places where basketball is uncommon.

39. For the most recent map of LDS membership distribution see: <http://www.lds.org/library/display/0,4945,198-1-168-12,FF.html>.

40. Leland A. Fetzer, "Tolstoy and Mormonism," *Dialogue* 6 (Spring 1971): 13–29; Gordon S. Wood, "Evangelical America and Early Mormonism," *New York History* 61 (Oct. 1980): 359–86.

41. Richard L. Bushman, *Joseph Smith and the Beginnings of Mormonism* (Urbana: University of Illinois Press, 1984), 131–33.

42. Harold Bloom, *The American Religion: The Emergence of the Post-Christian Nation* (New York: Simon and Schuster, 1992).

1

Soaring with the Gods: Early Mormons and the Eclipse of Religious Pluralism

Richard T. Hughes

To understand the genius of early Mormonism, one must first recognize that Mormonism was a profoundly primitivist tradition. But what did primitivism mean in the Mormon context? Answers to that question emerge when we compare early Mormonism with another primitivist movement that thrived in the early national period, the "Christian" or "Disciples" movement led by Alexander Campbell, Thomas Campbell, and Barton W. Stone.

The Mormon commitment to restoring first times was no less intense than that of the "Christians," though it took a radically different form. Indeed, Mormons rejected two central "Christian" premises, namely, that Baconian rationalism was the only proper lens through which the Bible should be viewed and that the New Testament was the only legitimate guide to the restoration task. Mormons looked instead to a constellation of sacred times, claiming that in Joseph Smith, their prophet, God had communed with earth again just as in the days of Adam, Abraham, Moses, and Jesus. Further, if the "Christians" took almost forty years to transform the lure of first times into a radically antipluralistic posture, that posture was inherent in the restoration vision of early Mormons from the very start. This essay, in part, seeks to explain how and why this was so.

❖ ❖ ❖

Sidney E. Mead observed in *The Lively Experiment* that one of the defining themes of American Christianity during the nation's early years was a profound sense of "historylessness," a perspective shaped by three assumptions: "the idea of pure and normative beginnings to which return was possible; the idea that the intervening history was largely that of aberrations and corruptions which was better ignored; and the idea of building anew in the American wilderness on the true and ancient foundations." Reinforcing this restoration perspective was the radical newness of the American experiment, which worked to erase continuity not only with Europe but also with the historic churches. Thus, many Christians imagined they were beginning again "at the point where mankind had first gone astray—at Eden, the paradise of man before the fall."[1]

Alongside this theme lay another that Mead developed in much greater detail, namely, the persistent refusal of many religionists in America to accept either the legitimacy or the premises of religious pluralism. Indeed, Mead argued that antipathy toward pluralism was especially strong in the early nineteenth century, when the religious premises for pluralism were "drowned in the great tidal wave of revivalism that swept the country" at that time.[2]

Mead noted the close connection between pluralism and primitivism in early nineteenth-century America. Each sect competed with all the others by claiming that it "most closely conformed to the Biblical patterns."[3] But the relationship between pluralism and primitivism was more intimate even than that. In the first place, while practically every sect and denomination used the appeal to biblical patterns as an effective weapon in denominational rivalry, some groups took upon themselves the restoration ideal as a defining characteristic, a raison d'être. This was the case, for example, with Mormons, Separate Baptists, Shakers, Disciples, and New Light "Christians" of both the West and the East. And in the second place, restoration among these sectarians often became the basis also for opposing both the fact and the premise of religious pluralism itself. Accordingly, many restorationists argued that a return to the ancient order of things would bring not only Christian unity but also civil unity under the lordship of Jesus Christ. Alexander Campbell, for example, argued that "there is now a scheme of things presented, in what is called the *Ancient Gospel,* which is long enough, broad enough, strong enough for the whole superstructure called the Millennial Church—and . . . it will alone be the *instrument* of *converting* the whole human race." Campbell added that this conversion finally would "subvert all political government," including that of the pluralistic American nation.[4] The Mormon missionary Parley P. Pratt foresaw in 1851 that through the progress of the Mormon restoration, all governments, kingdoms, and tribes would be "dissolved—destroyed—or mingled into *one*—one body politic—*one* peaceful empire—*one* Lord—*one* King—*one* interest all."[5]

How does one account for this radically ecumenical thrust with its antipluralist dimension? From a theological perspective, restorationists commonly appealed to Jesus' prayer for the unity of believers. But what prompted them to heed that prayer so devoutly, it seems, was the radical newness of the religious situation in America during that period. After all, early nineteenth-century Americans were not far removed in time from the established churches of the nations from which they had come. Those Old World environs provided *cosmos:* one knew where one stood, and one stood invariably in the bosom of the church. In contrast, the "brave new world"[6] launched on these shores was religiously chaotic. Clearly, one compelling way to bring order and cosmos to a messy, disorderly, and chaotic pluralism was to present the "ancient order of things" as a firm ecumenical foundation. Thus, as Mead observes, "It is notable that the most successful of the definitely Christian indigenous denominations in America, the Disciples of Christ, grew out of the idea of a 'new reformation' to be based, not on new insights, but on a 'restoration' of the practices of the New Testament church—on which platform, it was thought, all the diverse groups of modern Christianity could unite as they shed the accumulated corruptions of the Church through the centuries."[7]

While the Disciples may have been the most successful of the indigenous American traditions for their time, none presents to the historian a more richly textured restorationist-ecumenical perspective than does the Church of Jesus Christ of Latter-day Saints in its early years. And no single Mormon spokesperson more clearly explained the restorationist premise for Mormon antipluralism than did Parley P. Pratt, one of the original Twelve Apostles of the Latter-day Saints. It is therefore to the early Mormon understanding of restoration and its relationship to the problem of pluralism, and especially to Parley Pratt's understanding of these themes, that we now turn.

❖ ❖ ❖

The intimate connection between the early Mormon understanding of restoration and the problem of religious pluralism becomes apparent in the event that prompted the beginnings of this faith: the First Vision of Joseph Smith. Profoundly distressed by the competing claims of America's frontier sects, fourteen-year-old Smith retired to the woods in the spring of 1820 to ask the Lord which of the churches he should join. The Lord replied in a vision that he "must join none of them, for they were all wrong" and that "all their creeds were an abomination in his sight."[8] Following that vision, Smith became a seeker, earnestly searching for the one true church that once had flourished but now had disappeared from the face of the earth.

As a seeker, Smith was hardly unique. Seekerism as a religious phenomenon abounded in America in the 1820s, especially in upstate New York, where the Smith family lived. Typical was Solomon Chamberlain of Lyons, who had long been convinced that "faith was gone from the earth" and that "all Churches were corrupt," or Wilford G. Woodruff, who became convinced in 1830 that Christ's church no longer existed.[9] Joseph's father, Joseph Smith Sr., saw in a dream a barren earth that signified "the world which now lieth inanimate and dumb, in regard to the true religion, or plan of salvation." And Lucy Mack Smith, Joseph's mother, concluded that all the churches were "unlike the Church of Christ, as it existed in former days," and that there was not, therefore, "then upon the earth the religion I sought." Both Joseph Sr. and Lucy refused to "subscribe to any particular system of faith, but contended for the ancient order as established by our Lord and Saviour Jesus Christ, and his Apostles."[10]

For most of these seekers, religious pluralism was the source of their despair. George Burnham of Greenville, New York, bewailed the "multitude of sectarian divisions," which for him provided proof that American Christianity "is not the *house of God,* while thus divided against itself—and is not the *body of Christ* which cannot be divided."[11] And Joseph Smith himself in later years recalled the days of his youth when "the different religious parties . . . created no small stir and division amongst the people, some crying, 'Lo here!' and others, 'Lo, there!'" He wrote in his *History of the Church* concerning those early years that "so great were the confusion and strife among the different denominations, that it was impossible for a person young as I was, and so unacquainted with men and things, to come to any certain conclusion who was right and who was wrong. . . . In the midst of this war of words and tumult of opinion, I often said to myself, what is to be done? Who of all these parties are right; or, are they all wrong together?"[12]

Like Roger Williams two hundred years before, Smith concluded that they were "all wrong together." Indeed, the similarities between Smith and Williams are profound. Both concluded that the true apostolic and primitive church had vanished. Both concluded that the church had grown so completely corrupt over the centuries that no human being or group of human beings could possibly restore it to its original purity. And both longed eagerly for a latter-day prophet or apostle, bearing authority from the throne of God, who would restore the church to its first state.

But there the similarities break down, for Smith and Williams differed profoundly in two major respects. Most obvious is that Williams died a seeker, still longing and searching for the prophet and the restoration. In contrast, Smith himself became that prophet and by 1830 claimed that God, through him, had restored the Church of Christ once again to the earth. The other difference pertains to motivation. Williams found the church of his day a corrupt abomination and a gross departure from the primitive model precisely because it compelled and coerced the consciences of men and women. For Williams, therefore, the premise of religious freedom was essential to recovery of the apostolic church. Put another way, true religion, for Williams, was religion born of persuasion, not of coercion.[13] Ironically, however, it was the prevalence of persuasion in the competitive free market of souls that convinced Joseph Smith (and a host of other seekers in the new American nation) that the true church had disappeared. As Lucy Mack Smith said, the claims and counterclaims of the various sects made "them witnesses against each other." In this context of vacuous relativity, people needed authority—a clear word from God that would subdue the confused and errant words of men and women.[14]

The quest for authority was evident in the conversion of Parley P. Pratt. Living in Ohio in 1829, Pratt heard Sidney Rigdon, a follower of Alexander Campbell, proclaim faith in Jesus Christ, repentance toward God, baptism for remission of sins, and the gift of the Holy Ghost. "Here was the ancient gospel in due form," Pratt later wrote in his autobiography. Yet he was not content. By what authority could Rigdon establish this ancient gospel? He was neither prophet nor apostle. "Who is Mr. Rigdon?" Pratt asked. And "Who is Mr. Campbell? Who commissioned them?" On what basis could one determine that their ancient gospel was any more authentic than the ancient gospel of, say, the Baptists or of some other group with a primitivist orientation? What Rigdon and Campbell lacked, in Pratt's view, was "the *authority* to minister in holy things—the apostleship, the power which should accompany the form." After reading the Book of Mormon, however, and after learning that God had anointed Joseph Smith as his prophet in the latter days, Pratt exulted, "I had now found men on earth commissioned to preach, baptize, ordain to the ministry, etc., and I determined to obey the fulness of the gospel without delay."[15]

Indeed, for Pratt and for other early Mormons, the fact that God had restored to earth the ancient gospel through a latter-day prophet rendered entirely irrelevant the tumult of words, the contentions of preachers, and the strife of the sects. Campbell, Rigdon, the Baptists, and others might preach their *opinions* concerning the ancient gospel, but God had bestowed on Joseph Smith Jr. the authority of the priesthood both to baptize and to confer the gift of the Holy Ghost in the latter days. Further, God had communicated with Smith in visions and revelations, had called him to translate the Book of Mormon from the golden plates buried by ancient American Christians, and had anointed him both prophet and apostle. In this way, to the Mormon mind, God had established once again the true Church of Jesus Christ on the earth, sanctioned not by human opinion, or by the inventions of men, but by the authority of heaven itself.

This notion of restoration made it abundantly clear that God had sanctioned one true church and that all others were false. Allowing no room for abstractions, ambiguities, or shades of gray, this dichotomy found clear expression in the Book of Mormon, which asserts that "there are save two churches only; the one is the church of the Lamb of God, and the other is the church of the devil; wherefore, who so belongeth not to the church of the Lamb of God belongeth to that great church, which is the mother of abominations; and she is the whore of all the earth." From this premise it was only a short step to the conclusion that God's wrath would be "poured out upon . . . the great and abominable church of all the earth."[16]

Fundamental to this antipluralist posture was the peculiarly Mormon understanding of restoration. If Puritans, Baptists, and "Christians," for example, sought simply to emulate the faith and practices of the ancients, Mormons embraced a scheme of restoration that was cosmic in its scope, that penetrated space to the ends of the earth and the outer bounds of the universe itself, and that encompassed time from its very beginning to its end. Indeed, Mormons referred to their religion as the "restoration of all things."[17]

❖ ❖ ❖

In the annals of the Latter-day Saints, no one has articulated this vision more cogently and vividly than Parley P. Pratt. Born 12 April 1807 in Burlington, Otsego County, New York, Pratt moved in 1827 to Ohio, where he made common cause with Sidney Rigdon and the Campbellite "restoration movement" that Rigdon espoused. Returning to New York in 1830 on a preaching mission, Pratt discovered the Book of Mormon, converted, and was baptized by Oliver Cowdery on 1 September 1830 in Seneca Lake. From the time of that initiation into the fellowship of the Latter-day Saints, Pratt would become one of its most significant proponents. Ordained one of the Twelve Apostles on 1 February 1835, Pratt essentially was a missionary throughout his life. He preached throughout the United States and in England, Canada, the Pacific islands, and South America. On 13 May 1857, he was murdered while on a preaching tour near Van Buren, Arkansas.[18]

Pratt made his most lasting contribution through numerous pamphlets written in defense of the Mormon faith. In fact, many consider him the "Father of Mormon Pamphleteering."[19] Scholars generally acknowledge that two of his pamphlets in particular—A Voice of Warning and Key to the Science of Theology—furnished the most cogent noncanonical expressions of Mormon faith written in the nineteenth century. His 1837 work, A Voice of Warning, has been judged "the most important of all noncanonical Mormon books" and "the most important missionary pamphlet in the history of the church."[20]

While this was not the first Mormon tract, "it was the first systematic statement and defense of the fundamentals of Mormonism. More than this, it erected a standard for all future Mormon pamphleteers, setting down a formula for describing the tenets of Mormonism as well as biblical proof-texts, arguments, examples, and expressions that would be used by others for another century."[21] The *Times and Seasons* reported that by 1842 both a first edition of three thousand copies and a second edition of twenty-five hundred copies had been exhausted. Six more editions were printed by 1860. The editor of the 1978 edition suggests that this book "undoubtedly contributed to the conversion of thousands of seekers to Mormonism."[22]

Key to the Science of Theology, published in Liverpool, England, in 1855, was one of the earliest attempts to systematize the disparate elements of Mormon theology.[23] Clearly, it was among the most successful attempts, for the book was in great demand and remained through the early twentieth century "one of the leading statements of Church doctrine."[24]

Throughout his writings Pratt consistently cast Mormon theology in a restorationist mold. But what did he mean by this term *restoration?* Pratt addressed this question frequently and forthrightly. "Now we can never understand what is meant by restoration," he wrote, "unless we understand what is lost or taken away."[25] What had been lost, he explained, was dialogue with God and communion with heavenly beings. Thus he contrasted the ancients and the moderns in this regard: "Witness the ancients, conversing with the Great Jehovah, learning lessons from the angels, and receiving instruction by the Holy Ghost, in dreams by night, and visions by day, until at length the veil is taken off. . . . Compare this intelligence, with the low smatterings of education and worldly wisdom, which seem to satisfy the narrow mind of man in our generation."[26] The key to the science of theology, then, was for Pratt "the key of divine revelation," and it was this key Mormons claimed was restored.[27]

From this perspective, Pratt and his Mormon colleagues could view only as extraordinarily deficient the restoration efforts of Disciple leaders Thomas and Alexander Campbell. For Pratt, these "restorers" were part of the problem, not part of the solution, because they maintained that the gifts of the Spirit had expired with the original apostles. In their view, the object of restoration therefore was not recovery of the gifts of the Spirit or of divine revelation but rather recovery of the forms and structures the Spirit had inspired.

Armed with these convictions both Thomas and Alexander Campbell attacked Mormon claims to have restored the gifts of the Spirit. When Sidney Rigdon converted to the Latter-day Saints, Thomas Campbell challenged him to debate, claiming that he would demonstrate that "imposition of hands for communicating the Holy Spirit is an unscriptural intrusion upon the exclusive prerogative of the primary apostles."[28] And Alexander simply ascribed Rigdon's claims of spiritual gifts to insanity: "Fits of melancholy succeeded by fits of enthusiasm accompanied by some kind of nervous spasms and swoonings which he has, since his defection, interpreted into the agency of the Holy Spirit, or the recovery of spiritual gifts, produced a versatility in his genius and deportment which has been increasing for some time."[29]

Whether Pratt ever read these specific attacks is unknown, but he clearly responded to the common claim that spiritual gifts had ceased with the deaths of the apostles. To him, miraculous gifts partook of the essence of the Christian faith, and to claim that these gifts had ceased was tantamount to admitting that the church had ceased to exist. "When the miracles and gifts of the divine Spirit ceased from among men, Christianity ceased, the Christian ministry ceased, the Church of Christ ceased," he argued. Then he launched an attack of his own. "That ministry which sets aside modern inspiration, revelations, prophecy, angels, visions, healings, &c., is not ordained of God; but is Anti-Christian in spirit. In short, it is that spirit of priestcraft and kingcraft, by which the world, for many ages, has been ruled as with a rod of iron."[30]

From Pratt's perspective, the central defect of Protestant restorers such as Alexander Campbell was a narrow fixation on the Bible. For Pratt and his Mormon colleagues, the Bible was not the ultimate authority in religion, nor was it the final source of power or knowledge. Further, the Bible simply pointed beyond itself to the God who was the final arbiter of ultimate things. While the Scriptures are true and good and useful, Pratt argued, "they are not the fountain of knowledge, nor do they contain all knowledge, yet they point to the fountain, and are every way calculated to encourage men to come to the fountain and seek to obtain the knowledge and gifts of God."[31] The chief function of the Bible, Pratt argued, was not to provide guidelines or blueprints for forms, structures, or static institutions, but rather to demonstrate the divine power behind all forms, structures, and institutions. By this power, Pratt contended, Enoch was translated, Moses freed a nation, Joshua conquered the Canaanites, David excelled the wisdom of the East, and Jesus Christ himself conquered death and hell. And by this same divine power, "a Joseph in modern times has restored the fullness of the gospel; raised the church out of the wilderness; restored to them the faith once delivered to the saints."[32]

It was precisely because early Mormons pointed not to a book but to the divine power behind all books that Mormon theology could grow and evolve. Accordingly, Joseph Smith announced many revelations that continued from the First Vision until his death in Carthage, Illinois, in 1844. Those early Mormons who resisted theological change and defected to a more static tradition simply never understood the premises of the Mormon restoration ideal.

Indeed, Pratt specifically excluded from the Mormon faith the authority of a particular antiquity, even Christian antiquity. Mormons had no interest in patterning their faith and practice after a particular time, but looked instead to the God who had worked wonders in all times. Mormons "claim no authority whatever from antiquity," Pratt proclaimed; rather, "the Lord uttered his voice from the heavens, an holy angel came forth and restored the priesthood and apostleship, and hence has arisen the church of the Saints."[33] In contrast, traditional restorers had fixed their gaze on a particular institution—the church of the first century, for example—and had missed the divine reality that had inspired not only the primitive church but also the patriarchs, the prophets, and Christ himself. Pratt therefore criticized those traditional restorers as having "fallen into this one inconsistency, viz; of patching new cloth on to old garments; and thus the rent has been made worse." Alexander Campbell, for example, had "attempted to restore the ordinances without the priesthood, or gifts of the spirit."[34] In contrast, Pratt described the Church of Jesus Christ of Latter-day Saints as "a NEW TREE—NEW 'FRUITS,'—'NEW CLOTH,' and 'NEW GARMENTS,'—'NEW WINE' and 'NEW BOTTLES'—'NEW LEAVEN' and a 'NEW LUMP,' 'A NEW COVENANT' and spirit; and may it roll on till we have a new heaven and a new earth, that we may dwell forever in the new Jerusalem, while old things pass away, and all things are made new, even so. Amen."[35]

Pratt maintained that neither Campbell nor any other human being was capable of restoring the divine power and initiatives unless God had chosen him for the task. Like Roger Williams before him, Pratt believed that once the priesthood and spiritual gifts had been lost from the earth, they could be restored only at God's own initiative. Thus, "the man or men last holding the keys of such power . . . [must] return to the earth as ministering angels, and select . . . certain individuals of the royal lineage of Israel, to hold the keys of such Priesthood, and to ordain others, and thus restore and reorganize the government of God, or His kingdom upon the earth."[36] But this restoration would take place only in the fullness of times, or as Mormons liked to say, "the times of restitution of all things." Indeed, this latter phrase was part of the text by which Mormons typically justified their restoration efforts, Acts 3:20–21 (KJV): "And he shall send Jesus Christ, which before was preached unto you: whom the heaven must receive until the times of the restitution [restoration] of all things, which God hath spoken by the mouth of all his holy prophets since the world began."

God alone, Pratt believed, had determined this extraordinary time of restoration. Reformations, protests, and religious revolutions had failed time and again because their leaders had acted on their own, apart from the initiative from God. In a particularly cogent passage, Pratt wrote:

> Protests upon protests! Reforms and re-reforms; revolutions, and struggles, exertions of every kind, of mere human invention, have been tried and tried in vain. The science of Theology, with all its keys and powers, once lost, could never, consistent with the ancient Prophetic testimony, be restored to either Jew or Gentile, until the full time should arrive—"*The times of restitution of all things. ...*" Then, and not till then, could the science, the keys, the powers of Theology, be restored to man. No individual or combined human action could obtain or restore again these keys—this science. A mighty angel held the keys of this science for the last days.[37]

Pratt was convinced that he lived in these last days—"the times of restitution of all things"—and that God had anointed Joseph Smith as apostle and prophet in order to begin the restoration. Further, Pratt was convinced that the Mormon restoration was radically dissimilar to all other restoration attempts. If other would-be restorers focused on particular books, persons, or ancient times, Mormons treated all particular sacred manifestations as transparencies that pointed beyond themselves to ultimate reality. If other restorers, on their own initiative, sought to recover mere finite forms, God had called and enabled Mormons to recover communion with the infinite itself.

When viewed from this perspective, early Mormonism may well be understood as a romantic rejection of the Common Sense rationalist perspective so prevalent in America in the early nineteenth century.[38] The respective movements led by Alexander Campbell and Joseph Smith were both restoration movements, but there were distinct differences. Campbell's restoration movement was rational to the core, applying human reason to the biblical text and limiting authentic religion to that sphere. In so doing, the Campbellite movement was as clear an expression of the spirit of Common Sense rationalism as one could hope to find in early nineteenth-century America. On the other hand, Mormonism sought to transcend the cognitive and the rational and to soar with the gods in the realm of the infinite and the eternal. In this sense, Mormonism was an expression of romanticism in revolt against the constrictions of Common Sense.

The numerous defections from Campbell's Disciples to the Latter-day Saints illustrate well the nature of this revolt. In each instance, the converts despaired of Common Sense rationalism and longed instead to experience the Holy Ghost with power and authority from on high. Elizabeth Ann Whitney reports, for example, that "my husband, Newel K. Whitney, and myself were Campbellites. We had been baptized for the remission of sins, and believed in the laying on of hands and the gifts of the spirit. But there was no one with authority to confer the Holy Ghost upon us." When the Mormon gospel arrived in Kirtland, Ohio, therefore, the Whitneys readily converted. Eliza Snow "heard Alexander Campbell advocate the literal meaning of the Scriptures—listened to him with deep interest—hoped his new life led to a fulness—was baptized." But she soon discovered that Campbell had not been empowered by God and determined that "my baptism was of no consequence." In April 1835, therefore, she "was baptized by a 'Mormon' Elder, and in the evening of that day, I realized the baptism of the Spirit as sensible as I did that of the water in the stream."[39]

The case of John Murdock holds particular interest. A Seceder Presbyterian, Murdock had determined independently that baptism was for remission of sins. "I kept searching the Scriptures and looking to find a people that lived according to them," he wrote, "but could not find such a people." At last, however, he learned of Alexander Campbell, whose baptismal teaching struck Murdock as not only rational but also extraordinarily mechanistic. The Campbellites, he wrote, "promised any person remission of sins that would be baptized and that they had caught a whole Baptist Church in Mentor, and they would receive a drunkard or any profane person." Murdock found it "impossible that they should have caught that whole Baptist Church in such a gross error all at one haul," but he nonetheless submitted to immersion and joined the Disciples. Within three years, however, "finding their principal leader, Alex Campbell, with many others, denying the gift and power of the Holy Ghost, I began to think of looking me a new home." On 5 November 1830 he found his new home when Parley Pratt baptized him in the Chafrin River, "and the spirit of the Lord sensibly attended the ministration." At his confirmation several days later, Murdock wrote, "the Spirit rested on me as it never did before and others said they saw the Lord and had visions." The following summer Barton Stone visited a meeting of the Saints where Murdock was preaching "and tried to put us down by his learning." But Murdock proclaimed "the first principles of the gospel—Repentance and baptism for the remission of sins and the laying on of the hands for the gift of the Holy Ghost. . . . Priest Stone trembled, but would not yield."[40]

Many commentators on Mormonism have noted the literalism of the Mormon tradition. But literalism took second place to the romantic visions of the Spirit. Put another way, the Saints took quite literally a romantic theology that came to them in visions, dreams, and revelations, mediated through a latter-day prophet. But this was a very different sort of literalism from the rational,

New Testament–oriented literalism that characterized Alexander Campbell and his Disciples of Christ.

With this singular restoration vision, Mormons addressed the problem of religious pluralism that they found so disconcerting. In fact, religious pluralism, they thought, simply would not exist if the "science of theology"—communion with angels and gods—had not been lost. In their view, pluralism was merely the symptom of the human confusion that inevitably resulted when divine authority disappeared. Pratt wrote that "the reason for all the division, confusion, jars, discords, and animosities; and the reason of so many faiths, lords, baptisms, and spirits . . . is all because they have no Apostles, and Prophets, and other gifts, inspired from on high . . . , for if they had such gifts . . . they would be built up in one body, . . . having one Lord, one faith, and one Baptism."[41] Indeed, the final objective of the Mormon restoration was recovery of the one body, the one faith, and the one baptism.

This quest for *ultimate* power and *ultimate* authority, descending from the very heavens themselves, was the genius of the Mormon restoration ideal. Yet, it is undeniably true—and fundamentally important—that early Mormons sought recovery of infinite and ultimate authority precisely through recovery of the finite forms inspired by God in all ages past. Here was the meaning, then, of the phrase "restitution of all things": Mormons would restore "all things" from all God's epochs since the Creation itself. We now turn, therefore, to this other side of Mormon primitivism, the recovery of finite structures and forms, and the implications of this concrete, tangible restoration for Mormon attitudes toward religious pluralism in America.

❖ ❖ ❖

If Parley Pratt condemned Alexander Campbell for attempting to restore the outward ordinances without the gifts of the Spirit, he also condemned the Quakers for attempting to restore the gifts of the Spirit apart from outward ordinances.[42] Pratt's dual judgment in this regard is highly significant, for it symbolizes the inseparable relation of the finite and the infinite in the early Mormon imagination. Indeed, to encompass sacred, finite forms *was* to encompass the infinite precisely because, as Joseph Smith revealed in May 1843, "there is no such thing as immaterial matter. All spirit is matter."[43] Additionally, early Mormons argued that all matter is eternal. Thus Parley Pratt simply rejected creation ex nihilo. He asserted that "the original elements of matter are eternal" and "uncreated and self-existing." The very term *creation*, Pratt argued, is misleading: God no more created the world than he created himself; he simply organized preexisting elements into a coherent whole of universe.[44]

If inanimate matter was uncreated, Pratt contended, then obviously the same was true for humanity. Pratt scoffed at the Genesis notion that God made Adam from the dust of the ground and Eve from Adam's rib. Moses knew better, he said. But because humankind, immature as it was, could not view the Almighty face to face, Moses "was forced again to veil the past in mystery, and . . . assign to man an earthly origin." In so doing, Moses resembled a watchful parent who "would fain conceal from budding manhood, the mysteries of procreation . . . by relating some childish tale of new born life, engendered in the hollow trunk of some old tree." The real truth, however, which Moses refused to tell was that "man is the offspring of Deity."[45]

As the "offspring of Deity," humankind possessed the power to become the divine original from which it had sprung. Pratt therefore exhorted his readers to "burst the chains of mortality which bind thee fast; unlock the prison of thy clay tenement which confines thee to this groveling, earthly sphere of action; and robed in immortality, wrapped in the visions of eternity, with organs of sight and thought and speech which cannot be impaired or weakened by time or use; soar with me amid unnumbered worlds which roll in majesty on high."[46] Pratt even suggested that God's saints would, "like the risen Jesus, ascend and descend at will, and with a speed nearly instantaneous."[47]

This constellation of ideas—that spirit is matter, that matter is eternal, and that human beings sprang from God and can become gods themselves—constitutes the philosophic foundation for the early Mormon understanding of restoration. If the Saints ultimately would "ascend the heights" and "descend the depths" and "explore the lengths and breadths of organized existence"—something the gods themselves had done in the primordium—should not the Saints embrace this cosmic perspective in their restoration?[48] Unwilling therefore to confine themselves to a single book or to a single sacred epoch as did traditional restorationists, early Mormons sought "the restoration of all things." Like bees sucking nectar first from this flower and then from the next, early Mormons moved at ease from the primitive church to Moses to the prophets to Abraham to Adam and finally to the coming millennium. Many interpreters of Mormonism have commented on this amalgamation of sacred times, an amalgamation so complete that it appears as sheer confusion. To early Mormons such as Parley Pratt, however, it was far from confusion, resting instead on an inner logic that simply baffled those whose gaze was riveted to the finite particulars of religious faith.

To early Mormons, after all, the finite ordinances of every sacred age equally partook of the infinite. Nothing, therefore, could be more consistent than to practice Christian baptism in a baptismal font resting on twelve oxen symbolizing the twelve tribes of Israel. Likewise, Mormons saw no inconsistency in their intention to worship in a restored "Jewish" temple built on the site of the Garden of Eden. One must remember what motivated Mormons in the first place, namely, their quest for the infinite and therefore ultimate authority. To saturate themselves with the infinite by sucking the nectar of the infinite from the various finite blossoms of every sacred age only made sense.

Granted, this perspective made no sense to those whose restoration premises were governed by the rationalism of Common Sense. Alexander Campbell, for example, was appalled that Jews in the Book of Mormon were "called Christians while keeping the law of Moses, the holy sabbath, and worshipping in their temple at their altars and by their high priests" and that "the Nephites . . . were good christians, . . . preaching baptism and other christian usages hundreds of years before Jesus Christ was born!"[49] Likewise, Walter Scott, Campbell's colleague in their New Testament–oriented restoration, criticized the Book of Mormon for confounding "history with prophecy, . . . putting in the mouths of his fictious seers the language of the apostles."[50] From the Mormon perspective, however, neither Smith nor Pratt would have winced at these critiques, for to them these critiques failed entirely to speak to the heart of the Mormon faith. For Smith and Pratt, patriarchal polygamy, Jewish temple rites, and Christian baptism were all finite and material ordinances ordained by God during some sacred epoch. They all shared one function: to bring the power and authority of the infinite into the world of the Latter-day Saints. To Common Sense restorationists such as Campbell and Scott, this perspective was spiritual gibberish and religious nonsense.

It all made wonderfully good sense to early Mormons, however, for one fundamental reason—their conviction that they lived in the last days and on the threshold of the millennial dawn. Indeed, their millennial awareness lent both purpose and meaning to the Mormon restoration ideal. Pratt argued that "God has sent us . . . to prepare his way, and to make straight his paths—by gathering in the children of God from all the jarring systems in which they are now organized, and planting them in one fold by the ministration of the ordinances in their ancient purity." When that task was accomplished, Pratt proclaimed, "then shall the Lord Jesus Christ, the great Messiah and King, descend from the heavens in his glorified, immortal body, and reign with his saints, and over all the kingdoms of the earth, one thousand years."[51]

Further, this final age was not just one dispensation among others. Rather, as the last age, it would embrace all the others, tying together with cords of infinity the perfection of all previous sacred times. The Twelve Apostles therefore made it clear that "this [present] dispensation comprehends all the great works of all former dispensations."[52] Standing on the threshold of the age of infinite perfection, Mormons sought to reenact the sacred dramas of all prior ages and to saturate themselves with the infinite as it had manifested itself throughout the course of time. All of this made wonderful sense to those who stood in the shadow of the end.

To understand the early Mormon approach to religious pluralism, it is important to understand how Mormons consistently tied restoration of the infinite to restoration of particular, finite forms, rites, and institutions. Indeed, Mormons found in Zion and its temple an institutional complex that embraced all rites and ordinances of all sacred epochs, that encompassed time from beginning to end and earthly space from pole to pole, that obligated all men and women of all ages and nations to receive the Mormon gospel, and that provided means for their inclusion into the Mormon fold.

The city of Zion provided the link between heaven and earth and between primordium and millennium. Zion was no mere human concoction, but a city that literally would descend from heaven itself. According to the Book of Moses as it appears in the Pearl of Great Price, Enoch built the city of Zion, which the Lord took (with Enoch) unto himself, and which one day would descend to the earth as New Jerusalem, the center of the millennial kingdom. According to Joseph Smith in 1831, this heavenly city would be restored and rebuilt in Jackson County, Missouri, adjacent to the site of the primordial Garden of Eden in Davies County, Missouri, though in 1844 Smith proclaimed that "the whole of America is Zion."[53] Parley Pratt argued further that Zion served as the hinge between the ancient order of things and the millennial dawn and that restoration of this city must precede Christ's Second Coming. "When this city is built the Lord will appear in his glory, and not before," Pratt announced. "So from this we affirm, that if such a city is never built, then the Lord will never come."[54]

Further, Joseph Smith in 1833 envisioned the construction of city after city, all modeled after New Jerusalem and built in adjacent plots; in this way, he told the Saints, they would "fill up the whole world in these last days." Parley Pratt reflected this charge when, writing on behalf of the Twelve Apostles, he declared that God "has commanded us to . . . build up holy cities and sanctuaries—And we know it."[55] Thus, a British brother reported a dream in which he saw a conference of the Saints wherein "it was motioned by Joseph Smith and seconded by John the Revelator, 'That forty-eight new cities be laid out and builded, this year, in accordance with the prophets which have said, "who can number Israel? Who can count the dust of Jacob? Let him fill the earth with cities."'"[56]

While these visions all seem millennial, one must not forget their fundamentally restorationist underpinnings rooted in Enoch's Zion of old. Even in ancient times this Zion had stood opposed to religious pluralism and had symbolized unanimity rather than diversity, for, as the Book of Moses put it, "the Lord called his people ZION, because they were of one heart and one mind, and dwelt in righteousness, and there was no poor among them" (7:18).

Finally, during the Nauvoo period of Mormon history, Joseph Smith introduced into Mormon practice and theology two ordinances that made Mormonism more expansive still. Significantly, both ordinances could be performed only in the temple. The first was the doctrine of baptism for the dead, revealed on 19 January 1841, when Joseph also announced the Lord's command to build the Nauvoo Temple.[57] Not content to extend their restored, millennial kingdom through space, the Mormons by this doctrine might also extend the kingdom backward through time and thereby erase whatever religious pluralism existed in ages past. Regarding this doctrine Pratt proclaimed that "in the world of spirits . . . are . . . Catholics, and Protestants of every sect. . . . There is also the Jew, the Mohametan, the infidel. . . . All these must be taught, enlightened, and must bow the knee to the eternal king." In this way, as the Mormon historian Klaus Hansen has noted, the living and the dead would be linked together "in one gigantic chain of family and kinship that would ultimately bind together the entire human race."[58]

If baptism for the dead might potentially erase religious pluralism for ages past, the doctrine of celestial marriage promised the rule of the Saints on other worlds in ages to come. In a sermon of 16 May 1843, Joseph Smith declared that if "a man and his wife enter into an everlasting covenant and be married for eternity . . . , they . . . will continue to increase and have children in celestial glory." In the revelation of this doctrine, Joseph announced that those males who take a wife "by the new and everlasting covenant . . . shall inherit thrones, kingdoms, principalities, and powers, dominions, all heights and depths. . . . Then shall they be gods, because they have no end."[59]

Clearly, through this expansive, cosmic theology, early Mormons addressed the problem of religious pluralism not only for their own age but also for ages past and future. Their posture in this regard rested squarely on the issue of authority. Other reformers, even restorers, acted on their own, apart from divine authority, guidance, and direction. But the Latter-day Saints responded to God himself, who spoke to them through his prophet in dreams, visions, and revelations, as he had to saints of old. Restoration among Mormons, therefore, essentially meant soaring with the gods while others groveled on the earth. It meant appealing to the sacred while others could appeal only to the profane. It was appropriate, therefore, that the particular rites and ordinances that Mormons chose to restore were rites and ordinances that would bring heaven to earth, collapse both primordium and millennium into their own time and place, and tie the Saints to God's work in all time past. This perspective ultimately provided the theological basis for the political rule of the Saints.

❖ ❖ ❖

In 1841, Parley Pratt addressed a dire warning to Queen Victoria of England. He told the queen that the world was "on the eve of a REVOLUTION," that a "new nation will be established over the whole earth, to the destruction of all other kingdoms," that if the rulers of England would "hearken to this message, they shall have part in the glorious kingdom," but "if they will not . . . they will be overthrown with the wicked, and perish from the earth."[60] Earlier, in 1836, Pratt had incorporated these themes into his widely influential missionary tract *A Voice of Warning,* which was intended to be just that: a voice of warning. There Pratt proclaimed that the Mormon restoration "is the gospel which God has commanded us to preach. . . . And no other system of religion . . . is of any use; every thing different from this, is a perverted gospel, bringing a curse upon them that preach it, and upon them that hear it." Indeed, all who refused the Saints' message "shall alike feel the hand of the almighty, by pestilence, famine, earthquake, and the sword: yea, ye shall be drunken with your own blood . . . until your cities are desolate . . . until all lying, priestcrafts, and all manner of abomination, shall be done away."[61]

How can one account for such violent, coercive visions? This question is both underscored and complicated by the fact that Mormons consistently proclaimed the sanctity of religious freedom. A general assembly of the Saints voted unanimously in Kirtland, Ohio, in 1835 that governments should "secure to each individual the free exercise of conscience" and that human law has no right "to bind the consciences of men." That same declaration affirmed the total illegitimacy of mingling "religious influence with civil government, whereby one religious society is fostered and another proscribed." Further, as a candidate for the presidency of the United States in 1844, Joseph Smith promised to "open the prisons, open the eyes, open the ears, and open the hearts of all people, to behold and enjoy freedom—unadulterated freedom."[62]

Here, then, are two dominant threads in the intellectual garment of the early Saints: a coercive, sometimes even violent antipluralism alongside a ringing affirmation of the right of all people to freedom of conscience in matters of religion. How can one reconcile these two themes?

Two observations are in order. First, Mormons themselves suffered intense persecution, including physical violence, at the hands of other Americans and therefore took steps to defend their lives and property. Thus, the Kirtland Declaration of 1835 affirmed that "all men are justified in defending themselves . . . from the unlawful assaults and encroachments of all persons in times of exigency, where immediate appeal cannot be made to the laws, and relief afforded."[63] The persecutions they suffered and the steps they took for defense made violence, and the possibility of violence, a factor in their perspective. But how did they cross the line from the rhetoric and reality of defensive violence to a rhetoric of coercion?

Second, early Mormons such as Parley Pratt served as missionaries, whose task was made urgent by what they perceived as an imminent end to a profane and fallen world. In this apocalyptic context, it was God, not they, who would avenge the wicked and stiff-necked of this earth. Accordingly, many interpreters of Mormonism have rooted the Saints' coercive visions precisely in their apocalypticism. Thus, for example, Klaus Hansen viewed the creation of the Council of Fifty as a consequence of Mormon millennialism. And Grant Underwood, while faulting Hansen for rooting millennial perspectives in social deprivation, nonetheless concurred with Hansen on the point at issue and argued that "Mormon millennialism disposed the Saints to a . . . conspiratorial view which . . . leagued the whole sectarian world with Lucifer."[64]

But even these explanations, as helpful as they are, leave much unexplained. For what reason would God smite the wicked and exalt the Saints? To what final court would Pratt appeal for the legitimacy of his apocalyptic vision? And why would the God of a freedom-affirming people smite those of different faiths at all?

The fact is that the ideological basis for the coercive rhetoric of early Mormons was their restoration sentiment, not their millennialism. After all, early Mormons hardly could claim to differ from other religious groups on the basis of a millennium that was yet in the future. But they could—and did—put an infinite distance between themselves and their religious neighbors by identifying themselves with a constellation of sacred and primordial pasts while others confined themselves to the finite realm of history and time. By rooting themselves in the primal past, early Mormons simply removed themselves from history and the historical process and claimed instead that they had sprung full blown from the creative hands of God. In April 1830, they said, their prophet had restored to earth the ancient church with all its gifts, miracles, and visions.

This perspective spoke decisively to the Saints regarding the dilemmas posed by religious pluralism in American life. The Saints at one level were committed fully to freedom of conscience for all human beings so long as this fallen and profane world should last. But they believed that religious pluralism, as with other childish things, would be put away in the age of millennial perfection. In this scenario, millennialism was the source of neither Mormon perfectionism nor coercive rhetoric. The role of the millennium, instead, was to provide a stage on which the great cosmic drama, pitting the "church of the Lamb" against "the church of the devil," could be brought to its final conclusion.

In the meantime, the Saints could anticipate the coming age when, as Pratt predicted, "a universal Theocracy will cement the whole body politic. One king will rule. One holy city will compose the capitol. One temple will be the center of worship. In short, there will be one Lord, one Faith, one Baptism, and one Spirit."[65] And in anticipation of that golden age, they proceeded to establish the political kingdom of God, which one day would rule with Christ. As Orson Pratt, Parley's brother, wrote in 1851, "The kingdom of God . . . is the only legal government that can exist in any part of the universe. All other governments are illegal and unauthorized."[66]

One might argue that the doctrine of degrees of salvation, announced in a revelation of 16 February 1832, was in some sense an accommodation to religious pluralism. According to this doctrine, the faithful Saints would inherit celestial glory, while the "honorable men of the earth, who were blinded by the craftiness of men," would inherit a lesser, terrestrial glory.[67] Here, to be sure, non-Mormons would be saved, but hardly on equal terms with Mormons. Parley Pratt possessed a similar hierarchic vision. According to Pratt, the millennial kingdom would encompass the "heathen nations," but these nations would "be exalted to the privilege of serving the Saints. . . . They will be the ploughmen, the vine-dressers, the gardners, builders, etc. But the Saints will be the owners of the soil, the proprietors of all real estate, . . . and the kings, governors, and judges of the earth."[68] One finds in these visions evidence of the tension of a people who, at one level, valued religious pluralism but who, at another level, anticipated its final collapse. In any event, the pluralism inherent in these visions is hardly the kind of pluralism implicit in the First Amendment and plowed into the history of the American experience.

The fact is that early Mormons ultimately rejected the ideal of religious pluralism as that ideal has been understood by most Americans. Further, that rejection finally rested on the notion that through their restoration, early Mormons burst the bonds of time, history, and finitude that for centuries had imprisoned humankind. As Parley observed, they had "burst the chains of mortality" and now soared with the gods "amid unnumbered worlds which roll in majesty on high." Here indeed was a radical form of that common nine-teenth-century vision Mead described as "building anew in the American wilderness on the true and ancient foundations."

Notes

1. Sidney E. Mead, *The Lively Experiment* (New York: Harper and Row, 1963), 108, 111, 110. On this theme, see also Sidney E. Mead, "The Theology of the Republic and the Orthodox Mind," *Journal of the American Academy of Religion* 44 (Mar. 1976): 105–13.

2. Mead, *Lively Experiment*, 53.

3. Mead, *Lively Experiment*, 110.

4. Alexander Campbell, "Millennium—No. 1," *Millennial Harbinger* 1 (Feb. 1830): 55–56; Alexander Campbell, "An Oration in Honor of the Fourth of July," *Popular Lectures and Addresses* (St. Louis: John Burns, 1861), 374–75.

5. Parley P. Pratt, "The Millennium," in *Writings of Parley Parker Pratt*, ed. Parker Pratt Robinson (Salt Lake City: Parker Pratt Robinson, 1952), 259–60.

6. Sidney E. Mead, *The Old Religion in the Brave New World* (Berkeley: University of California Press, 1977).

7. Mead, *Lively Experiment*, 111.

8. Joseph Smith, *History of the Church of Jesus Christ of Latter-day Saints,* ed. B. H. Roberts (Salt Lake City: Deseret Book, 1927), 1:6.

Marvin Hill also has observed the close and intimate connection between primitivism and antipluralism in the Mormon experience. In his 1968 Ph.D. dissertation, Hill wrote that most interpreters have "failed to see that within the primitive gospel beliefs was an anti-pluralistic tendency, largely resulting from a reaction to the fiercely divisive and strife promoting effects of sectarian revivalism." See "The Role of Christian Primitivism in the Origin and Development of the Mormon Kingdom, 1830–1844," Ph.D. diss., University of Chicago, 1968, 4. Hill also recognized the antipluralistic dimensions of the First Vision, observing that through this vision Joseph Smith "in effect turned his back upon the prevailing religious pluralism in the United States, rejecting it as the source of confusion and religious doubt in his own mind" (55). Hill's dissertation was written under the direction of Sidney E. Mead.

Arguing along similar lines, Gordon Pollock saw early Mormonism as a response to the social, economic, and religious chaos that characterized early nineteenth-century America. See "In Search of Security: The Mormons and the Kingdom of God on Earth, 1830–1844," Ph.D. diss., Queen's University, 1977, 6ff. Regarding the Mormon response to religious pluralism, Pollock wrote: "The intense competition between sects was the application to religion of the free market system which characterized the American economy. . . . In the face of quarrelling and competing sects those who became Mormons did so because they accepted its claim to be the one, true and authoritative religion in the world" (22–23).

For the other assessments of the restoration theme in early Mormonism, see Richard L. Bushman, *Joseph Smith and the Beginnings of Mormonism* (Urbana: University of Illinois Press, 1984), esp. 179–88; Peter Crawley, "The Passage of Mormon Primitivism," *Dialogue* 13 (Winter 1980): 26–37; Marvin Hill, "The Shaping of the Mormon Mind in New England and New York," *Brigham Young University Studies* 9 (Spring 1969): 351–72; Jan Shipps, *Mormonism: The Story of a New Religious Tradition* (Urbana: University of Illinois Press, 1985), esp. 67–85; and F. Mark McKiernan, Alma R. Blair, and Paul M. Edwards, eds., *The Restoration Movement: Essays in Mormon History* (Lawrence, Kans.: Coronado Press, 1973).

9. Bushman, *Joseph Smith*, 149–50; Thomas G. Alexander, "Wilford Woodruff and the Changing Nature of Mormon Religious Experience," *Church History* 45 (Mar. 1976): 2. For a more expansive delineation of seekerism in the Smith milieu, see Hill, "Role of Christian Primitivism," 49–61.

10. Lucy Mack Smith, *History of the Prophet Joseph* (Salt Lake City: Improvement Era, 1902), 55, 33, 45.

11. George L. Burnham, *Voice of Truth*, July 27, 1844, quoted in David L. Rowe, "A New Perspective on the Burned-Over District: The Millerites in Upstate New York," *Church History* 47 (Dec. 1978): 415.

12. L. Smith, *History*, 1, 3–4. The statistics of Laurence Yorgason point further to the pervasiveness of seekerism among early Mormons. He found that 62 percent of those who became Mormons had earlier changed their church affiliation at least twice. See "Some Demographic Aspects of One Hundred Early Mormon Converts, 1830–37," M.A. thesis, Brigham Young University, 1974, 49–50, cited in Alexander, "Wilford Woodruff," 3.

13. On the restoration vision of Roger Williams, see C. Leonard Allen, "'The Restauration of Zion': Roger Williams and the Quest for the Primitive Church," Ph.D. diss., University of Iowa, 1984.

14. Mario S. De Pillis has argued that the quest for authority was from the beginning the fundamental issue in Mormonism. See "The Quest for Religious Authority and the Rise of Mormonism," *Dialogue* 1 (Mar. 1966): 68–88.

15. Parley P. Pratt, *The Autobiography of Parley Parker Pratt, One of the Twelve Apostles of the Church of Jesus Christ of Latter-Day Saints*, ed. Parley Parker Pratt (Chicago: Law, King, and Law, 1888), 32, 42.

16. 1 Nephi 14:10, 17.

17. Jan Shipps has argued that Mormonism was not, like the "Christians" or Disciples, a mere imitation of primitive Christianity, but rather a radical tear "across history's seamless web to provide humanity with a new world wherein God is actively involved" (*Mormonism* 72). It is largely for this reason that she describes Mormonism as a "new religious tradition."

18. See P. Pratt, *Autobiography;* and Andrew Jenson, *Latter-day Saint Biographical Encyclopedia* (Salt Lake City: Andrew Jenson History Company, 1901), 1:83–85. Parley P. Pratt had converted Elenore McLean, who became convinced that Gentile marriages were il-

legitimate since they lacked priesthood authority. She therefore left her husband, Hector, and became Pratt's wife. Hector then murdered Pratt. See Richard S. VanWagoner, *Mormon Polygamy: A History* (Salt Lake City: Signature Books, 1986), 43–44.

19. David J. Whittaker, "Early Mormon Pamphleteering," Ph.D. diss., Brigham Young University, 1982, 58. Whittaker cites as the source of this designation of Pratt an unpublished essay by Peter Crawley, "Parley P. Pratt: The Father of Mormon Pamphleteering."

20. Parley P. Pratt, *A Voice of Warning and Instruction to All People, Containing a Declaration of the Faith and Doctrine of the Church of the Latter Day Saints, Commonly Called Mormons* (New York: W. Sanford, 1837); Crawley, "Passage of Mormon Primitivism," 33; and introduction to *Key to the Science of Theology/A Voice of Warning* (Salt Lake City: Deseret Book, 1978), i–ii.

21. Crawley, "Passage of Mormon Primitivism," 33.

22. Whittaker, "Early Mormon Pamphleteering," 59n.30; introduction to *Key to the Science of Theology*, i.

23. Parley P. Pratt, *Key to the Science of Theology: Designed as an Introduction to the First Principles of Spiritual Philosophy; Religion; Law and Government; as Delivered by the Ancients, and as Restored in This Age, for the Final Development of Universal Peace, Truth, and Knowledge* (Liverpool, England: F. D. Richards, 1855).

24. Introduction to *Key to the Science of Theology*, ii; Whittaker, "Early Mormon Pamphleteering," 62–63.

25. P. Pratt, *Voice of Warning*, 147.

26. Ibid., 154–55.

27. P. Pratt, *Key to the Science of Theology*, 26–27.

28. Thomas Campbell, "Open Letter to Sidney Rigdon," *Painesville (Ohio) Telegraph*, 15 Feb. 1831, quoted in Frances W. Kirkham, *A New Witness for Christ in America: The Book of Mormon* (Independence, Mo.: Press of Zion's Printing and Publishing, 1942), 2:93.

29. Alexander Campbell, "Sidney Rigdon," *Millennial Harbinger* 2 (7 Feb. 1831): 100.

30. P. Pratt, *Key to the Science of Theology*, 108–9.

31. P. Pratt, "The Fountain of Knowledge," *Writings*, 20–21.

32. Ibid., 19–20.

33. Parley P. Pratt, *Late Persecution of the Church of Jesus Christ of Latter Day Saints: Ten Thousand American Citizens Robbed, Plundered, and Banished; Others Imprisoned, and Others Martyred for Their Religion . . . Written in Prison* (New York: J. W. Harrison, 1840), iii; Parley P. Pratt, "Grapes from Thorns, and Figs from Thistles," *Writings*, 303.

34. P. Pratt, "Grapes from Thorns," 303.

35. Ibid., 303–4.

36. P. Pratt, *Key to the Science of Theology*, 70.

37. Ibid., 18–19.

38. This is a very different argument from that made by Robert N. Hullinger in

Mormon Answer to Skepticism: Why Joseph Smith Wrote the Book of Mormon (St. Louis: Clayton, 1980). Hullinger argues that Mormonism was essentially a response to skepticism and deism.

39. Edward Wheelock Tullidge, *The Women of Mormonism* (New York: Tullidge and Crandall, 1877), 41–42; Eliza R. Snow, *Eliza R. Snow: An Immortal: Selected Writings of Eliza R. Snow* (N.p.: Nicholas G. Morgan Sr. Foundation, 1957), 1:5ff.

40. John Murdock, *An Abridged Record of the Life of John Murdock, Taken from His Journal by Himself*, 4–10, copy loaned by Milton V. Backman, Brigham Young University.

41. P. Pratt, *Voice of Warning*, 118–19.

42. P. Pratt, "Grapes from Thorns," 303.

43. Doctrine and Covenants 131:7.

44. Parley P. Pratt, "Immortality and Eternal Life of the Material Body," *Writings*, 28; Parley P. Pratt, "The World Turned upside Down," *Writings*, 28, 65. Likewise, Joseph Smith had declared in 1833 that "the elements are eternal" (Doctrine and Covenants 93:33).

45. P. Pratt, *Key to the Science of Theology*, 30.

46. P. Pratt, "Fountains of Knowledge," 18. Cf. P. Pratt, *Key to the Science of Theology*, 32–33.

47. P. Pratt, *Key to the Science of Theology*, 155–56.

48. P. Pratt, "Fountains of Knowledge," 18.

49. Alexander Campbell, "Delusions," *Millennial Harbinger* 2 (7 Feb. 1831): 93, 87.

50. Walter Scott, "Mormon Bible—No. 1," *Evangelist*, n.s., 9 (1 Jan. 1841): 18–19.

51. P. Pratt, *Late Persecution*, 171; P. Pratt, "Proclamation of the Gospel," *Writings*, 163.

52. "An Epistle of the Twelve Apostles, to the Brethren Scattered Abroad on the Continent of America," in J. Smith, *History of the Church*, 4:437.

53. Moses 7, esp. verses 21, 23, and 62–65. For Jackson County, Missouri, as Zion, see J. Smith, *History of the Church*, 1:189, and Doctrine and Covenants 57:1–3. For America as Zion, see J. Smith, *History of the Church*, 6:318–19. For Davies County as the Garden of Eden, see Doctrine and Covenants 107:53–57, 116.

54. P. Pratt, *Voice of Warning*, 177.

55. J. Smith, *History of the Church*, 1:358; Parley P. Pratt, "Proclamation of the Twelve Apostles," *Writings*, 13.

56. *Millennial Star* 6 (1845): 140–42, quoted in Robert Flanders, "To Transform History: Early Mormon Culture and the Concept of Time and Space," *Church History* 40 (Mar. 1971): 111–12. Flanders's article is a germinal statement of early Mormon attempts to collapse both space and time into their restored millennial kingdom.

57. J. Smith, *History of the Church*, 4:277; Doctrine and Covenants 124:27–39. Cf. Robert Bruce Flanders, *Nauvoo: Kingdom on the Mississippi* (Urbana: University of Illinois Press, 1965), 190–91.

58. P. Pratt, *Key to the Science of Theology*, 128–29; Klaus J. Hansen, *Mormonism and the American Experience* (Chicago: University of Chicago Press, 1981), 103.

59. J. Smith, *History of the Church,* 5:391–92; Doctrine and Covenants 132:19–20. The revelation on celestial marriage was never made public by Joseph Smith during his lifetime, but only in 1852 by Brigham Young. See Flanders, *Nauvoo,* 274–75.

60. Parley P. Pratt, "A Letter to the Queen," *Writings,* 97, 100, 108.

61. P. Pratt, *Voice of Warning,* 140–42. This chapter, which is the pivotal "warning" section of *Voice of Warning,* has been deleted from the 1978 edition.

62. Doctrine and Covenants 134; J. Smith, *History of the Church,* 6:208–9.

63. Doctrine and Covenants 134:11.

64. Klaus J. Hansen, *Quest for Empire: The Political Kingdom of God and the Council of Fifty in Mormon History,* rev. ed. (Lincoln: University of Nebraska Press, 1974), 23. Grant Underwood faults Hansen's social deprivation perspective in "Early Mormon Millenarianism: Another Look," *Church History* 54 (June 1985): 222–23. But see also Grant Underwood, "Millenarianism and the Early Mormon Mind," *Journal of Mormon History* 9 (1982): 45.

65. P. Pratt, *Key to the Science of Theology,* 135.

66. Orson Pratt, *The Kingdom of God* (Liverpool, England, 1851), 1. The antipluralism implicit in the early Mormon vision of the kingdom of God should not be surprising, especially given the Old Testament theocratic roots of this vision. Indeed, Richard Bushman has argued effectively that the "templates for Book of Mormon politics" were biblical, not American. Bushman notes that "Book of Mormon government by Jacksonian standards was no democracy. . . . Looking at the Book of Mormon as a whole, it seems clear that most of the principles associated with the American Constitution are slighted or disregarded altogether." Bushman concluded that "Book of Mormon political attitudes have Old World precedents, particularly in the history of the Israelite nation." See "The Book of Mormon and the American Revolution," *Brigham Young University Studies* 17 (Autumn 1976): 16–19.

67. Doctrine and Covenants 91:6–7.

68. P. Pratt, *Key to the Science of Theology,* 134.

2

Mormons

Dean L. May

The Mormons are perhaps the only American ethnic group whose principal migration began as an effort to move out of the United States. Moreover, this migration of the main body of Mormons from western Illinois to the Rocky Mountains in the late 1840s imprinted upon the group a self-consciousness gained through prior experience in the Midwest. The Mormons have been influenced subsequently by ritual tales of privation, wandering, and delivery under God's hand, precisely as the Jews have been influenced by their stories of the Exodus. A significant consequence of this tradition has been the development of an enduring sense of territoriality that has given a distinctive cast to Mormon group consciousness. It differentiates the Mormons from members of other sects and lends support to the judgment of the sociologist Thomas F. O'Dea that the Mormons "represent the clearest example to be found in our national history of the evolution of a native and indigenously developed ethnic minority."

Origins

The Mormons are the product of a religious movement begun in 1830 by Joseph Smith Jr. (1805–44), third son in an upstate New York farming family. Disturbed by the competing claims of various churches to divine favor, Smith in 1820 prayed for guidance. The ensuing religious experiences reported by Smith served to unify his own family and those of his friends in a new faith seen by his followers as a "restoration" of primitive Christianity in preparation for the return of the Savior. Within a short time Smith had gone beyond the millennialist and restorationist concerns of such contemporaries as William C. Miller and Alexander Campbell. He claimed that as part of his prophetic mission he had been instructed to restore "all things," by which he meant God's most significant communications to people, from all previous

Judeo-Christian revelatory epochs or "dispensations." In maintaining that Christ's earthly ministry was pivotal but not an all-encompassing or final revelatory epoch, Smith made himself a pariah among the divines of restorationist and millennialist sects.

Smith began to draw heavily from the Old Testament and over the next several years instituted the building of temples, an elaborate temple ritual, the practice of plural marriage (technically polygyny, but commonly referred to as polygamy), and a series of related doctrines and practices. He drew also from precedents in the Book of Mormon, an additional book of Scriptures he claimed to have translated from records inscribed on goldlike plates provided by an angel, which described the religious history of a pre-Columbian group of New World Christians. For the rest of his life Smith endeavored to build the disparate thousands who became his followers into a unified, orderly, covenanted society. He taught that the Latter-day Saints, as they called themselves, were a people whose special relationship to God through their prophets would prepare them for a unique and critical role in the Christian eschatological scheme. Smith's early followers seemed to be seeking within the authoritarian structure and social order of the prophet's revealed religion a haven from the chaotic and centrifugal tendencies they saw about them in Jacksonian America. Profoundly attracted to the liberal, republican ideologies of antebellum America, they nonetheless feared the social consequences of such ideologies and sought refuge in Mormonism.

The Midwest Migrations

Smith's earliest activities as a religious leader took place near his parents' home in Manchester Township, New York, and the home of his parents-in-law near Harmony in north-central Pennsylvania. The Book of Mormon was printed in Palmyra, New York, in the early spring of 1830, and on 6 April of that year Smith and a few friends formally incorporated as the Church of Christ (changed in 1838 to the Church of Jesus Christ of Latter-day Saints).

Four of Smith's disciples undertook the first major missionary journey in the fall of 1830. Traveling through newly settled farming areas in northeastern Ohio, they preached to several congregations of Alexander Campbell's followers and attracted more than one hundred converts, including an important minister, Sidney Rigdon (1793–1876). Within a short time there were more followers of the new faith in Ohio than in New York. In December 1830 Smith announced a revelation commanding the New York congregations to migrate to Ohio. (Smith's revelations, often recorded verbatim, were regarded by himself and his followers as direct communications from God.) This first Mormon migration, of perhaps seventy persons, was accomplished in the early months of 1831. The region around Kirtland, Ohio, a few miles east of Cleveland, became a major center of Mormon activity for the next seven years; the prophet himself resided there during most of the period.

Smith made it clear as early as February 1831, however, that the Ohio settlements were staging areas for a more important migration to a site he would designate as "Zion" or "The New Jerusalem," which was to be a millennial administrative center. Revelations in July 1831 named Jackson County, Missouri, which encompasses present-day Kansas City, then America's westernmost frontier, as the place where the Saints were to "gather." Migration and the purchase of land in Missouri began immediately.

Mormons gathering to Missouri from all parts of the country were asked to enter into a communal order called Consecration and Stewardship. Their different social values and rapidly increasing numbers quickly caused concern among earlier, non-Mormon Missouri settlers. The Mormons—almost all New Englanders, clannish, communal, and generally opposed to slavery—threatened to take over an area previously pioneered by migrants from the hill countries of Tennessee and Kentucky. The pro-slavery earlier settlers, unsuccessful in legal attempts to dislodge the newcomers, resorted to mob action in July 1833. They destroyed the Mormon press and threatened further violence if the Saints did not leave the country. By October the mob made good its threats; twelve hundred or more Mormons fled northward across Missouri into Clay County. In 1836 they were asked to move again and reached an informal agreement that a new county, Caldwell, would be created in which they could settle.

Mormons settled in considerable numbers in Caldwell County and built a capital city, Far West, which by 1838 had an estimated population of five thousand. Early in that year the Kirtland Saints arrived; they had fled the Ohio center because of financial difficulties and bitter feelings arising from the failure of a bank sponsored by Mormon leaders. By autumn political differences between Mormons and non-Mormons in Missouri led to mutual distrust and hostility and in October the governor ordered that the Mormons be "exterminated or driven from the state." After numerous confrontations and several dozen deaths, Smith and a few close friends were taken into custody, and mobs once again moved into Mormon settlements. This time the Saints fled northeastward into Iowa and Illinois.

Smith escaped from prison in April and found his followers in Illinois gathering near an undeveloped tract of land called Commerce. The Mormons renamed the site Nauvoo and began immediately to build a city. Under a liberal charter and fed by a stream of immigrants converted through remarkably successful missionary efforts in England, Canada, and the United States, Nauvoo grew rapidly. In 1844 secret plans were laid for establishing a political kingdom of God, to be governed by a Council of Fifty which would include some non-Mormons and would be responsible for civil and temporal affairs generally. Early that same year Smith, unable in conscience to support either Henry Clay or James K. Polk for the U.S. presidency, declared himself a candidate. By that time, however, dissension between Mormons and non-Mormons was rising, stirred by apostates offended by the clandestine introduction in the early 1840s of the practice of plural marriage. In June Smith was taken into custody. On 27 June an armed mob broke into the Carthage, Illinois, jail where Smith was confined and killed him and his brother.

The Exodus

The ensuing struggle for succession led to considerable splintering, but Brigham Young (1801–77), president of the Council of the Twelve Apostles, quickly gained the confidence of most of Smith's followers and assumed leadership of the church. However, the prophet's death did not resolve the basic differences between Mormons and non-Mormons in western Illinois. By February 1846 relations between the two groups had become so critical that abandonment of Nauvoo could no longer be delayed. The Mormons, feeling that U.S. officials had failed to protect their constitutional rights, began to organize wagon trains and cross the Mississippi westward into Iowa.

Variously estimated at between ten thousand and fifteen thousand people, the group moved across Iowa, settling temporarily along the Missouri in the present Omaha and Council Bluffs area. In the spring of 1847 migration began to an area then known as Upper California in Mexican Territory. Pioneer trains arrived in the Salt Lake Valley in late July. Some months later, in February 1848, the new homesite became part of the United States through the Treaty of Guadalupe Hidalgo. Subsequent migration brought most of the refugees from Missouri to the Great Basin by 1852. Mormon converts from Europe and North America continued to follow the same route overland until 1869, after which time most traveled by rail.

Tales of "the exodus" or "the trek" occupy a large place in Mormon folk tradition. Whether or not their ancestors were involved in the migration, most Mormons can recall stories of sacrifice and heroism associated with the experience. Although the eight-hundred-mile overland journey was arduous, the Mormons probably suffered a lower mortality than non-Mormon companies making the same trip, because from the outset their migration was well planned to minimize hazards. Brigham Young announced a revelation in January 1847 that commanded organization of the "Camps of Israel" into groups of ten, fifty, and one hundred wagons supervised by appointed captains at each level, a pattern paralleling that of the ancient Israelites and followed in most subsequent Mormon migrations. Farm implements, seeds, tree cuttings, and other necessities for successful colonization were included among the supplies. Poor families were distributed among the trains so that a number of the better provided would be able to share responsibility for their well-being.

Transporting the residents of the Missouri River settlements to the Great Basin severely taxed the Mormons' resources but did not prevent church leaders from setting up at the same time an elaborate system for bringing European converts to the newfound Zion. Most European immigrants sailed from Liverpool on ships chartered by the church. In the United States, Mormon agents were stationed at port cities and along the overland route to make arrangements each season for transportation of complete immigrant companies to Salt Lake City. In the late 1860s, as the Transcontinental Railroad extended westward, church teams were sent to the railhead to escort the immigrants to the Mormon capital. Church officials assumed responsibility for placing new immigrants in temporary homes and jobs until permanent settlement could be arranged. Completion of the railroad in 1869 eased the logistical problems of transporting immigrants to Utah and greatly changed the nature of the migration and its impact upon its participants.

Through the Perpetual Emigrating Fund the church contributed considerably to the costs as well as the logistics of migration. This revolving fund was established in 1850 and continued in use until 1887 when the federal government, during an antipolygamy campaign, revoked the church's charter and seized its assets. During its nearly forty years of operation the fund directly assisted some 50,000 European immigrants. Movement from the areas of Mormon mission activity occurred in distinct phases, paralleling the general migration to the United States from those same areas. Emigration from England, Scotland, and Wales began shortly after the first Mormon mission to England in 1837 and remained fairly strong throughout the rest of the century. Scandinavian emigration began in the 1850s, reached large numbers in the 1860s, and remained strong through the 1880s. Mormon missionaries of the period traveled through most of Europe, Asia, and Oceania but were most successful in Protestant countries, especially the British Isles, Scandinavia, and Germany. Total Mormon emigration from these areas up to 1957 is estimated at some 54,000 from Great Britain, 28,041 from Scandinavia, and 13,755 from

Germany. Since the nineteenth-century missionaries urged their European converts to gather to Zion, the resultant emigration caused local congregations to be unstable and impermanent. Most European Mormons of the period accepted fully the spirit of a contemporary Mormon hymn, "Oh Babylon, Oh Babylon, we bid thee farewell, / We're going to the mountains of Ephraim to dwell."

Settlement in the Great Basin

To these many thousands, dwelling amidst the mountains of Ephraim was far less pleasant in fact than it had been in prospect. The Great Basin was isolated, eight hundred miles in either direction from the nearest settlements. The high cost of imported goods made self-sufficiency a necessary goal, but the environment did not favor such an effort. Timber was scarce, the annual rainfall averaged only twelve to fifteen inches, there was little arable land, and much of the area was inhabited by Shoshonean-speaking Indians. The most promising valleys of the region stretched along the western edge of the Wasatch Mountains, which run north and south through the middle of what is now Utah. Rising abruptly several thousand feet above the valley floors, they trap winter snows and distribute them evenly during the summer along a network of small rivers and streams—a system ideally suited to irrigated agriculture.

Colonization spread from the Salt Lake Valley to low valleys lying northward as far as Brigham City and southward to the subtropical region around present-day St. George. Outlying colonies were founded in the early 1850s in San Bernardino, California; Las Vegas and Carson Valley, Nevada; and on the Salmon River in Idaho. But most of these settlements faltered for various reasons; those still viable in 1857 were abandoned and their inhabitants recalled when a federal army was sent to quell an alleged uprising among the Mormons and install the territory's first non-Mormon governor. Despite such setbacks the population grew rapidly, increasing from 11,000 in 1850 to 41,000 in 1860 and 87,000 in 1870. As the early sites filled and began to strain the resources of the immediate environment, higher mountain valleys were settled until, beginning in the 1870s, it became necessary to send colonizing missions to Arizona, Nevada, New Mexico, and Wyoming, as well as Alberta, Canada, and Sonora and Chihuahua, Mexico. The normal pattern was to found a central town under church "call" and direction that then served as a base for the settlement of satellite villages. The last church-sponsored migration, beginning in 1900, was to the Big Horn Basin in northern Wyoming.

As Mormons colonized area after area, they developed a pattern of settlement that was replicated in nearly every colonization venture through the turn of the century. When the Mormons planned a colonizing mission, church authorities "called" specific families to participate in the venture, making certain that the group included people who possessed the skills and trades necessary to the colony's success. Church and often civil government for the new location were organized before departure (the two were in fact nearly indistinguishable). Leaders planned and organized the supplies and equipment, and the whole company departed on a prearranged date from a designated staging site. Once the colonists reached the new territory, they immediately began to survey and lay out the town and the farm plots, which, following instructions Joseph Smith had given in 1833, were outside of town. Thereafter, the colonists did their private work (the plowing of individual parcels or building a home) during time left from assigned public work—the building of canals, mills, fences, churches, and schools. After this initial planting, smaller towns were founded in the vicinity on a more individualistic basis. The physiognomy of Mormon towns was remarkably uniform because of the need to find land, water, and timber nearby and because the same layout and planning procedure were used in founding both "called" and spontaneously settled towns.

The practice of living within the town and farming outside it, rarely seen in the United States outside New England and Spanish-settled areas, fostered an intense social and religious life. The strong communal sentiment of the townsfolk was reinforced by doctrines contained in Smith's revelations and by deliberate church policy. Many of these towns remained only slightly altered until the 1920s, their traditional pattern of life established and reinforced over three generations. The western Mormon towns nurtured a provincial and religious self-consciousness into an incipient ethnicity.

Almost from its initial settlement, the limited resources of any one locality encouraged further migration of those forming new families. In the twentieth century, however, the direction of this movement shifted from founding new agricultural towns to further populating the urban centers of Salt Lake City, Provo, and Ogden. In the 1930s and 1940s there was also substantial migration to cities in neighboring states, especially California. Nonetheless the proportion of Mormons in Utah's population continued to grow, aided by the return migration of the 1960s and 1970s and a continuing high birthrate. Mormons made up 56 percent of the Utah population in 1920 and 72 percent in 1970. Mormon settlement did not observe state lines. One authority has coined the term "Deseret Mormons" for the central body of Mormons raised in those areas of the West where Mormon influence predominates—primarily Utah; much of southeastern Idaho; Star Valley, the Bear River Valley, and the Big Horn Basin in Wyoming; the San Luis Valley in Colorado; the Ramah Valley in New Mexico; the Little Colorado River Valley in northern Arizona and certain towns in the Salt and Gila River valleys; a few towns in Chihuahua and Sonora, Mexico; extensive parts of southern Alberta, Canada; and a few localities in Washington, Oregon, and California. Deseret was the Mormon name for the state planned by Brigham Young shortly after the Mormons settled in the Great Basin, an entity much larger than the present boundaries of Utah.

During the nineteenth century, European converts to Mormonism were expected to leave their homeland and go to Deseret, where they were utterly dependent upon the Utah church leaders for both temporal and spiritual guidance. Under these circumstances the immigrants rapidly assimilated and use of their native languages soon died out. An early Mormon apostle expressed this rapid assimilation as an avowed aim of church leaders. After visiting a settlement where ethnic differences seemed to be inhibiting the development of a native iron industry in 1852, he reported: "We found a Scotch party, a Welch party, an English party, and an American party and we turned Iron Masters and undertook to put all these parties through the furnace, and run out a party of Saints for building up the Kingdom of God."

Brigham Young, in his efforts to counter the appeal of California in the 1840s, spoke of the Great Basin as a "good place to make Saints." He referred not just to the growth of piety, but to the development of a people sufficiently distinct in values and traditions from other Americans to be regarded as a separate nation; he even went so far as to encourage the development and use of a new alphabet to facilitate written communication among Saints and widen the gulf between Deseret and the rest of America. The present distinctiveness of the Mormon core or culture region suggests that Brigham Young succeeded in this effort better than he might have expected. In the twentieth century, however, rapid growth outside the Deseret area has caused some observers to suggest that Mormon distinctiveness may eventually be lost through too great a geographic diffusion. Certainly there are gradations in the degree to which members of the church are imbued with the Mormon culture, but several factors seem to favor perpetuation of Deseret influence over the entire church membership for the foreseeable future. There were almost 4 million Mormons throughout the world in 1977; of these, over 1.4 million (36 percent) were from Utah, Idaho, Wyoming, Arizona, Nevada, Colorado, and New Mexico. This substantial minority exercises a commanding influence upon the church and church members elsewhere in the world.

Deseret Mormons are almost always agents in conversion to Mormonism, a process which in most cases results in the converts' abandoning old social relations and forming new ones within the church; converts are cut off from old values and historical roots and establish new ones within the context of the newly acquired religion. Throughout this process Deseret Mormons are the dominant role models. The missionaries who encourage conversion, the presidents of mission areas, and the central church leaders who visit the missions periodically are for the most part Deseret Mormons. The voice of the predominantly Utah-born central church leadership—the "general authorities," as they are known to church members—seems to strike at least as strong a resonance in mission areas as it does in Deseret. The degree to which an individual participates in Mormon culture is influenced partly by length of membership in the church but is affected more strongly by the amount of interaction with other Mormons. Interaction in turn is determined primarily by commitment to the church and activity in its various programs. Nonparticipating Salt Lake City Mormons are often less acculturated than recent Nashville converts. Although it was formed in a particular region by particular circumstances, Mormon society is constantly being revitalized in mission areas.

Not all followers of Joseph Smith shared in the Utah experience. At the time of the founder's death several splinter groups formed, some of which still exist, most with only a few members. In the 1850s followers of several such groups began to unite as the Reorganized Church of Jesus Christ of Latter Day Saints. The prophet's widow Emma and her family had not moved West and Smith's descendants became the leaders of the "Reorganization." As the historian Jan Shipps has noted, Latter-day Saints who joined the Reorganization were attracted more by the Christian primitivism in Smith's teachings than by the neo-Judaic Christianity evidenced in temple rituals, polygamy, and the political kingdom concept. Because they did not participate in the exodus west and escaped the traumatic experiences of the pioneer Utah period, the membership of the Reorganized church is culturally less distinctive than that of the Utah church. Now centered in Missouri, the church has over 213,000 members.

Mormon Culture

Rapid assimilation of ethnic groups entering the Mormon Zion has led to considerable uniformity in cultural expression. European immigrants were not moving out of their old life into relative freedom, as happened elsewhere in the American West, but rather into tightly structured, hierarchical, closely knit villages where pressures to conform were great. Anti-Mormon writers of the nineteenth century saw Mormon society as a form of oriental despotism, and although most Mormons, then as now, voluntarily accepted the pervasive influence of the church in their lives, critics quite rightly saw the system as alien to the more liberal and individualistic forms of social organization prevailing elsewhere in America. Most forms of creative expression were sponsored by the church, related to religion, and stressed group rather than individual achievement. Even in contemporary Mormon society there is discernibly greater emphasis on the performing arts than on the visual arts. There is widespread emphasis on group singing, in choirs and in congregations; the well-known Mormon Tabernacle Choir is a great source of local pride and the epitome of Mormon cultural expression. Musical ensembles, especially bands, have been widespread among the Mormons since the mid-nineteenth century. The brass bands that were used to encourage members of immigrant trains crossing the plains became a symbol of determination and cheerfulness in the face of hardship. Musical training programs begin early in Utah public schools and are well developed in high school curriculums.

Plays and theatrical productions have also been a favorite cultural activity of the Mormons. The Salt Lake Theater, built in 1861, was long the center of drama in the Rocky Mountain West, a source of so much community pride that Salt Lake City now boasts two replicas of the original structure. The church continues to sponsor theatrical productions by the youth of each congregation and until the 1980s subsidized the Promised Valley Playhouse in downtown Salt Lake City. Church members in several areas produce extravagant pageants depicting the Mormon past. The most famous is the pageant at the Hill Cumorah near Palmyra, New York, reported by Joseph Smith as the site where he acquired the records from which the Book of Mormon was translated. As of 1980 Salt Lake City supported six professional theater companies, an impressive number for a metropolitan area of five hundred thousand people. Dancing has also been popular since the nineteenth century both as a social activity and as a form of creative expression. The city's five dance companies have made Utah a center for dance in the West. Ballet West and the Utah Repertory Dance Theater have national reputations for excellence.

More individualistic forms of creative expression have not received the widespread support given to performing arts. Mormon painters have produced numerous portraits of church leaders, murals to decorate the interiors of temples and churches, and traveling shows to illustrate church history. Representational painting has been patronized almost to the exclusion of abstract art. There are four notable public galleries in all of Utah: the Utah Museum of Fine Arts on the University of Utah campus in Salt Lake City, the Salt Lake Art Center, the Museum of Art on the Brigham Young University campus, and the

Springville Art Museum south of Provo, a remnant of WPA activities during the Great Depression.

Both the domestic and the church architecture of the Mormons are largely derivative—adaptations of styles popular in the greater United States. There is a growing emphasis in church or "meetinghouse" architecture upon the plain and practical over the decorative. The meetinghouses demonstrate the social nature of Mormon life: in addition to a chapel for worship they always include a gymnasium with a stage for both theater and sports, numerous classrooms, a room for women's activities, a fully equipped kitchen, a library, a Scout room, and a chapel for small children. Mormons have a strong tradition of landscape architecture and give considerable attention to beautifying church and public buildings with shrubs, lawns, and trees. The relative scarcity of timber in Utah and the early teaching of Joseph Smith favoring stone or brick over frame construction have led to the widespread use of brick for houses. In the twentieth century Chicago and California have been the main sources of innovation in Utah's domestic architecture.

Temples are special structures reserved to the faithful for the most sacred rituals, and as such are very different in character from the spare functionalism of the meetinghouses. Mormon architects have used contemporary architectural styles in the temples, but their desire to make a significant statement in a stone structure of considerable size often gives the temples a distinctive, exotic character. Most temples in recent use have been lavishly decorated with murals, carved woods, and ornate and costly furniture and appointments, although those designed in the 1960s and 1970s show traces of the utilitarianism that characterizes Mormon meetinghouses.

Mormon writers, like Mormon painters, have worked within a fairly narrow range of acceptable forms. There are a number of excellent and powerful Mormon hymns. Periodical literature was produced in quantity at every Mormon stopping place from Missouri to Utah, and even in remote Utah towns manuscript newspapers were laboriously transcribed and circulated among the townspeople. The most important publications include the *Evening and Morning Star* (Independence, Missouri, 1832–33; Kirtland, Ohio, 1833–34), the *Times and Seasons* (Nauvoo, Illinois, 1839–46), the *Millennial Star* (Liverpool, England, 1840–1970), the *Frontier Guardian* (Kanesville, Iowa, 1849–52), the *Deseret News* (Salt Lake City, f. 1850), the *Woman's Exponent* (Salt Lake City, 1872–1914), and the *Improvement Era* (Salt Lake City, 1897–1970). At least fourteen newspapers and as many magazines have been printed by church members as organs of the church since 1832. Most served primarily to communicate events of interest to other Mormons, church doctrine and policy, and didactic stories and messages. The first journal addressing itself to Mormon scholars was *Brigham Young University Studies* (f. 1959); in 1966 *Dialogue: A Journal of Mormon Thought* was founded in the face of strong disapproval by many in the church hierarchy. *Dialogue* was followed by the *Journal of Mormon History* (f. 1974), *Exponent II* (f. 1974), and *Sunstone* (f. 1975), the latter two serving especially Mormon women and college students. None of the scholarly journals is an official organ of the church; in fact all but *Brigham Young University Studies* and the *Journal of Mormon History* are printed by small groups without official sponsoring organizations. Creative writing became a Mormon literary endeavor relatively late, perhaps partly because the early church disapproved of novels. Vardis Fisher (1895–1968) is the most powerful novelist to write from a Mormon background. Many of his works, beginning with *Toilers of the Hills* (1929), are set in the Mormon West, and some, such as *Children of God* (1939), deal directly with the Mormon experience. Other novelists of Latter-day Saint background who have used Mormon themes are Samuel W. Taylor (1907–97), Virginia Sorensen (1912–91), Maurine Whipple (1904–92), and Levi S. Peterson (b. 1933). Non-Mormons Dale L. Morgan and Wallace Stegner have also contributed significantly to the literature of Mormonism.

There is a strong tradition of folk expression in Mormon literature. Personal journals and life histories abound, many of them eloquent and compelling. Stories of persecution, migration, and deeds of the pioneers are told and retold in a form which has become almost a Mormon litany. Stories of miraculous healings, visions, and visitations—and especially of such experiences on missions—are recited often. Most of these, like the writing of hymns and the periodical literature, serve to reinforce commitment and belief among the faithful; indeed a whole genre of such stories has developed, called by church members "faith-promoting experiences." There is also a notable collection of humorous stories and songs, some containing elements of self-ridicule, but these are not as pervasive in the folk repertoire as the more serious themes.

What Mormons may lack in creative writing they make up in technological innovations. It is paradoxical that a group that historically has been hostile to the outside world and its influences has always embraced technology fully. The arid Utah climate forced Mormons into pioneering the use of irrigated agriculture as the base of a region-wide economy. Speculators in other arid western areas pointed to Mormon accomplishments in the 1880s and 1890s as models of what could be accomplished through irrigation. The many streams flowing west from the Wasatch Mountains did not require costly large-scale dams and canals, however, and Mormon achievement rested more with evolving institutions for the control and apportionment of water than with developing the technology of surveying, designing, and constructing dams and irrigation works.

In other enterprises, however, the Mormons assiduously borrowed technologies already developed by others. In the mid-1850s, long before the sugar beet industry was established in America, church leaders purchased machinery for a sugar factory in France, had it shipped across the Atlantic and up the Missouri, then had it hauled by wagon across Nebraska and Wyoming to Utah in an unsuccessful effort to develop a native sugar industry. Similarly Mormons attempted without success to establish an iron industry in southern Utah in the 1850s. A successful paper plant was set up in 1851 and small textile mills were established in many Utah towns; some mills operated into the twentieth century. The state was among the first to extend electrical service to rural areas. The church uses the latest computer systems in handling population, mission, and financial data. Numerous church visitors' centers feature electronic displays as teaching and proselytizing devices. Perhaps most remarkably, parts of sacred temple rituals are now generally presented on film to participants.

Economic Institutions

Although the Mormon church invests successfully in the markets that sustain the American economy and there is much rhetoric about devotion to free enterprise, economic institutions functioning within the church are still strongly flavored by communal laws contained in Joseph Smith's revelations. The prophet's Law of Consecration and Stewardship stressed self-sufficiency, simplicity in living, and consumption according to need but preserved some elements of individualism—particularly the vision of entrepreneurial activity as an engine of economic progress and the marketplace as chief allocutor of goods and services. It also placed capital investment in the hands of church leaders and gave special attention to an internal system of poor relief.

Under Smith's plan, a new male communicant entering the system would agree to the "consecration" of all his possessions to the church and receive in return, as a lifetime lease contingent upon faithfulness, a "stewardship" consisting of materials and property needed to pursue a chosen trade and to domicile a family. The member was to use individual initiative to improve his stewardship during the ensuing year and report his progress to the bishop at the end of each year. During this "stewardship interview," any surplus above the "wants, needs, and circumstances" of the family was to be defined and given voluntarily to a general fund for relief for the poor, for general church expenses, and for providing stewardships to new members and those coming of age. The system was practiced in Missouri in 1831–33, but failed. It was replaced in the 1840s by the "lesser law" of tithing, until, as church leaders explained, the Saints could demonstrate their worthiness to live the higher law.

Though organized under Consecration and Stewardship for only brief periods, the church has consistently taken an interest in and considerable responsibility for the temporal as well as the spiritual aspects of the lives of Mormons. Brigham Young assumed much of the burden of directing the development of Utah's economy during his lifetime. Between 1848 and 1852 the church minted gold coins and issued its own currency. Under Young's guidance the church established a large public works program to alleviate unemployment, especially for converts newly arrived in Utah who had not yet found permanent situations. It was under church call that strenuous efforts were made to develop industries in Utah in the 1850s.

Nor were the teachings of Joseph Smith forgotten in the rush to develop the newly settled land. Encouraged by some church leaders, a movement to consecrate private possessions and property to the church began in the mid-1850s. Perhaps as many as half the family heads executed deeds assigning their possessions to the church, although the church never actually took possession of the consecrated property. The cooperative movement of the late 1860s established cooperative retail stores in most Mormon towns and cooperative manufacturing establishments in many localities. Some of the retail stores lasted into the 1930s, and Zion's Cooperative Mercantile Institution (f. 1869), or ZCMI, long since shorn of its cooperative aims, is one of Utah's major department stores.

Some church leaders saw the cooperative movement as a preliminary step toward full practice of Joseph Smith's communalism. A more dramatic move in that direction took place in 1874, when the aging Brigham Young attempted to place the whole economy under the United Order of Enoch, his own version of Smith's system. In that year the economic resources of over two hundred Mormon towns were organized into some form of the United Order. The aims were to combine capital, promote regional and local self-sufficiency, divide labor, equalize consumption, and generally to "unite the temporal and spiritual interests of the Saints." Although most United Orders failed almost immediately, efforts to make the system viable continued until the mid-1880s, when they were abandoned by a new church leadership less committed to communalism and under strong pressure from the U.S. government to abandon distinctive Mormon economic and social practices. Mormons have remained strongly impressed with the notion, instilled by a century of preaching and exhortation, that they are under obligation to prepare for a time when they might be asked to live the United Order again.

The Welfare Program, a church-sponsored cooperative undertaking, shares many aspects with the United Order. The Welfare Program was organized in 1936 as a response to the Great Depression and continues to expand. Under the plan diocesan organizations called "stakes" purchase and maintain cooperative manufacturing or farming ventures that produce essential household commodities. These products are shipped to regional or central warehouses, where they are available for bishops to draw upon for the poor within their jurisdictions. Most labor on welfare projects is voluntary, supplied through local church congregations. Welfare commodities are also drawn upon to provide relief to victims of disasters such as floods, earthquakes, or war.

Another Mormon economic practice is the contribution by church members of an amount equivalent to or greater than the cost of two meals missed in a spiritual fast on the first Sunday of each month. These "fast offerings" are used to care for the local poor. Any excess is forwarded to church headquarters to help maintain an elaborate system of social and economic welfare services. In addition, for many years all Mormons have been advised to develop a personal or family program of food storage sufficient to sustain themselves for a full year if necessary. Church leaders claim that a major purpose of these various programs, including tithing, is to teach church members sufficient selflessness to be able to live under Consecration and Stewardship at some future time.

Ethnic Consciousness and Religious Organization

A related set of doctrines has strongly influenced the development of a Mormon ethnic consciousness. Mormons have believed since the 1830s that Christ will soon return to the earth to initiate a millennial reign. Therefore, the "restoration" of the true church and authority, lost from the earth through apostasy, was accomplished expressly for the purpose of preparing a covenanted people to administer world government under Christ. The Saints were selected from the nations so that they might be trained in moral precepts and necessary administrative skills. Missionary work has always been the primary vehicle of this selection process. In the nineteenth century the missionaries taught that the faithful should physically remove themselves from worldly influences and gather to Zion, where, concentrated in one geographical area, they could be instructed and reinforce one another in preparing to live the Law of Consecration and Stewardship and other celestial laws. Rapid growth of church membership outside Utah in the twentieth century has made physical gathering of this sort impractical, but the church still fosters a number of teachings and practices which tend to separate faithful Mormons from non-Mormons, wherever they reside.

The religious hierarchy extends into every Mormon household, even those not involved in church activity. The primary unit of church organization is the "ward," or local congregation of three hundred to six hundred members. A bishop oversees each ward and counsels his congregation in both religious and secular affairs. He is assisted by the Women's Relief Society, first organized by Joseph Smith in Nauvoo, and by the men and boys as members of the various priesthood quorums—high priests, seventies, and elders in the higher, or Melchizedek, priesthood and priests, teachers, and deacons in the lower, or Aaronic, priesthood. Boys enter the hierarchy at the age of twelve as deacons. Each rank has specific responsibilities; most assist in "home teaching"—making visits in pairs at least once a month to an assigned four or five families and reporting back to the bishop. Thus the ward, whether rural or urban, is like a village, with geographic boundaries (not commitment to church activity) defining membership and with considerable mutual solicitude.

Church organization ascends to the "stake" (several wards), presided over by a stake president, his two counselors, and a high council composed of twelve high priests. The next level is the region, a jurisdiction created in response to rapid church growth; it is presided over by a regional representative of the Twelve Apostles. Above the region is the churchwide level.

Those who hold high positions on a churchwide level are referred to as "general authorities." They are for faithful Mormons quite literally "general" authorities, exercising worldwide authority in ecclesiastical affairs and commanding respect and obedience when they offer advice on religious and secular matters. They include the Presiding Bishop of the church, the First Quorum of the Seventy, the Patriarch of the Church, the Quorum of the Twelve Apostles, and the three-member First Presidency. The principal figure in the First Presidency is the prophet or president of the church, regarded as the mouthpiece of God upon the earth.

The church organization offers responsibility and authority at some level to all members willing to accept positions. All men hold offices in the lay priesthood, and all members are subject to "calls" for staffing a wide variety of religious, cultural, social, welfare, and recreational activities for both sexes and all age groups. Demonstration of faithfulness by living according to church teachings is officially required for calls to church positions; in practice, however, different positions require different levels of faithfulness, so that almost anyone willing to accept a position is likely to be offered one. Thus members are involved in the organization through assuming responsibility for communicating general policies and teachings to others within their calling, and their involvement generates a high degree of loyalty to the broader system. It is difficult to obtain estimates on the number of "inactive" or nonengaged members—sometimes referred to as "Jack Mormons"—they probably range between 25 and 35 percent of the total church membership. Anyone baptized in the church is retained in the membership files wherever he or she goes and regardless of participation. The membership record is discontinued only upon formal request.

Education

Mormons see piety and priesthood as the main qualifications for leadership and the right to make pronouncements on doctrinal matters. There has never been a systematic rationalization of Mormon doctrines or canon of essential beliefs beyond a brief general statement by Joseph Smith in 1842. Communicants are expected to believe in Jesus Christ's redeeming mission and to accept the roles of Joseph Smith and his successors as present-day spokesmen for God. Scriptures, including the Book of Mormon and the compilation of Smith's revelations called the Doctrine and Covenants, are interpreted freely and variously by church members. This amorphous lay theology has reinforced a widespread disregard for some forms of higher education among the Mormons. Yet, paradoxically, education in general is highly prized, and a favorite maxim from the Doctrine and Covenants, "the Glory of God is intelligence," is often used to support the contention that intellectual endeavor is divinely sanctioned. Utah has an excellent public school system; public school expenditures total more than 11 percent of the personal incomes of Utah citizens, a proportion exceeded by only two other states. In addition, the proportion of college-age youth attending college is among the highest in the nation. The church subsidizes Brigham Young University, Ricks College, and other church schools. Most college-trained Mormons tend to be involved in public education and in practical trades or professions, such as business, law, or medicine, or in applied science; general church leaders and members alike regard intellectual curiosity with suspicion unless it is directed toward a practical end or clearly infused with a religious and moral perspective.

In pioneer Utah, schooling was the responsibility of the local wards, and the meetinghouse often served as both school and church. Mormons did not support public schools because they believed that moral and religious instruction was an integral part of a child's education and that federal influence would prevent such instruction from being part of a public school curriculum. Because of the lack of public schools, non-Mormons in Utah established private denominational schools; these were so superior to the Mormon schools that many Saints enrolled their children in them. Church officials then reversed their policy and pushed for improved free grammar schools, which the Saints could control through their numerical majority. The teaching of moral values in high school remained a concern of the church leaders, however, and in the 1870s a number of church-maintained "academies" were established in heavily Mormon localities. They proved costly and redundant, and in the 1920s were given up in favor of a program that provided religious instruction at the seminary (high school) and institute (college) levels in buildings erected and maintained by the church close to public schools. If local laws do not permit Mormon youth to attend seminary classes during the school day, the program is adapted to provide religious instruction in the early morning and late afternoon.

Mormon involvement in higher education began in Nauvoo, where a university was founded and a few classes taught in the 1840s. The University of Deseret (now the University of Utah) was founded by the Mormons in 1850 but has since become a tax-supported state institution. Brigham Young University was established as a secondary school in 1875 and has grown into a major university with a student body of more than twenty-five thousand; it is wholly owned and operated by the Mormon church.

Politics

In politics as in education the Mormons have had difficulty defining appropriate boundaries between religious and secular affairs. Much of the trouble encountered by the early church in Missouri and Illinois was political and arose in part from the Mormons' tendency to vote as a block and when possible to elect church leaders to government positions. The Council of Fifty, organized in Nauvoo as an instrument of secular government under church control, retained influence throughout the nineteenth century.

When the federal government imposed territorial status upon Utah, it set off a half-century of conflict between the Saints and federal authorities. Mormons felt that the Washington appointees did not represent local interests. Moreover, some federal officials were openly anti-Mormon; they cast aspersions on the morals of Mormons and vowed to diminish church influence in the territory. After some officials complained that the Mormons were ungovernable and disloyal, President James Buchanan in 1857 appointed a non-

Mormon governor and sent a 2,500-man military force to install him. The Mormons, who had received little communication regarding the purpose of the expedition, chose to see it as an invading force and conducted guerrilla warfare against the troops, who camped on the plains of Wyoming during the winter of 1857–58. Eventually a compromise permitted the army to establish a post in a sparsely settled area forty-five miles southwest of Salt Lake City. Before the army was allowed to march through the city to its new quarters the Mormons evacuated the area, filled homes and orchards with straw, and appointed men to stand by ready to set fire to the settlement should the army commence any hostile actions. This army was recalled at the outbreak of the Civil War. In October 1862 uncertainty as to Mormon loyalty to the Union led to the establishment of Fort Douglas on the outskirts of Salt Lake City. The commander, Colonel Patrick E. Connor, encouraged publication of a virulently anti-Mormon newspaper, the *Union Vedette*, and attempted to dilute Mormon influence in the territory by fostering gold and silver mining.

Federal officials denounced the entire social system of the Mormons, including their communal activities, their hierarchical church government, and the remarkable loyalty of the general membership to church leaders. Outsiders saw the Mormons as the antithesis in almost every respect of what patriotic Americans should be and viewed the Mormon system as more akin to oriental despotism than to American democracy. This exotic image was enhanced by Mormon polygamy, practiced secretly since the 1840s and openly after 1852. Congress passed a series of antipolygamy laws between 1862 and 1887, when the Edmunds-Tucker Act provided instruments for destroying the economic and political power of the Mormon church. This act disincorporated the church and declared all church-owned property in excess of $50,000 escheat to the federal government. It dissolved the Perpetual Emigrating Fund Company in an effort to cut off the flow of Mormon converts from Europe. It undermined Mormon political strength by denying citizens of Utah the right to vote, serve on a jury, or hold public office until they had signed an oath pledging support of and obedience to all antipolygamy laws. The act further reduced Mormon political power by denying the franchise to women, who had been given the right to vote by the territorial legislature in 1870.

Initially the church avoided the full impact of the financial provisions of the Edmunds-Tucker Act by entrusting church property to individuals or associations. However, church leaders wished to challenge the law before the Supreme Court as quickly as possible; to avoid delays in lower courts they agreed to turn over to the federal receiver $800,000 in real and personal property in exchange for a promise that no more claims would be pressed against church property.

Properties in downtown Salt Lake City, including even the temple block, were rented by the church from the receiver until the matter was resolved.

In the meantime church leaders, forced underground to avoid prosecution, submitted to Congress a request for statehood and prepared a constitution that outlawed polygamy and required separation of church and state. Their petition was denied in committee. Hopes for redress were dashed in May 1890 when the Supreme Court sustained the Edmunds-Tucker Act. Finally, in August 1890, the church president, Wilford Woodruff, announced the "Manifesto," which recommended that Mormons no longer contract marriages contrary to federal law. After a period of adjustment the Mormons entirely abandoned polygamy. It is presently practiced only by members of what Mormons call "fundamentalist" groups, who are excommunicated by the main church when such practices are discovered.

Elections in Utah during the pioneer period featured a one-party slate with church leaders filling civil positions often analogous to their church positions. A growing non-Mormon, or Gentile, population united in the 1870s with a dissident Mormon faction to form the Liberal party, which was countered by the pro-Mormon People's party. In national politics the Mormons, sensitive to states' rights issues, tended to vote Democratic. So one-sided were politics in Utah that a federal commission appointed in 1882 to administer territorial elections demanded a viable two-party system as a condition of statehood; in order to achieve the recommended political balance Mormon leaders encouraged some of their followers to become Republicans. Statehood was granted in January 1896, forty-six years after Brigham Young began his efforts toward that end. In the process Utah had undergone a "reconstruction" not unlike that experienced in the South after the Civil War.

Up to the end of World War II Utah residents did not consistently support any one political faction. Since that time some church leaders have outspokenly favored conservative positions on key issues, reflecting a long-standing bias against federal interference in local affairs and a protracted response to charges of un-Americanism in the late nineteenth century. Despite this, however, voting has for the most part followed national trends, although voting on local issues is usually conservative.

Social Structure

A conception of themselves as a "covenant people" has been reinforced by other doctrines that encourage Mormons to make the primary division in their social world between Mormon and Gentile. Mormon children grow up with a conflict between their identity as Mormons and their national identity similar to the conflict experienced by youth in ethnic minorities throughout the world. Even converts who have not been in Utah are commonly ostracized by former associates, which encourages them to develop new ties almost exclusively within the church.

The most important social stratification within Mormonism is by church office. But despite much nepotism at the higher levels, particularly in the past, the system as a whole is strongly egalitarian in character. Callings to church office are tendered on the basis of piety and diligence in church service rather than wealth or occupational status, and there is considerable rotation in all offices but those of general authorities. General church, stake, and ward offices nonetheless carry overtones connoting status within the community.

Since the mid-nineteenth century the ward has been the fundamental social group for both urban and rural Mormons, and understanding its structure and function is necessary to an understanding of Mormon society. The ward defines the neighborhood in cities and the town in rural areas. Moreover, these ward "villages," whether in downtown Salt Lake City, suburban Dallas, or Berlin's Dahlem, are very similar. Church classes throughout the world study the same material on roughly the same schedule; the same attitudes toward the general church leadership prevail everywhere; distinctive use of particular words or phrases, or the equivalency in translation, is evident; meetinghouses even have the same architecture. Although many find the uniformity stifling, newcomers to a ward usually experience an immediate sense of community approaching kinship (Mormons refer to one another as "brother" and "sister"), which has distinct social and organizational advantages. Mormons feel themselves a part of an extensive family that transcends geographic and social boundaries; they are clannish and inward looking, acutely attuned to important happenings within their world, and not greatly interested in external affairs. Active Mormons have little social contact outside the ward in which they reside and even less outside the stake of which their ward is part.

Family and Kinship

Joseph Smith's First Vision was in part a result of anxiety over division within his own family on matters of religion. Since his time Mormonism has been preoccupied with family structure and family relationships. "Sealing," or eternal marriage, initiated by Smith in Nauvoo, clearly has the function of promising to secure family unity beyond life on earth. In Mormon temple marriages partners are pronounced husband and wife for all eternity rather than for just their mortal lives, with the promise that worthy parents and children will associate as a family in the hereafter. Similarly, a sealing ceremony is performed in temples for deceased families, with descendants or other Latter-day Saints assuming the names of the deceased and acting as proxies for them during the ceremony. Mormons believe that once the earthly ordinances are performed for the deceased in the temple, the dead, now residing in a spirit world where individuals still exercise free will, can decide whether or not to accept the sealings, baptisms, and other temple work performed in their interest by living persons. Such ceremonies provide the rationale for massive genealogical programs that make it a religious obligation for church members to reconstruct family history at least four generations back and further if records permit.

Implicit in the doctrine of eternal marriage is plural marriage, for several wives sealed to a man serially in this life would all be with him in the afterlife. Plural marriage was practiced secretly by Joseph Smith and a few close associates in Nauvoo. Until 1852, when the Saints were safe in Utah, church leaders issued carefully phrased denials to charges that polygamous marriages were taking place; in reality, however, polygamy was common from the early 1840s until 1890.

Although studies of Mormon polygamy have generally been based on samples overrepresenting elites, some reasonably reliable facts have emerged. Most studies indicate that 8 to 12 percent of married men had more than one wife. In one southern Utah town, however, 24 percent of the inhabitants were members of polygamous households, a figure which perhaps is more significant in understanding the importance of polygamy in the society. Census schedules for other areas suggest that this figure is not unusual. Samples of lists of polygamous families show that about 70 percent of the men had two wives, 21 percent had three, and 9 percent had four or more.

Apparently polygamy was never sufficiently widespread among the Mormons to prevent single young men from finding wives; studies indicate that there was always a reserve of unmarried persons of both sexes at all age levels. The sociologists James L. Smith and Phillip R. Kunz have concluded that because a significant number of the wives entering polygamous marriages were older than wives entering monogamous ones, they were women who had "survived" the monogamous marriage market. It is apparently not true that each polygamous union doomed some men to unwilling bachelorhood. The common practice of taking widows and spinsters into polygamous families indicates that polygamy had the effect of diminishing the importance of romantic love as a consideration in family formation. It also reduced the possibility that some women might remain involuntarily outside a family group, an important consideration, given the great stress church leaders placed on the family as the fundamental unit of an ordered society.

Polygamy was of far greater importance in shaping non-Mormon attitudes toward Mormons than the numbers involved suggest. Non-Mormon political leaders and churchmen, opposed to the Mormon system generally, were shocked by polygamy and saw it as an issue that could be used to bring about anti-Mormon feeling throughout America and destroy the movement. Thus strong attacks were launched against Mormon polygamy, especially in the 1880s. Instead of eliminating the division between the Mormon and non-Mormon worlds, these attacks increased it by causing all Mormons, polygamous or not, to unite in defense of their system.

Another aspect of Mormon preoccupation with the family is the law of adoption, begun under Joseph Smith and practiced until the 1890s. Church members without Mormon parents were "adopted" into the families of church leaders in a transaction that entailed both filial and paternal obligations and often formed the basis of lifelong associations. Modern vestiges of these concerns are evident in the prevalence of family organizations and reunions among Mormons, activities strongly urged by high church leaders. Mormons are aware of and often identify others by the family or clan to which they belong.

Church authorities have issued solemn declarations on the importance of family and spent vast sums on media spots and programs to promote the teaching that stable family relationships are fundamental to a healthy society. Pornography, sexual permissiveness, gay liberation, liberal divorce laws, abortion, and women's liberation are opposed by Mormon leaders as threats to family stability. They also oppose birth control, but rather than preach against it they have consistently taught that children are a blessing and that parenthood is an essential lesson in Christian giving. Indeed, Mormons believe that the highest celestial blessings cannot be obtained outside the marriage union. In consequence, Mormon fertility remained over twice as high as American norms in the mid-1970s. In 1976 the Mormon birthrate was 29.8 per thousand, and the national average was 14.7.

The emphasis on family and family values has helped shape the response of many Mormons to the women's liberation movement, particularly the Equal Rights Amendment (ERA). The Latter-day Saint church has always been strongly patriarchal in its organizational structure and has emphasized the importance of women's roles as homemakers. All worthy men are ordained to the priesthood, but not women. Leadership in all church organizations except those that exclusively serve women, small children, and teenage girls is reserved to men. Surprisingly, given this fundamental aspect of church government, nineteenth-century Mormon women were encouraged to enter professions and take responsibilities outside the home. Apparently the pressing need for workers in a developing economy momentarily overcame the fundamental belief that women should be primarily guardians of home and family. Prominent Mormon women of the nineteenth century, such as Brigham Young's daughter Susa Young Gates (1856–1933) and Emmeline B. Wells (1828–1921), were active in the suffrage movement and were well acquainted with its national leadership. Utah women, who received the vote in 1870, were among the first in the nation to be given full suffrage. Twentieth-century church leaders, however, observing changes in societal values that they believe to be destructive to the family, have increasingly advised women to make nurturing children and building a family their first responsibilities in life. The leaders have seen the women's liberation movement generally and the ERA particularly as causes that divert women from their primary role. The position of the church undoubtedly influenced Utah's negative response to the ERA.

Intergroup Relations

Mormon-Gentile conflict remains a muted but real aspect of life in heavily Mormon areas, where the social world is clearly divided into Mormon and Gentile realms that have little interaction or common understanding. The tendency to regard all non-Mormons as Gentiles has diminished Mormon awareness of other ethnic groups; sizable Greek and Italian communities exist in Utah with little evidence of ethnic tension beyond that common in Mormon relations with all Gentile groups.

Blacks and American Indians, however, are exceptions. Until 1978 Mormons denied blacks ordination to the lay priesthood and access to temple rituals, both of which were open to males of all other races. There was no clear doctrinal rationale for this exclusion, which was applied only to Africans; ironically, it apparently arose as a reaction to criticism of Mormon opposition to slavery in the 1830s.

Occasional comments by past church leaders indicated that future revelations might change the practice, a promise fulfilled in June 1978, when church president Spencer W. Kimball (1895–1985) announced a revelation extending the right of ordination to all worthy male members of the church. The membership responded warmly, and no significant dissent has been evident. The small number of blacks in Utah minimizes overt expression of racial tension, and it is therefore difficult to assess its effect on race relations in heavily Mormon areas. Blacks in such localities claim that exclusion was not the only expression of racial prejudice, but one sociological study has indicated that Mormons are no different in their racial attitudes from non-Mormons in the West.

Mormon doctrine teaches that American Indians are remnants of a Book of Mormon people—the Lamanites—a race descended from a migrant band of ancient Israelites with a tarnished past but great promise and a specific mission in the Mormon millennial scheme. The first major missionary effort of Mormons, in 1830, was directed toward American Indians. Strenuous efforts to "redeem" the Lamanites have continued since that time.

Indian skirmishes took place in the 1840s, 1850s, and 1860s, but Brigham Young's overriding policy was to avoid conflict and fraternize as much as possible in order to "civilize" the Indians and help them adjust to modern white society. Early Mormon settlements in areas frequented by Indians commonly set aside "Indian farms" or plots of land for their use. In the nineteenth century numerous efforts under church auspices to establish farms, reservations, and settled communities for local tribes were made independently of federal Indian policies. Such efforts often soured relations between Mormons and federal Indian agents but led generally to good relations between Mormons and Indians, many of whom submitted to Mormon baptism and differentiated between Mormons and other whites. Mormons teach that Polynesians are likewise descendants of Book of Mormon peoples, and missionary efforts have been remarkably successful among the Maori of New Zealand and in Tonga, Samoa, Tahiti, and Hawaii. Church records indicate that in 1970 over 15 percent of all Tongans, 14 percent of all Samoans, and nearly 5 percent of all French Polynesians were Mormons. During the 1960s and 1970s members of these groups immigrated to Salt Lake City and other Mormon areas in substantial numbers.

The Mormon Indian placement program of the twentieth century is clearly an extension of nineteenth-century efforts to change the lifestyle of the Indians and help them adapt to modern society. Under this program Indian children whose parents so decide were taken for the school year into Mormon homes, often far from the parental home, treated as family members, and sent to local public schools. Difficulties of adjustment and fear that children will be alienated from their native culture persisted. The program was modified in an attempt to meet these problems and eventually abandoned. Brigham Young University has a remarkably successful record of keeping the dropout rate for first-year Indian college students far below that of other universities with sizable Indian minorities. Mormon-Indian relations have historically been fair to excellent in contrast to the hostile relations prevailing in neighboring western states.

Group Maintenance

Several circumstances have served to erect and maintain social boundaries between Mormons and others. Partly by design, Mormons were physically isolated from Gentiles from the earliest periods of Mormon history; where possible, the Saints lived together in separate communities. Their early difficulties resulted in part from insufficient isolation, and the choice of the Great Basin as a new settling place in 1847 was deliberate: even the waters there did not mingle with those of the outside. For a quarter-century Mormons were free to work out their own particular lifestyle. Even after 1869, when the Transcontinental Railroad began to bring Gentiles to Utah, the newcomers stayed for the most part in the cities or in separate mining camps. Thus the isolation continued well into the twentieth century.

Social isolation has reinforced the physical isolation of Mormons. The persecutions created an initial wall of hostility and distrust; a generation later, plural marriage became an equally divisive issue that taught Mormons to regard outsiders as enemies. The desire for isolation led to Brigham Young's call in 1854 for creation of the Deseret alphabet, a phonetic system based on Pitman shorthand. Schoolbooks, newspapers, official church documents and papers, and parts of the Book of Mormon were printed in this alphabet between 1854 and 1867. One of Young's wives, Eliza R. Snow (1804–87), designed and attempted to introduce distinctive styles of dress in order to free Mormon women from outside fashion trends. Neither the new alphabet nor new dress styles were widely adopted or of lasting effect.

After abandoning or modifying plural marriage, communal life, and other distinctive aspects of the group character, church leaders began to place greater stress on the Word of Wisdom—the Mormon health law proscribing alcohol, tea, coffee, and tobacco. The Word of Wisdom was revealed by Joseph Smith in 1831 but was not rigidly observed until the 1920s. Now that strict adherence is required as a condition for entrance into the temple, the Word of Wisdom makes Mormons uncomfortable at cocktail parties, coffee breaks, and other such gatherings which serve the rest of American society as important occasions for social interaction. The Word of Wisdom is in some measure to twentieth-century Mormons what polygamy was to those of the nineteenth century—a mark of peculiarity setting them apart from much of the rest of American society.

In addition Mormon youth, especially young men, are taught from childhood to prepare to fulfill a two-year mission that totally removes them from normal young adult society; they spend this time teaching and defending

Mormonism, clearly an effective way of building a life-long loyalty and commitment. There is also strong pressure to marry in Mormon temples. Because only faithful Mormons can enter the temples by obtaining a certificate of worthiness from their bishop and stake president, the importance attached to temple marriage limits teenage dating and other contact with non-Mormons. Statistics for the United States are unavailable, but a study of Canadian Mormons reported that 80 percent of rural and 70 percent of urban youth marry other Mormons. Provision of a full range of church-sponsored social activities in each ward and the maintenance of church universities, seminaries, and institutes serve to decrease outside contact and to increase opportunities to marry within the group. In addition, ward activities permit the fully engaged Mormon little time for outside social engagements. Thus, devout Mormons have always kept considerable distance, both physically and socially, from non-Mormon society.

Accommodation and Ethnic Commitment

In the years since the bitter decades attending resolution of the polygamy issue, Mormon accommodation to greater American society has been more apparent than real. Traits remain that caused much criticism of Mormons in the nineteenth century: unreserved obedience to church authority, difficulty in making distinctions between secular and religious realms, commitment to cooperative and communal activities, and devotion to the church above all other loyalties. The remarkable success of present-day general church programs depends to a considerable degree upon precisely those traits that made the system so tenacious and successful in the past. Most such programs take place within a purely religious framework, but the welfare program extends into the economic sphere and provides a model for broader expansion into the secular realm should church leaders deem it necessary. Moreover, the voluntary responsiveness of Mormons to the calls and counsel of church leaders may be even more pronounced than it was in the nineteenth century and thus permits continued flexibility in the system. If the need arose, these avid proponents of capitalism and free enterprise might well lead their people into a communal life where rewards would be determined by need, and contribution by ability.

Mormon society during the first two-thirds of the twentieth century was relatively outward looking and open to external influence. Since the 1960s, this trend has been reversing and a more defensive attitude similar to that prevailing in the nineteenth century has developed, partly as a reaction to a perceived

disintegration of moral values in the greater society, particularly as they relate to sexual mores and family life. Perhaps more important, however, a people committed to unity and order as prime social virtues are reacting to what
they see as an increasingly chaotic outside world. Over the next few decades,
the Mormons, despite an aggressive missionary program and commitment to
build a worldwide church, may move toward making even sharper the boundaries dividing their world from that of the Gentiles.

Bibliography

Brief general introductions are Leonard J. Arrington and Davis Bitton, *The Mormon
Experience: A History of the Latter-day Saints* (New York: Knopf, 1979); and James B.
Allen and Glen M. Leonard, *The Story of the Latter-Day Saints* (Salt Lake City: Deseret
Book, 1976). Thomas F. O'Dea, *The Mormons* (Chicago: University of Chicago Press,
1957), is written from a sociologist's perspective; and Leonard J. Arrington, *Great Ba-
sin Kingdom: An Economic History of the Latter-day Saints, 1830–1900* (Cambridge,
Mass.: Harvard University Press, 1958), adds that of an economic historian. Aspects of
the early experience are discussed in David Brion Davis, "Some Themes of Counter-
Subversion: An Analysis of Anti-Masonic, Anti-Catholic, and Anti-Mormon Literature," *Mississippi Valley Historical Review* 47 (Sept. 1960): 295–324; Robert B. Flanders,
"To Transform History: Early Mormon Culture and the Concept of Time and Space,"
Church History 40 (Mar. 1971): 108–17; and Klaus J. Hansen, *Quest for Empire: The Political Kingdom of God and the Council of Fifty in Mormon History,* rev. ed. (Lincoln:
University of Nebraska Press, 1974). The struggle between the Mormons and the federal government is described in Gustave O. Larson, *The "Americanization" of Utah for
Statehood* (San Marino, Calif.: Huntington Library, 1971). Rewarding insights can be
found in Austin Fife and Alta Fife, *Saints of Sage and Saddle: Folklore among the Mormons* (Bloomington: Indiana University Press, 1956).

  Aspects of the Mormon West are treated in Donald W. Meinig, "The Mormon Culture Region: Strategies and Patterns in the Geography of the American West, 1847–
1964," *Annals of the Association of American Geographers* 55 (1965): 191–220; and Evon
Z. Vogt and Ethel M. Albert, eds., *People of Rimrock: A Study of Values in Five Cultures*
(Cambridge, Mass.: Harvard University Press, 1966; reprint, New York: Atheneum,
1970).

  For the role of town life in Mormon society, see Charles S. Peterson, "A Mormon
Village: One Man's West," *Journal of Mormon History* 3 (1976): 2–12; Dean L. May, "The
Making of Saints: The Mormon Town as Setting for the Study of Cultural Change,"
Utah Historical Quarterly 45 (Winter 1977): 75–92; and Dean L. May, *Three Frontiers:
Family, Land, and Society in the American West, 1850–1900* (New York: Cambridge
University Press, 1994). See also John L. Sorenson, "Mormon World View and Amer-
ican Culture," *Dialogue* 8, no. 2 (1973): 17–29; Jan Shipps, "The Mormons: Looking

Forward and Outward," *Christian Century* (16–23 Aug. 1978), 261–66; and Gordon C. Thomasson, "Teaching across Dispensations: A Comparative Perspective on the Challenges of Being a Worldwide Church," in *Mormonism: A Faith for All Cultures,* ed. F. LaMond Tullis (Provo: Brigham Young University Press, 1978).

The major collection of source materials on Mormonism is in the Library-Archives, Historical Department, Church of Jesus Christ of Latter-day Saints, Salt Lake City. Other important collections are in the University of Utah, Brigham Young University, and Utah State University libraries and the Utah State Historical Society Library in Salt Lake City. Other holdings are in the Coe Collection, Yale University; the Huntington Library, San Marino, California; the Bancroft Library, University of California, Berkeley; the Houghton Library, Harvard University; and the New York Public Library. An important aid is Chad J. Flake, ed., *A Mormon Bibliography, 1830–1930* (Salt Lake City: University of Utah Press, 1978).

3

Is Mormonism Christian?
Reflections on a Complicated Question

Jan Shipps

Since I, a staunch member of the First United Methodist Church in Blooming-ton, Indiana, have been studying the Latter-day Saints for close to forty years, it is perhaps not surprising that I am frequently asked whether Mormons are Christians and whether Mormonism is Christian. Put to me by journalists, ac-ademics, denominational bureaucrats, participants in adult forums in various local Protestant and Catholic churches, active Latter-day Saints, bona fide anti-Mormons, my students, and a variety of other interested people, the query comes in both forms. Whatever the form, a forthright yes or no seems to be expected.

Because many people think the two questions are one and the same, inquir-ers are often startled when I respond by asking if they wish to know whether Mormons are Christians or whether Mormonism is Christian. Moreover, since their question, whatever its form, seems so straightforward to so many, inquir-ers are surprised—and sometimes impatient—when I attempt to determine the framework within which the question is being asked. Yet before I can for-mulate a response, I must know both the substance of the question and its context.

The two queries are essentially the same if the inquirer's main concern is analogical (Is the LDS Church like the Presbyterian church, for example, or are Mormons similar to Catholics?), analytical (How is Mormonism related to other forms of Christianity?), or historiographical (What have historians said about the connection between Mormonism and Christianity?). If the framework for the inquiry is more theological and religious than theoretical and academic, these are not simply two versions of the same question. While they are obviously related, quite different theological propositions inhere in them. Inquirers who want to know whether Mormons are Christians signal their assumption that a divine determination is made about individuals on a case-by-case basis. The more usual query—"Is Mormonism Christian?"—

presumes a divine economy in which redemption depends on an individual's membership in a true or authentic "body of Christ."

To discover whether an inquiry is more theological and religious than theoretical and academic or vice versa, I respond to all inquiries about this issue with a series of counterqueries whose answers will allow me to determine what sort of question I have been asked. Does the inquirer wish to know, for example, whether some particular Mormon—say Marie Osmond, Orrin Hatch, Hugh Nibley, or Paul Edwards—is a Christian? Or is it a matter of whether some particular group of Mormons is Christian—say the members of the Reorganized Church of Jesus Christ of Latter Day Saints or the Mormon fundamentalists in Colorado City? Alternatively, is the question a normative one? Am I being asked whether Mormon theology is congruent with some particular form of Christian theology; whether the institutional structure of the LDS (or RLDS) Church is sufficiently similar to the institutional structure of the Christian church in New Testament times to make it Christian; whether Mormon doctrine is compatible with traditional Christian doctrine; or whether Mormon rituals and worship forms are comparable to Christian rituals and worship forms?

If the inquirer answers yes to any of these questions, I ask for more information about presuppositions that underlie the query: by what standard does the inquirer believe that individuals, organized groups of persons, or institutions are accorded status as Christians? Does one proceed in the Protestant fashion and look to the Bible, assuming that words speak for themselves? Or does one look to authority and tradition, as Catholics do, asking someone who, like the pope, can speak ex cathedra? If not, how about asking a prophet who can add "thus saith the Lord" to his or her words?

By responding to these queries with such counterqueries, I point to my conviction that definitive answers to normative questions assume the reality of discoverable norms (rules or sets of standards that can be authoritatively established). Within human communities, however, authority always rests on a base of cultural support. In the absence of a single source of authority whose nature is universally respected, humanity has to struggle along with provisional rules and standards. Thus, I conclude that definitive answers to normative questions are not forthcoming in the sort of pluralistic situation in which the contemporary world finds itself. All my years of study notwithstanding, if the question of whether Mormonism is Christian is a normative one, I do not presume to provide a normative answer.

It is nevertheless obvious that my continuing—even strengthened—Methodist commitment over the many years in which I have had an opportunity to learn more about Mormonism is a negative answer to the question of whether I believe that the Church of Jesus Christ of Latter-day Saints or one of the other institutional forms of this tradition is *the only* legitimate Christianity now present on the earth. This negation has proved frustrating to some of my Mormon friends, something I first learned when the late Richard Poll asked somewhat sorrowfully, "How can you know so much and not believe?" But many Saints have apparently recognized that my own religious commitment has allowed me to develop a deeper appreciation of their tradition as I have become more familiar with it. I believe they are right.

Because I was doing research during the "Arrington Spring," soon after Leonard Arrington was first installed as church historian and when access to the LDS documentary record was as open as it had ever been and is ever likely to be again, I had access to the central texts related to the founding of the faith. My closeness to those early Saints—as I have become acquainted with them and their church through the historical record—and those who live in the present has made me equally unwilling to say that Mormonism is not *a* legitimate form of Christianity. Actually, even in my earliest writing about the Saints, I never said that Mormonism is not Christian. But up to now, in addition to writing Mormon history, I have mainly addressed historiographical and analytical issues connected to it.

Those I have addressed at length. For example, the essay I wrote for the *Encyclopedia of Mormonism* surveyed the historiographical situation.[1] It describes what historians have said about this matter from the middle of the nineteenth century, when Robert Baird erroneously classified Mormonism as a liturgical form of Protestantism—presumably something like Lutheranism—up to the renewal of old charges that Mormonism is a non-Christian cult. I also investigated and commented at great length on the early recording of the Mormon prophet's story in a careful consideration of the account based on what Joseph Smith's mother said about what occurred.[2] Much more recently, during the 1999 Sunstone Symposium I served as the respondent in a session in which Klaus Hansen presented an overview of the writing of those historians whose work is a part of the "new Mormon history." My commentary surveyed the writing of Mormon history from the 1830s onward, showing how historians have been making arguments for and against the legitimacy of this as a Christian movement from the time its history was first recorded.[3]

I also provided my own classification of the movement in *Mormonism: The Story of a New Religious Tradition*. This book begins and ends with analogy. It opens with an observation that just as the early Christians believed they had found the only proper way to be Jewish, so the early followers of the Mormon prophet believed they had found the only proper way to be Christian. It closes with my conclusion that the Mormonism of the Church of Jesus Christ of Latter-day Saints is best understood as a form of corporate Christianity that is related to traditional Christianity—in other words, the forms of Protestantism, Catholicism, and Eastern Orthodoxy that existed in the first third of the nineteenth century—in much the same way that early Christianity was related to Judaism. I did not say the same about the Mormonism of the Reorganized Church of Jesus Christ of Latter Day Saints, since it appears to me that it can be classified as an idiosyncratic form of Protestantism. This "Josephite" body never accepted "the restoration of all things," and in the years since my book was written, RLDS emphasis on the importance of patriarchy, which is central to the notion of "the restoration of Israel," has been dramatically attenuated by the selection of someone not in the direct Joseph Smith family line as its prophet-president.[4]

In saying I am unwilling to provide normative answers when the framework of an inquirer's question is theological or religious, however, I do not mean to say I am unwilling to confront this issue in a religious setting. From time to time, I am invited by various church groups to talk about the Mormons. (Since most Protestants have not caught up with changes in nomenclature, they nearly always speak of "the Mormons" rather than the Latter-day Saints.) When I accept such invitations, I am confronted with a real challenge—even if the members of the group that extended the invitation have not seen one of the *Godmakers* videos. While those who invite me to talk usually tell me that the Mormons are "really nice people" who "take care of their own" and "have a great choir," most of the members of these groups know very little about the Saints' history (except that they practiced polygamy), and they know even less about Mormon doctrine and LDS theology.

The task I set for myself in such situations is not merely connecting Mormonism to Christianity—after all, I am talking about a church of Jesus Christ. The task also involves showing how this connection "plays out" in the Mormonism of the Church of Jesus Christ of Latter-day Saints and in the Reorganized Church. As I do so, I sometimes try to clarify the distinction with a speculative comparison. In view of Mountain Mormonism's historic emphasis on the restoration of Israel, it could well be the sort of Christianity that might have developed if the outcome of the Jerusalem conference (Acts 15:1–30; Gal. 2:1–10) had favored St. Peter rather than St. Paul, that is, if potential converts to Christianity had been required to first become a part of the "chosen people."[5] "Missouri Mormonism" may well signal what Christianity might have been without the conversion of Constantine and the subsequent integration of religious and political authority. With this comparison, I make the point that both of these churches in the Mormon tradition are forms of Christianity, yet both differed from the Christianities that existed in 1830—and they still do.

As is well known, the extent of the difference was first manifested in a dramatic manner when the followers of the Mormon prophet responded to the revelations to "gather" by establishing settlements in Kirtland, Ohio; in Independence, Far West, and elsewhere in Missouri; and in Nauvoo, Illinois. The very existence of these Mormon "kingdoms" set the Saints apart. This contrast was spectacularly intensified when a large body of Joseph Smith's followers fled to the Intermountain West after the prophet's murder and introduced the public practice of plural marriage.

Acceptance of the plural marriage principle, regardless of whether one adhered to it, became the most obvious testimony that the Saints who followed Brigham Young gave assent to a truly distinctive set of beliefs. It bound the Saints who went west together and provided them with a means of identification that kept them from being confused with members of the many other innovative Christian movements that originated in the United States in the nineteenth century. For the "Josephites" and many of the other Saints who did not go west, plural marriage became a standard against which they could define themselves. Proving that the practice was not part of Mormonism became important to them as a means of identification, as significant a negative marker for them as it was a positive marker for the "Brighamites."

If plural marriage told LDS people, whose church prescribed its practice, who they were and if it told RLDS people, whose church proscribed its practice, who they were, plural marriage told everyone else in Victorian America who the Mormons were not. If they practiced polygamy or even believed in its practice, they could not possibly be Christian.

The Mormon fundamentalists, who refuse to relinquish polygamous practice, believe that the LDS Church jeopardized its birthright—its exclusive claim, its very Mormonness—when it surrendered the practice of plural marriage in response to pressures from the U.S. government. I think they are wrong if they believe that the LDS Church renounced the essence of Mormonism by giving up plural marriage. However, it is possible that this renunciation could prove to have been an early signal pointing to an eventual relinquishing of enough of the LDS Church's distinctiveness to bring it into what some might call the traditional Christian fold. If something like that proves to be the case, I will obviously need to reexamine my interpretation of this movement as one that cannot be fully comprehended in Troeltschian categories.[6] But that is a matter that will have to be dealt with in my next book on Mormonism, not in this one.

❖ ❖ ❖

What I do here is confront directly the question of whether Mormonism is Christian by examining the situation from a different and fairly complicated angle that calls for looking at the significance and implications (and even the pluses and minuses) of labeling and naming in culture and religion. Doing so requires me to associate this matter of labeling and naming with the zero-sum game that results when exclusive claims are set forth so that they create situations in which churches claiming that theirs is the only legitimate form of Christianity are forced to hold that all other forms of Christianity are illegitimate. After noting the active and ongoing naming and labeling shift occurring within the Church of Jesus Christ of Latter-day Saints as it moves away from the Mormon moniker, I consider two possible connections central to the way the Mormonism Christian question is being worked out: (1) the connection between the growth and geographical expansion of the LDS Church and its move from Mormon and Latter-day Saint to Christian definitions of the church and its members; and (2) the connection between the growth and increasing social and political significance of conservative Christianity and its need to have something to define itself over and against, a need that defining Mormonism as not-Christian helps satisfy. Finally, in a more personal vein, I return to the main question of the essay. After pointing to the obvious yet usually overlooked reality that the "Is Mormonism Christian" question is in some sense a generic question, I suggest the following: if the members of one group of people gathered into a community that calls itself Christian are permitted to decide that a person or everyone gathered into a different community that likewise calls itself Christian is not Christian, then some pretty unChristian defining is going on.

❖ ❖ ❖

Teeming with an almost incredible variety of European immigrants superimposed on a much older Anglo-Dutch Yankee culture, New York City's Lower East Side in the early decades of the twentieth century produced a childhood archetype known as the "Dead End Kid." A youngster of this ilk, familiar to aficionados of gangster movies of the 1930s and 1940s, survived in the bewildering metropolitan milieu by becoming cocky, impudent, resourceful, and extremely suspicious.

No logical connection exists between those B-movie urban urchins and the matter of whether Mormonism is Christian. Yet every time I try to organize my reflections on how the question of whether Mormonism is Christian has been answered, I remember snatches of dialogue from the films in which the Dead End Kids appeared:

> Adult to scruffy looking pre-adolescent: "What's your name, kid?"
> Kid: "Who wants ta know?" Or "What's it to ya?"

Despite such questions, the Dead End Kids themselves were always asking for the "monikers" of newcomers, which is not surprising since names were extremely important in their polyglot neighborhood. Names established identities, determined boundaries, and sent encoded messages about how the members of one of these clusters of preadolescent first-generation Americans ought to treat the "new kids on the block" who came from different immigrant stocks.

The same principle holds for religion. Names matter. They matter a lot. For that reason, whenever people I do not know ask me if Mormonism is Christian, a little computer inside my head starts sorting out possibilities. Who wants to know? What's it to 'em? Or to put it another way, is there a hidden agenda?

In the past thirty years, certain conservative Christians, charging that Mormonism is not Christian, have established a sometimes bitter adversarial relationship with Mormons. During the same period, one finds everywhere within Mormonism—in the *Church News* and the *Ensign,* in the public statements of LDS officials, in Sunday School lessons, and in talks the Saints give in ward sacrament meetings, as well as in private conversations—an escalating emphasis on the suffering of the Savior, the atonement of Christ, personal salvation, and so on. In view of these conflicting convictions about whether Mormonism is Christian, I often get the feeling that I am being asked for my opinion so that the inquirer can use what I say to score points for either the Latter-day Saints or those who oppose them.

And why not? If one looks at LDS history from the perspective of the Saints' perception of themselves and others' perceptions of them, it has always been thus. An agenda has always existed, and it has never been hidden.

When the Prophet Joseph Smith and his followers first appeared on the American religious scene, the new nation was becoming as religiously diverse as the Lower East Side would later be ethnically varied. In this case, however, the newcomers spoke a very familiar language. They came preaching repentance, calling on their hearers to listen to the words of Jesus Christ, and reminding those who had ears to hear that the "Lord your Redeemer suffered death in the flesh" and afterward rose "from the dead that he might bring all men unto him."[7] The prophet's followers said that by the spirit of prophecy and revelation, Jesus had directed them to establish an ecclesiastical organization headed by Joseph Smith Jr., who was "called of God and ordained an apostle of Jesus Christ."[8] They named their new fellowship the Church of Jesus Christ.

Its name and straightforward proclamation of the uniquely salvific significance of the suffering of Christ notwithstanding, this new ecclesiastical association never became a party to the informal denominational compact that, in the eyes of a majority of American citizens, turned the Christian church in this new nation into a pan-Protestant body. But this was not an instance of membership tacitly sought and implicitly denied. Sufficient reason on both sides kept the Church of Jesus Christ that Joseph Smith led from becoming a member of this larger body of Christ. For one perhaps unfamiliar example of the lack of ecumenical feeling on the prophet's part, listen to how Apostle William E. McLellin described a sermon preached on December 14, 1834: "President Smith preached . . . three hours in Kirt[land] during which he exposed the Methodist Dicipline in its black deformity and called upon the Elders in the power of the spirit of God to expose the creeds & confessions of men— His discourse was animated and Pointed, against all Creeds of men—."[9]

Such total refutation of the doctrines of every other Christian body reflects the extent to which the claims of this particular church of Jesus Christ were exclusive. Its members asserted that their church was set apart from all other churches that were called Christian because theirs was the only restored church of Jesus Christ that had been on the earth since the days of the "Great Apostasy." They maintained that their way of being Christian was the only legitimate way to be Christian. They also believed that in becoming members of this restored church, they had become as Christian as Christians had been in New Testament times.

These "New Testament Christians" or latter-day Saints, as they soon called themselves, believed that theirs had to be the only authentic church of Jesus Christ because it was the only church in which men who held the restored Aaronic and Melchizedek priesthoods presided. It quickly became a tenet of their faith that men who were not ordained members of these priesthood orders could not legitimately act for God in space and time.

Still, Smith's followers were by no means the only ones whose preaching of the crucified Christ was coupled with exclusive institutional claims. In the same year that Smith's followers established their church of Jesus Christ, another new Christian church was also established in the United States. This church was organized by the adherents of Thomas Campbell and Alexander Campbell, who called themselves Disciples of Christ. Like the members of the church headed by the Mormon prophet, the members of this newly "restored" church were committed to the doctrines and practices found in the New Testament.

Members of both churches expected an imminent millennium, and in each case, the members believed that through their church—and only through their church—a "restoration of the ancient order of things" would be accomplished.

Exclusivity, then, was not the claim forming the barrier that kept the Saints outside the denominational compact. The Book of Mormon was a much more serious stumbling block. By accepting this found text as testimony to the truth of gospel claims, the Saints rejected *sola scriptorum,* the Protestant principle of vesting final authority in the Word only as it was manifested in the Old and New Testaments. Moreover, the Saints' church was the only Christian church of substantial size that was headed by a prophet, one who also assumed the role of church president and high priest. Theirs was a church that—in terms whose meaning was specified in the work of the sociologist Max Weber—made neither office nor tradition definitive, settling ultimate authority instead on charisma adhering in a single individual. This practice was anathema to Protestants in the United States.

The Saints' obedience to the revelations directing them to "gather" to Zion moved the Saints away from the prevailing Protestant congregational pattern and toward the creation of independent LDS enclaves that could (and sometimes did) function as virtually autonomous political, economic, and cultural units powerful enough to challenge the separation of church and state in the United States. But the movement's true distinctiveness was not always recognized in the early years, and many observers failed to realize that this new church of Jesus Christ would withstand the centrifugal pull of Protestant hegemony long enough to become something other than an idiosyncratic Protestant denomination. That it did so is surely related to the Saints' possession of the Book of Mormon, the gathering, the leadership of the prophet, and all of Mormonism's other singular factors, including, after 1852, the publicly acknowledged practice of plural marriage.

But another reason—one that might be called "product labeling" in contemporary parlance—probably helped Mormonism escape the fate that awaited the Campbellites. The original aim of the Disciples of Christ was to be the church to end all churches, the ecclesiastical institution that, by the force of its theological claims, would attract all other Protestant churches to merge with it, bringing an end to denominationalism.[10] In claiming the name Christian, the Campbellites found themselves drawn into the Protestant compact and could only watch as their "true" church—the one supposed to end all churches—gradually lost so much of its distinctiveness that it turned into yet one more Protestant denomination—or into two if the Christian/Disciple schism is taken into account.

A close reading of Apostle McLellin's journals prompted me to reconsider this labeling matter as Joseph Smith's followers had to work through it in the 1830s. These valuable documents provide firsthand evidence that historians who write about a religious marketplace in the early republic are not simply using an effective metaphor. In the 1830s, an actual religious marketplace existed in towns, villages, and hamlets all across the nation. Preachers of every stripe proclaimed the Christian gospel in the schoolhouses, courthouses, meetinghouses, and even barns that formed the public square of that day. This competition for converts meant that Baptist preachers had to find a way to distinguish themselves from Congregationalist and Presbyterian ministers, Disciples, and similar groups; Methodist circuit riders had to find a way to distinguish themselves from all the other evangelists; and so forth. Since the texts for their sermons were drawn from the same scriptures (the Bible) that all the other preachers used, what to call themselves and their message posed a real problem for Saints on the religious hustings.

It was not simply a question of using common scriptural texts. Although Mormon missionaries usually told their listeners about the Book of Mormon and generally directed those who responded to their gospel presentations to "gather to Zion," the basic LDS message was, at many points, virtually the same message that Protestant ministers were preaching. Most particularly, according to Richard Bushman, the Mormon message often coincided with what members of the new Disciples of Christ were preaching.[11]

But Bushman, in his delineation in *Joseph Smith and the Beginnings of Mormonism* of the difference between the Mormon prophet's followers and this group whose members were confiscating the Christian label by calling their church "the Christian Church," did not explore the implications of the Disciples' rapid appropriation of this label for either the Disciples or the Saints. Yet the fact that another group challenged the Saints' appropriation of the name Christian appears to have been important in the formation of Mormon distinctiveness and possibly even a factor in Mormonism's survival as a movement whose adherents became a "peculiar people."

Scholars usually report that Smith's followers shortened to "Mormon" the derisive "Mormonite" appellation their opponents had given them. Not so often mentioned, but equally consequential, is their taking Eber D. Howe's scornful naming of the movement in his anti-Mormon work *Mormonism Unvailed* and turning it inside out so that, by 1839, in an epistle from Liberty prison, Joseph Smith himself could proclaim that "truth is 'Mormonism.'"[12] Adopted by his followers, this distinctive label sent a signal to potential converts that this church was not a Christian church in the usual sense of the term, even if the Mormons who were licensed to preach the gospel contended on reasonably equal terms with all the other preachers who were proclaiming the gospel of Christ.

Today, members of the Church of Jesus Christ of Latter-day Saints may be sorry that the need to distinguish themselves from the Campbellites forced the early Saints to forego calling themselves Christians, thereby relinquishing the only name that could have provided Mormonism with an unambiguous Christian identity. But from the standpoint of the identity construction critical to the preservation of distinctiveness, the adoption of an alternative label in their early formative stage worked to the Saints' advantage.

While the Mormon gospel was Christian, it was not the same gospel being preached by Methodists, Baptists, Presbyterians, and representatives of all other existing forms of Christianity. Those who accepted the gospel, repented, and were baptized under the hands of Mormon missionaries did not simply become Christians. They were convinced they were the Saints that God promised (through revelation to Joseph Smith) to gather out from "among the Gentiles."[13] As such, they understood themselves to have become members of a chosen lineage, a peculiar people. It is therefore not surprising that the prophet's followers erected a sturdy rhetorical fence between themselves and those who were not part of the group. Naming the *other*, they denominated as "Gentile" all those who had not yet heard the Mormon gospel and especially those who had heard it and refused to accept it. This naming became a primary means of establishing the distinctiveness of the LDS Church.

In the light of a contemporary rhetorical shift that seems to be turning Mormon into an adjectival modifier used to signify a particular kind of Christian, I may seem to be making too much of the fact that at a critical juncture in the establishment of their church, the Saints accepted and came to relish Mormon and Mormonism as alternative labels. But there can be little doubt that their embracing the label Mormon in lieu of being called Christian contributed to a perception that Mormonism is not Christian.

The Saints' naming of those who would not hear the LDS message also figured in the conception of Mormons as non-Christian. Writings about Mormonism penned in the nineteenth century by Catholics as well as Protestants reveal that Christians in both those camps were stung by the "Gentile" label. Their understanding was (and is) that the primary purpose of Christ's life and ministry was to extend the gospel to the Gentiles. It therefore seemed to them both strange and ironic that these upstart Saints would use this particular term to imply that Christians who were not Mormons remained outside the gospel bounds, especially since the negative naming was being done by the members of an institution that bore the name of Jesus Christ.

Distinguishing so plainly between themselves and those outside the community was nevertheless useful and perhaps even necessary during the decades of fortress mentality that characterized the kingdom period of Mountain Mormonism. While opposition to this flourishing movement was not entirely—or even primarily—grounded in religion, between 1850 and 1890 the Saints had to face intense political and legal harassment that was nearly always explained in religious terms. That they believed all their opponents were Gentiles must have helped them slough off charges that Mormonism was the very antithesis of Christianity. Considering the source as Gentile surely helped them ignore indictments that the Saints were not only un-Christian because some of them engaged in the practice of plural marriage but also un-American because they were all helpless pawns in the hands of tyrants who had turned a U.S. territory into a theocratic state. In view of such negation of all they held dear, the Saints' confidence that they were a chosen people and that, as such, they were the only true Christians must have sustained and comforted the LDS community.

The LDS political kingdom and the practice of plural marriage were the most public and hence visible evidences of that part of the "restoration of all things" that rooted Mormonism in the Old Testament as well as the New. When coerced to give up both at the end of the nineteenth century, the LDS Church started what was at first an almost imperceptible transfiguration that would ultimately lift once again to public view the Christianity that had always been at the base of Mormonism. Following the publication of the 1890 Manifesto that renounced the church's sanction of plural marriage, the Saints started to move away from—or at least to deemphasize—the Hebraicism appended to Mormon Christianity in Kirtland, Missouri, and Nauvoo, Illinois. Not, however, until after the mid-twentieth century did the Saints start to give up labeling outsiders—whether Christian or not—as Gentiles.

This turn away from labeling outsiders as other has coincided with the dramatic turn to which I referred earlier, a turn toward Christian rhetoric and Christian themes, not only in Mormonism's official presentation of itself to the world but also in Mormon life generally. I located these shifts by closely analyzing the LDS missionary lessons since the 1960s and the contents of the *Ensign* since 1971, but all sorts of other church publications provide evidence of the commanding presence of Christian rhetoric in modern Mormonism. I regard the casual manner in which Mormons are increasingly referring to themselves as Christians as even more convincing evidence that Mormons are coming to think of theirs as the Church of Jesus Christ more than they are thinking of it as the Mormon or LDS Church.

I keep a notebook of examples of linguistic signals that show how rapidly this shift is taking place. One of the items recounts a three-way conversation among a graduate student who was a true-blue birthright Latter-day Saint, the chancellor of our university, and me in the early 1990s. I am sensitive to the shift and often anticipate altered LDS rhetoric, but I must admit that I was somewhat surprised to hear my young friend explain that her husband had learned Japanese when he was "serving a Christian mission" in Japan.

This change in how the Saints think of and talk about themselves and how they think of and talk about those who are not Saints suggests to me that having attained a firm LDS identity during 125 years or so of creating and living in a separate and distinct Mormon culture, the Saints no longer have a sociological need for Gentiles. They do not need an *other* to set themselves apart either rhetorically or categorically. If this reading of what is happening is correct, it calls into question the somewhat cynical notion that is sometimes articulated, even by Latter-day Saints, that the paramount reason for the increasing level of the Saints' collaboration in ecumenical efforts to relieve distress, hunger, and suffering in the world is that the LDS Church wants to improve its public image as a Christian organization. The interreligious activities reported in the *Church News* and described nearly every week on the *News from the Church of Jesus Christ of Latter-day Saints* audiotape, which the church distributes to media outlets, signal instead the self-confidence of a people whose identity is now fixed and steadfast enough that they no longer need to be segregated from other denominations.

❖ ❖ ❖

Saints, however, are not being universally welcomed into the Judeo-Christian fold. Several reasons may account for this. While such ecumenical bodies as the National Conference of Christians and Jews and various interchurch relief organizations are pleased to have a new cooperative partner, some mainstream Protestant denominational bodies seem reluctant to accept a newcomer on equal terms, perhaps because they have been, in the sociologist Wade Clark Roof's words, "hemorrhaging members."[14] Some mainline churches are clearly worried about the impact of the success of the LDS missionary program on the size of their congregations. But this pragmatic consideration, at least among the Methodists, is of less importance than the LDS Church's doctrinal insistence that all Christian baptisms are null and void except those performed by properly ordained holders of the LDS priesthood. I expect this negative reaction exists in most of mainstream Protestantism for this subject seems to have become a matter of particular touchiness since Vatican II, when the Roman Catholic church accepted Protestant baptisms as legitimate.

Notwithstanding the refusal of the Presbyterians to accredit Mormonism as Christian, many members of the old Protestant "establishment" seem willing to make a place for the Saints in the American religious mosaic. Furthermore, if the signals from Salt Lake City—where the Tabernacle Choir gave a concert to celebrate the renovation and rededication of the Cathedral of the Madeleine—are at all indicative of a larger pattern, the same may be said of the nation's Roman Catholic community. But the same cannot be said for most of the neo-evangelicals and Protestant fundamentalists who form the conservative Christian coalition. For them, the matter of "sheep stealing" is extremely important, as are various doctrinal issues. But, to return to my main theme, I believe that neither of these matters is as potent as labeling. This time, however, the issue is turned on its head. As the Saints' need for an *other* has been steadily diminishing during the past quarter of a century, such a need has been escalating in conservative Christianity. That need is being satisfied by the Latter-day Saints, although they are by no means the only ones serving as negative markers of conservative Christian identity.

For the most part, Christians in this fundamentalist-evangelical-Pentecostal coalition share an emphasis on the critical need for an experiential encounter with Jesus Christ (being "born again"), and they likewise share acceptance of the Bible as both "inerrant" and the only source containing the revealed Word. Moreover, many of the members of the independent congregations belong to such ecumenical organizations as Youth for Christ. In the National Association of Evangelicals, the coalition has its own ecumenical organization. Yet the various constituencies in this conservative Christian coalition differ so much among themselves over significant points of doctrine and ritual, as well as the proper form of church organization, that finding a unifying descriptor (one that at once includes and excludes) has turned out to be a formidable task.

To the dismay of members of the mainstream Protestant denominations that have always regarded themselves as evangelical, the neo-evangelicals have practically succeeded in taking possession of the evangelical designation. (Some Methodists are also bothered because many of these new evangelicals have also been trying to take exclusive possession of John Wesley.) Since not all fundamentalists describe themselves as evangelicals and not all evangelicals are fundamentalists, capturing this label has not proved sufficient. As a result, at least some conservative Christians have been engaging, with some success, in a two-pronged effort to take exclusive possession of the Christian label.

In their most wide-ranging and sustained attempt to de-Christianize those who do not agree with their position on the inerrancy of the scriptures and other "fundamentals," many Christians in the conservative coalition condemn the liberal stance of the National Council of Churches (successor to the Federal Council of Churches of Christ in America), making it obvious that they question the "real" or "true" Christianity of members of the historic Protestant denominations that maintain membership in a body concerned with inclusiveness and the social gospel. More important, conservative fundamentalists, neo-evangelicals, and Pentecostals characterize as potentially apostate any Christian willing to surrender one whit of Christianity's exclusive claim. They often place beyond the pale Christians who affirm the existence of other legitimate ways to be religious.

According to many conservative Christians, however, the ultimate heresy of liberal Protestantism is not its inclusiveness. Its greatest heresy is its tendency to acknowledge the validity of modern scholarship, especially the work of the scholars in the so-called Jesus Seminar who question the historicity of the virgin birth and all the others who place early Christianity in cultural context and study it as a social movement, but also those who question the historicity of the Bible's Old Testament books—the Book of Daniel in particular. No matter what the intensity of such people's commitment to the cause of the gospel of Jesus Christ, the right wing of the neo-evangelical/fundamentalist coalition describes such Christians as secular humanists and reads them right out of Christianity.

A somewhat different, but equally exclusivist, approach may be seen in modern evangelicalism's renewed embrace of old charges that America's indigenous religions (Seventh-day Adventism, Mormonism, Christian Science, and Jehovah's Witnesses) are non-Christian cults. Such charges were a staple of Protestant journalism in the nineteenth century, when Protestants and Catholics believed that the responsibility to carry the gospel to the heathens and pagans included an obligation to carry the gospel to "benighted" Mormons, Adventists, Christian Scientists, and Jehovah's Witnesses. The home missionaries, as they were called, who undertook such assignments assumed it was also their place to warn the members of traditional Christian bodies—and anyone else who would listen—against these new movements.

Even after the Saints renounced the practice of plural marriage and gave up their political kingdom, some efforts were still made to warn Americans about the danger Mormonism posed to the nation. Yet for almost half a century, there was a clear break in Protestant efforts to convert Latter-day Saints away from Mormonism. Soon after the end of World War II, however, certain conservative groups renewed the attempt to take the Protestant version of the gospel to participants in all sorts of "new religious movements," including those that would increasingly be described by evangelicals and fundamentalists as the four "major American cults," the largest of which was Mormonism.[15] Significantly, however, this "mission ministry" began not as a campaign to warn potential converts away from these "new" movements but as an effort by conservative Christians, who were convinced that they were the only ones with access to "true truth," to share the gospel with those in darkness.

Although those who have succeeded the Southern Baptist minister John L. Smith, the first publisher of the *Utah Evangel,* are now trying to keep people from becoming Mormon as much as seeking to induce Latter-day Saints to leave their faith, Smith's early ministry seems to have been primarily directed to converting members of the Utah Mormon church away from Mormonism and into evangelical Protestantism. To a lesser extent, this was true of the ministry of the Reverend Wesley Walters, a Presbyterian clergyman whose reporting of research into the early life of Joseph Smith was aimed as much at convincing LDS believers that Smith was not a prophet as at warning Presbyterians away from Mormonism. Early efforts of Ex-Mormons for Jesus and several other groups of dissident Saints were also directed to Saints whose faith appeared to be wavering. Convincing Saints that they have been deceived seems to have been the primary objective animating Jerald Tanner and Sandra Tanner, Mormon converts to Protestant fundamentalism who publish the *Salt Lake City Messenger* and have produced a mass of exposé material designed to prove that Joseph Smith, Brigham Young, and LDS leaders from the 1830s onward all had or have clay feet. But because there were other evangelists who mounted similar ministries to Adventists, Christian Scientists, and Jehovah's Witnesses at about the same time, it is clear that the Mormons were by no means the only—or even always the principal—domestic target of conservative Protestantism.

As I read it, this mission started to change in the 1970s for two quite different reasons. First is the set of interrelated elements that propelled post–World War II Mormonism out of its intermountain sanctuary, away from the sidelines, and onto the nation's cultural and religious main stage, where it challenged conservative Protestantism on its home turf. A second and more complex reason is related to the creation of the Moral Majority and the sense of danger conservative Christians felt when they realized they shared with the Saints a common social and political agenda. This very closeness caused evangelicals and fundamentalists to pull back and led many of those who had theretofore eschewed the anti-Mormon crusade to take strenuous measures to define Mormonism as beyond the Christian pale.

So far as their distinctiveness in the mainstream white American culture is concerned, the Saints started to lose their status as peculiar people sometime between 1950 and 1970. Evidence of this shift includes the ubiquitous presence of the Tabernacle Choir on radio and television and in almost every American home equipped at that time with a sound system and roundtable for playing the "new" LP records; the gradual ascent into the nation's consciousness of an array of attractive, distinctly Mormon personalities from the political, sports, and entertainment scenes (Ezra Taft Benson, George Romney, Johnny Miller, the Osmonds); integration of "those amazing Mormons" into the idealistic representation of American culture found in middlebrow print media (*Coronet, Reader's Digest*); and the depiction of Mormons—although not always so identified—in a series of low-key radio and television spots that espoused and connected the Saints to American family values. Both because the church worked at its image so hard and because the media's purposes were served by pointing to real-life Leave-It-to-Beaver families (at least in the 1950s and 1960s), the LDS image was transformed during these middle decades from exotic outsider to inordinately wholesome, "squeaky clean" insider.

On the religious scene, the remarkable success of the LDS missionary program in the 1950s, 1960s, and 1970s was news, but so was the success of Adventist missionaries and Jehovah's Witnesses. Because the exceptional rate of growth of conservative Christian congregations was also newsworthy, it was perhaps inevitable that the heralds of the several movements would seek out the same audiences. Evangelical and fundamentalist missionaries from the United States were challenged by Adventists and Witnesses as often as by Latter-day Saints in overseas mission fields, but the Mormons were the ones who appeared to be making the most headway at home. Mormon proselytizing was especially successful in suburbia, the field whitest to the harvest, where LDS missionaries contended most directly with conservative Protestantism and where the Saints often seemed to be winning.

Yet neither Mormonism's increasing visibility and acceptability in the culture nor the news about its fantastic rate of growth was the main source of the perception that Mormonism might really be a threat to American Protestantism. That came with the growing realization that Mormonism was no longer "out there" somewhere. The appearance—apparently sudden and seemingly everywhere—of new LDS meetinghouses, easily identified as Mormon because they were all built according to standard architectural plans, signaled that Latter-day Saint success was not likely to be temporary.

This emergence of the Saints on the American religious landscape was actually not as precipitous as it looked, for the Saints had long been present in many areas of the nation. But before World War II, local Mormon organizations outside the Intermountain West and California were nearly all associated with the geographical headquarters of regional LDS missions, which, for the most part, were housed in Victorian mansions or other substantial dwellings in residential areas. Although signs identified them as LDS mission headquarters, these structures did not resemble churches and therefore did not advertise the existence of LDS congregations outside Utah. While a number of LDS ward houses had been built in southern California and all along the West coast before 1941 and while several substantial meetinghouses were located in the larger urban areas of the nation, these buildings also did not effectively advertise the presence of LDS congregations, for the structures' architecture was not peculiarly Mormon.

This situation changed dramatically between 1945 and 1965 as LDS men from the Intermountain West, most of whom were members of the church's lay priesthood, settled with their families in many different areas of the United States. Joining branches of longtime relocated "Mountain Saints" and the rapidly expanding cadre of LDS converts who had never "gathered to Zion," these "Utah Mormons" provided the lay leadership critical to the organization of LDS stakes and wards all across the country. The formation of these basic congregational units of the church called for building meetinghouses on an unprecedented scale.

In what turned out to be a brilliant decision from the standpoint of the maintenance of LDS identity in an altered situation, leaders of the church decreed that the church's standard building plans would be used for all these LDS structures. Their edict, which appears to have been made on practical and economic grounds, has been much maligned on aesthetic grounds. But in view of the significance of place to the Saints, the sagacity of the decision that led the Saints to build structures giving the appearance of a new religious "franchise" is evident in retrospect.

The reason this is the case is fairly obvious. Members of virtually all of these newly formed "mission field" stakes and wards included western Saints who had been born in the church. They had been reared in a Mormon culture rooted as firmly in a sense of place (Zion in the tops of the mountains) as in the sense of unity and order implicit in a world whose structure rests on a coherent "plan of salvation" and a clearly defined system of ecclesiastical hierarchy. In many of these newly organized units, there were also members who were lifelong Saints or longtime converts who had never moved west but whose religious imagination and institutional life revolved around Salt Lake City, Mormonism's center place.

The new LDS congregations also included substantial and sometimes overwhelming proportions of recent converts; they needed a special place where the "Mormonizing" process could go forward. No matter what their physical location, the neat, utilitarian, multifunctional structures built according to the church's standard plan were distinctively Mormon places. The very fact that these clearly identifiable LDS structures could be found in town after town and suburb after suburb cultivated among the Saints what might be called a Zionic sense, making the LDS meetinghouses themselves agents of assimilation and signals that wherever the Saints gather, there Zion is.

The Saints were not the only ones able to read this signal, however. It was also read by evangelicals and fundamentalists—and by some members of churches in the Protestant mainstream—who surmised that the growth of Mormonism, which they regarded as non-Christian, was endangering Christianity itself. As suggested, their worry was strengthened in the early 1980s after the television evangelist Jerry Falwell moved from the religious to the political arena and created the Moral Majority, into which he welcomed the Latter-day Saints, whose social and political agenda was correctly perceived to coincide almost precisely with that of conservative (evangelical and fundamentalist) Protestantism.

Students of culture as well as religion have identified and started intensive study of a cross-cultural phenomenon they describe as "fundamentalism." Fundamentalist movements are characteristic of those cultures in which change, rather than stability, has become the normal condition. Specialists in the study of these movements say that in whatever culture they appear, the people who are attracted to them are threatened by the blurring of gender, race, and all the other apparently inborn status distinctions emblematic of traditional cultures. As indicated by Martin Marty and Scott Appleby, directors of the massive Fundamentalism Project at the University of Chicago, a critical identifying element of such a fundamentalist movement is not merely its construction of an *other,* over and against which it can stand. An *other* must be constructed whose properties and attributes are very close to, but not exactly the same as, the properties and attributes of those in the movement. Because the primary function of the *other* is creating clarity where confusion might reign, it cannot be truly foreign.[16]

The Reverend Jerry Falwell was not wrong when he concluded that many of the Latter-day Saints and the members of the conservative Christian coalition shared similar values, lifestyles, and political preferences. They are for traditional family values, and they stood firmly against the Equal Rights Amendment. They define homosexuality as aberrant and homosexual practices as sinful, they are against abortion—although the LDS position is less rigid and more nuanced—and they oppose the ordination of women. They express their distaste for long hair (on men), short skirts (on women), and rock music. They even share a strong preference for the King James Version of the Bible.

What they do not share is a theology and a plan of salvation. This difference is, at base, the reason for the activities of Concerned Christians, Inc., an organization that seeks to accomplish its goals by propagating the messages in the *Godmakers* books and films prepared and distributed by Ed Decker and Dave Hunt. It also explains the accelerated rekindling of anti-Mormonism by all the other groups who oppose the Mormons by arguing they are a non-Christian cult. Mainly composed of evangelicals and fundamentalists, these groups are sometimes joined by ex-Mormons, but their ministry is not aimed primarily at the Saints. It is directed first and foremost to those who are not Mormon. As various advertisements of their films and publications explain, these groups believe that they serve the Christian community by "exposing and bringing to full knowledge the real doctrines of false prophets and teachers of the Mormon Church." Their purpose is providing conservative Christians with information that will allow them to discriminate effectively between "false truth" and "true truth."

Decker and Hunt's rabid book and appalling films, which feature cartoon-like renderings of temple ceremonies, have been widely shown and appreciatively received in hundreds, perhaps thousands, of evangelical and fundamentalist congregations. These groups seem grateful to have the *other* named and classified. Although no means of precisely determining the source of most of the support of these and other anti-Mormon efforts exists, and while there is no way to identify the purchasers of the books and pamphlets that purport to reveal the secrets of the "temple cult," the appeal of works in this genre, including *Secret Ceremonies,* a best-selling book by Deborah Laake, is certainly not their artistic merit or reportorial excellence.[17] Rather it is that they touch on the point where Mormonism diverges most dramatically from traditional Christianity, thereby providing evangelical and fundamentalist readers and viewers of video presentations with negative confirmation of their own conservative Christian faith.

❖ ❖ ❖

I am certain the charge that Mormons are members of a non-Christian "temple cult" must be as distressing to Latter-day Saints as the charge that liberal Protestants are secular humanists is disturbing to Methodists like me. But my study of Mormon history has helped me put these charges in perspective: there was a time not long ago when the label "Mormon" was not always enclosed in parentheses when it was used by members of the Church of Jesus Christ of Latter-day Saints. By reminding the members of the LDS Church that they were God's chosen people, that label enclosed the Saints within communal bounds and signaled that those who remained outside were Gentile. As an identifying label, "Christian" (even "conservative Christian") cannot do the work of including only those who ought to be included within the boundaries of the neo-evangelical/fundamentalist/Pentecostal coalition nearly so well as the label "Mormon" once worked to include Saints and only Saints in the LDS community.

The designations conservative Christians use to exclude those who are not adjudged worthy to be drawn inside their particular Christian circle are less parsimonious than the Saints' designation of outsiders. They are likewise less charitable and more offensive. Yet it seems to me that when I am described as a secular humanist and members of the Church of Jesus Christ of Latter-day Saints and the Reorganized Church of Jesus Christ of Latter Day Saints are described collectively as non-Christian, what is really being said to us all ultimately has less to do with our Christian faith or lack of it than with the fact that, to those who make such charges, we are Gentile.

A final personal observation: even though I suppose I can understand why people keep indicting liberal Christianity for its openness, its social activism, and its failure to accept the principle of inerrancy; even though I think I am able to comprehend why the same people or others like them keep trying to tear Mormon Christianity down by endeavoring to prove it not true; and even though I appreciate the positive function of negation and refutation, I regret that such things have come to pass because I am certain that winners and losers alike will be drawn within the circle of God's love someday. I am convinced that the time will come when Christians will no longer need to choose up sides and come out fighting. Meanwhile, when I am asked by one set of Christians whether I think they ought to be warning people away from another set of Christians, I refer to Matthew 13 and the parable of the wheat and the tares: "So when the plants came up and bore grain, then the weeds appeared also. . . . And the servants . . . came and said to [the Lord], . . . do you want us to go and gather them? But he said 'No, lest in gathering the weeds you root up the wheat along with them.'"[18]

In the fullness of time, a decision will be made in a higher court as to whether the Holy Catholic church that evolved from the apostolic church described in the New Testament managed to stay Christian; whether the Protestants, including the Anglicans, who separated from the Roman church maintained their status as Christians; whether the Methodists who separated from the Anglicans continued to be Christian; and whether the new Christian movements that evolved in the United States in the nineteenth century—Mormonism, Seventh-day Adventism, Christian Science—are authentically Christian. Till then, as one who sees "in a mirror dimly," I withhold judgment, counting within the definition of Christian any church, sectarian movement, liberal or conservative coalition, or new religious tradition that gathers persons together in the name of Christ and, in so doing, creates genuine community wherein women and men may—to use Methodist phraseology—take up the cross and follow him.

Notes

1. Jan Shipps, "Mormonism: An Independent Interpretation," in *Encyclopedia of Mormonism,* 5 vols., ed. Daniel H. Ludlow (New York: Macmillan, 1992), 1:248–50.

2. Jan Shipps, *Mormonism: The Story of a New Religious Tradition* (Urbana: University of Illinois Press, 1985), 87–107.

3. The title of the session was "Mormon History and the Conundrum of Culture." While not available as a printed text, both Hansen's paper and my remarks are conveniently accessible from Sunstone in an audiotape format.

4. In its selection of Grant McMurray as church president in 1993, the RLDS Church cut the line, up to that point unbroken, of having as prophet-president a direct descendant of Joseph Smith.

5. Whether this historic emphasis will continue is an open question.

6. Ernst Troeltsch, one of the earliest and most influential sociologists of religion, characterized Christian institutions as either churches or sects. The way this classification relates to Mormonism is discussed in Lawrence A. Young, "Sect," in *Encyclopedia of Mormonism,* 3:1291–92.

7. Doctrine and Covenants 18:11–12.

8. Ibid. 20:2.

9. Jan Shipps and John W. Welch, eds., *The Journals of William E. McLellin, 1831–1836* (Provo, Utah, and Urbana: *BYU Studies* and University of Illinois Press, 1994), 152.

10. William A. Clebsch, "Each Sect the Sect to End All Sects," *Dialogue* 1 (Summer 1966): 84–89, speaks of the "morphology" of American religion and points to his be-

lief that the exclusivist tendency in American religion has made every group hope, at some time or other, to be "the sect to end all sects." Certainly this was the initial goal of the Campbellite organization.

11. Richard L. Bushman, *Joseph Smith and the Beginnings of Mormonism* (Urbana: University of Illinois Press, 1984).

12. Eber D. Howe, *Mormonism Unvailed* (Painesville, Ohio: By the author, 1834); Joseph Smith Jr., *Teachings of the Prophet Joseph Smith,* comp. Joseph Fielding Smith (1938; reprint, Salt Lake City: Deseret Book, 1976), 139.

13. Doctrine and Covenants 133:12.

14. Wade Clark Roof, "Mainline Protestantism," in *Taking Stock and Charting Change: Religious Reconfigurations in America since the Sixties,* ed. Jan Shipps and David Smith (Indianapolis: Privately printed on the occasion of the retirement of Robert W. Lynn from the head of the Religion Division of Lilly Endowment, Inc., 1990), 6–12. Roof used the phrase "hemorrhaging members" in a public presentation of the material in this chapter.

15. Anthony A. Hoekema, *The Four Major Cults* (Grand Rapids, Mich.: Eerdmans, 1963).

16. Martin Marty and Scott Appleby, "Conclusion: An Interim Report on a Hypothetical Family," in *Fundamentalisms Observed,* ed. Martin Marty and Scott Appleby (Chicago: University of Chicago Press, 1991), 842.

17. Deborah Laake, *Secret Ceremonies: A Mormon Woman's Intimate Diary of Marriage and Beyond* (New York: W. Morrow, 1993).

18. Matt. 13:27–29 KJV.

4

"This Great Modern Abomination": Orthodoxy and Heresy in American Religion

Terryl L. Givens

> Therefore let everyone who can, smite, slay, and stab, secretly or
> openly, remembering that nothing can be more poisonous,
> hurtful, or devilish than a rebel.
> —Martin Luther, 1525

> O merciful God, who hast made all men, and hatest nothing that thou
> hast made: have mercy upon all Jews, Turks, and HERETICS.
> —frontispiece to Reverend Henry Caswell's *City of the Mormons,* 1842

> There is scarcely the faintest notion anywhere that unbelief might be
> changed directly into what the church calls false belief. No, where
> there is heresy, orthodoxy must have preceded. For example, Origen
> puts it like this: "All heretics at first are believers; then later they
> swerve from the rule of faith."
> —Walter Bauer, *Orthodoxy and Heresy in Earliest Christianity,* 1971

The heretic has always been a much graver threat to spiritual solidarity than
the infidel. Contamination, seduction, corruption, insinuation are hallmarks
of the first; mere difference the mark of the second. The fires of the Inquisi-
tion scorched the lapsed Christian or deviant believer, not the professing Jew
or the Muslim. In the context of sociocultural difference, we have seen that
threatening categories often invite a representational response that would emphasize or invent otherness as a means of establishing a tolerable distance. In
the religious realm, heresy reflects a similar need to exaggerate disparity so that
boundaries can be imposed and enforced. To speak in these terms is to recognize the constructed, artificial, and highly malleable nature of categories like
heresy and orthodoxy. Of course, ideology often conceals its own foundations.
For example, if the believer accepts whatever *is* as originary or primary, then

anything else is schism or apostasy from the primal, sanctioned order, and authority may legitimately identify and censure such deviance wherever it occurs. This is the implication of the seeming truism that Walter Bauer cites, that where there is heresy, orthodoxy must have preceded. Heretics are those who swerve from the *rule* of faith.

In reality, orthodoxy comes into being only after there are choices to be made, with competing, and mutually exclusive, options. Heresy is the choice that loses. Ecclesiastical history, like any other, is written by the victors. In the case of American religious history, the situation grows more complicated, however. In colonial times, heresy and orthodoxy were simple matters. Ecclesiastical authority, buttressed by the arm of the state, was centralized and arbitrary. Thus in 1659, the official church of Massachusetts (Puritan Congregationalism) had no difficulty in trying a number of Quakers for heresy, finding them guilty, and hanging them for their nonconformity. Two went to the gallows in that year, and one each in 1660 and 1661.[1] With the constitutional rupture of the church-state alliance, orthodoxy and heresy persisted as categories, but sanctions were restricted. Heresy, that difference sufficient to prompt excommunication rather than benign censure or correction, marks the limits of religious freedom which any one particular community will tolerate. Outside the borders of that religious community, the designation is meaningless—or so it would seem.

In the absence of a state religion, and in spite of an American predilection for religious diversity, heresy has persisted as a category that transcends narrow denominational boundaries. By general nineteenth-century consensus, Mormonism was self-evidently beyond the pale of mere difference, a fit candidate for the label of heresy. As Ruth Alden Doan has pointed out, excommunication from orthodox churches of that period was not practiced for "fine distinctions": "The cases that came to trial tended to point to rather obvious disagreements—acceptance of universal salvation, for example, or 'imbrasing the *Mormon heresy* [sic].'"[2]

Such trials were common among the Baptists and Congregationalists. Thus we have the experience of the recently converted Mormon Isaac Haight, who records that "in the fall of 1839 the Baptist Church sent their priest to labor and reclaim me from the error of my ways. . . . [He] requested me to meet with the church and answer for myself before the deacons. I gladly accepted the invitation and on the day appointed I met with the church to be tried for heresy."[3] And in the same period, the Mormon William Seichrist was "excluded from the fellowship of this [Baptist] church [of Allegheny, Pennsylvania] for embracing and maintaining a heresy,—to wit, doctrines peculiar to a late sect called Mormons or Latter-day Saints, that miracles can be wrought through the instrumentality of faith; that special revelations from God are now given to men; and that godly men are now endowed with the gift of prophecy."⁴ Such efforts to enforce doctrinal conformity within a community of believers are, to some extent, common to most religious groups. The case of Mormonism, however, presents us with a problem of ampler magnitude. In the rhetoric of the nineteenth century, what is at stake is not merely parish purity, but the national soul. The characterization of Robert W. Beers was typical: Mormonism "is acknowledged to be the Great Modern Abomination, the most pernicious heresy of this century."⁵

Heresy and Pluralism

Given the American tradition of innovation and independence, and of hostility toward authoritarianism and conformity, attacks of heresy in general, and Mormonism's "heresies" in particular, seem odd. In a society characterized by such religious pluralism, how do we distinguish diversity from heresy? When does a sect become a "cult" (a related term of opprobrium used even today of Mormonism)?⁶ And what weight or legitimacy does a label like heresy have in a democratic culture? If Mormonism is heresy, what is the American religious orthodoxy from which it deviates? The weight of such unarticulated orthodoxy is considerable. For individualism, even religious individualism, may be an American inheritance, but when religious innovation passes the threshold of the heretical, the rights of the individual have often been overridden by the greater claims of orthodoxy, as witnessed so abundantly in the religious history of the Mormons.

Clearly, to say that excommunication was not practiced for "fine distinctions" will not get us very far. Not only does such a statement beg the question of how heresy is constructed, it suggests that heresy can be correlated with departure from fundamental Christian dogma. In other words, it suggests that we can identify the core of *essential* Christian belief, make that constitutive of orthodoxy, and consider variations from *accidental* features of Christianity to explain denominational differences. Unfortunately, the historical status of Mormonism does not accord with such a mechanical model of analysis. Rodney Stark and Charles Y. Glock, for example, in their study *American Piety*, after acknowledging the virtual impossibility of finding any "universally acceptable standards" of orthodoxy,⁷ selected four "belief items" from which they constructed an "Orthodoxy Index." They were "existence of a personal God, the divinity of Jesus Christ, the authenticity of biblical miracles, and the existence of the Devil." For good measure, they included as "other central Christian tenets: life beyond death, the virgin birth, and Christ's walking on water."[8] In all seven cases, Mormon belief is in unambiguous accord with these core beliefs. Almost entirely lacking from nineteenth-century accusations of Mormon heresy are charges that they deny those beliefs, the Bible, or the Christian sacraments. It would seem, if Stark's and Glock's criteria are valid, that Mormon "heresy" was not a simple matter of rejecting orthodoxy.

That Mormons claimed to *add* scripture, or reintroduce discarded elements of the Christian tradition, they acknowledged readily enough. But given the dynamics of Protestant church history, the inescapability of tradition, convention, and doctrinal formation all serving to add layer upon layer of accretions to religious institutions, deviation or innovation per se are obviously useless categories for identifying the construction of heresy. And as the historian David Steinmetz reminds us, "Christians have argued, often passionately, over every conceivable point of Christian doctrine from the filioque to the immaculate conception. There is scarcely an issue of worship, theology, ethics, and politics over which some Christians have not disagreed among themselves."[9]

In any case, as the religious scholar Stephen Robinson has demonstrated, Mormons are labeled heretics "for opinions and practices that are freely tolerated in other mainstream denominations."[10] To take one example, a favorite target or reproach among Mormon doctrines is the belief that human beings can become gods. In the Mormon prophet Lorenzo Snow's words: "As man now is, God once was; As God now is, man may be." Robinson points out that this is a virtual paraphrase of Saint Clement's teaching that "the Word of God became a man so that you might learn from a man how to become a god." Saint Irenaeus, Justin Martyr, Athanasius, and Augustine, as well as the popular Christian apologist C. S. Lewis, proclaimed the same principle.[11]

So at least some Mormon heresies can make a claim to have once been Christian orthodoxies and are, as Truman G. Madsen has demonstrated from the other side of history, in many cases making their way back into the Christian mainstream. In his survey of Mormon doctrines from the nature of God to continuing revelation Madsen argues that a number of Mormon "heresies" anticipate positions articulated by dozens of theologians and philosophers from Dietrich Bonhoeffer and Charles Hartshorne to Avery Dulles and Dean Turner.[12]

At the same time, many Christian tenets that Mormonism rejects were patently alien to early Christianity as well—even doctrine as fundamental as the Trinity, as sources as disparate as the *New Catholic Encyclopedia* and *Harper's Bible Dictionary* acknowledge. According to the *Encyclopedia:* "The formulation of 'one God in three Persons' was not solidly established, certainly not fully assimilated into Christian life and its profession of faith prior to the end of the 4th century. . . . Among Apostolic Fathers, there had been nothing even remotely approaching such a mentality or perspective." From *Harper's*, we have the assertion that "the formal doctrine of the trinity as it was defined by the great church councils of the fourth and fifth centuries is not to be found in the New Testament."[13]

A more facile solution to the problem of defining heresy is suggested by any number of sociologists of religion who equate heresy with what is new. Frederick Sontag notes that "obviously, existing religions must consider [any] new religion as heresy."[14] Rodney Stark agrees that by definition, "since all new religions begin in obscurity," they are in their "formative days . . . tiny, deviant, and insignificant."[15] Finally, Martin Marty also observes that all major religions were considered heresy in their earliest stages.[16]

The difficulty with this explanation is twofold. First, it does not address the problem this work began by posing—why a violent response to the Mormon "heresy" out of proportion to all other antireligious expressions directed at contemporary heterodoxies? Second, it does nothing to explain why, after a century and a half, the church is still labeled "heresy" (or "cult" or "non-Christian") by its detractors. In fact, according to Gordon Melton, director of the Institute for the Study of American Religion, some four hundred "anti-cult" groups are currently aimed specifically at Mormonism.[17] Many contemporary examples could be cited, but the following is typical of the form such intolerance takes today:

> [In Vail, Colorado,] local churches were forced by high land prices to build an ecumenical chapel overlooking the slopes. Members of the Catholic, Lutheran, Baptist, Episcopalian, Presbyterian, Christian Science, and Jewish congregations all worship there après-ski. The centerpiece is a small cross fashioned out of two ski-tips. When Jews hold services, the cross is easily moved aside, but when the Vail ward of the Church of Jesus Christ of Latter-day Saints applied to use the chapel for its services, the request was denied by a 7–3 vote in 1985 of the Vail Religious Foundation, which oversees the chapel. "This is an interfaith chapel, not an intercult chapel," . . . [a] minister told the *Rocky Mountain News*.[18]

One (non-Mormon) researcher noted: "How easy it is for one person's faith to be another's heresy. Indeed, that was the basis of my early work on religion and anti-Semitism. . . . Thus I continue to be astonished at the extent to which colleagues who would *never* utter anti-Semitic, anti-Catholic, or even anti-Moslem remarks, unselfconsciously and self-righteously condemn Mormons."[19] Not only is the church no longer a recent religious innovation, it stands, in the words of this same researcher, "on the threshold of becoming the first major faith to appear on earth since the Prophet Mohammed rode out of the desert."[20]

So, rather than equate heresy with doctrine deviance or threatening novelty, it may be more useful to examine the cumulative *effect* the Mormon innovations had on challenging the very bases of Christianity as it had come to exist by Joseph Smith's day. Discovering how this heresy was constructed, we may thereby come to understand the orthodoxy that it challenged. It is easy to pinpoint the aspects of Mormonism that early detractors found most pernicious. The Reverend Diedrich Willers had found offensive the belief in supernatural visitations and continuing revelation, and the Baptist church that excommunicated Seichrist voiced similar objections, mentioning charismatic gifts, in particular. Forty years later, the Mormon leader Orson Pratt defiantly concurred about the nature of Mormon heresy: Ministers, he wrote, "from the first century down to the present time . . . have denied new revelation. . . . To believe that God would again speak and call men by new revelation . . . was in their idea a heresy, and they were not to believe in anything except it was bound in their ancient books."[21]

The fairly obvious implication, of course, is that from Pratt's perspective, the entire Christian tradition amounts to one vast heresy. Indeed, three years earlier, the Mormon apostle George Q. Cannon had proclaimed the "pure Gospel [was] lost because of the propagation, for centuries, by so-called Christian ministers, of the soul destroying and damnable heresy that God cannot or will not speak to man again from the heavens; that God will not reveal his will, send his angels, or exercise his power in the affairs of earth as much as he did in ancient days."[22] In this light, Mormonism's controversial status as a Christian sect may depend on whether "Christian" is taken to refer to a historical tradition or a mode of Jesus-centered discipleship, however idiosyncratic its articulation. The recurrent charge of orthodoxy, even today, is that Mormons are not Christian. Mormons, or members of "the Church of Jesus Christ of Latter-day Saints," as they remind their orthodox critics, officially and personally find the accusation repugnant, erroneous, and hurtful. But for Mormons to insist on their Christianity, given that label's evolution as a historically conditioned category of belief and practice, is to minimize Mormonism's innovations and to subvert its own insistence that restoration rather than mere reformation was necessary. For Pratt's and Cannon's claim that Christendom has persisted almost two thousand years in a state of apostasy is tantamount to declaring that Christianity so-called is a misnomer. Harold Bloom is correct in saying Mormonism's hallmark is its deliberate obliviousness to two millennia of Christian tradition.[23] So Mormonism could be considered, in the context of ecclesiastical history, emphatically not Christian.

Mormonism has chosen the other rhetorical route, however, asserting its claim to the Christian label, while basing that claim on its unique vision of primitive Christianity. This course is equally daring in its own way. To insist that Mormons are Christian, but in a sense peculiar to them, is to appropriate the term to their private meaning and to impudently assert that heresy is orthodoxy, and orthodoxy heresy. Such a move is not difficult for a religion that has long persisted in referring to the Jews as Gentiles.[24] But such claims do suggest that heresy in American religious discourse is not merely a function of additions, accretions, fine points of doctrine, or institutional practices. Rather, Mormonism sees itself as redefining in a radical way the essence of Christianity, and both Mormonism and its critics deny the possibility of accommodation because of the way Mormonism reconceptualizes religion itself.

Ineffability and the Sacred

Only taken in the collective do the assaults on Mormonism's heresies reveal their common theme: the disintegration of that distance that separates the sacred and the profane, that defines religious experience as unfathomable mystery, that constitutes religious feeling in the presence of the ineffable, that renders such terms as holiness, worshipfulness, and reverence as the very essence of religion. Such distance comes close to being the sine qua non of all Western religious faith and practice.

Rudolf Otto is emphatic on this point. In *The Idea of the Holy,* he insists that this category of experience, this *mysterium tremendum,* is not merely an attribute of divinity, but "the deepest and most fundamental element in all . . . religious devotion." It is something "beyond conception or understanding, extraordinary and unfamiliar, . . . before which we therefore recoil in a wonder that strikes us chill and numb." In sum, the mysterious is "that which lies altogether outside what can be thought, and is, alike in form, quality, and essence, the utterly and 'wholly other.'"[25]

Such mystery has not traditionally been characterized as merely incidental to God's nature or to our fallen condition. In Emil Brunner's words, "God's revelation of Himself always occurs in such a way as to manifest more deeply his inaccessibility to our thought and imagination. All that we can know is the world. God is not the world. . . . He is Mystery."[26] As Elizabeth A. Johnson writes:

The history of theology is replete with this truth: recall Augustine's insight that if we have understood, then what we have understood is not God; Anselm's argument that God is that than which nothing greater can be conceived; Hildegard's vision of God's glory as Living Light that blinded her sight; Aquinas's working rule that we can know that God is and what God is not, but not what God is; Luther's stress on the hiddenness of God's glory in the shame of the cross; Simone Weil's conviction that there is nothing that resembles what she can conceive of when she says the word *God;* Sallie McFague's insistence on imaginative leaps into metaphor since no language about God is adequate and all of it is improper.[27]

A sense of the sacred is inseparable from a sense of radical discontinuity, be it temporal, rational, experiential, or a combination of the three. The mystification that is usually a concomitant of such discontinuity is at the very heart of the Christian tradition especially. Whether it takes the form of Tertullian's reputed *"credo quia absurdum est"*[28] or the more subtle form of fundamentalism's ahistorical canonicalism, distance is the guarantor of the sacred's status as sacred. The difference between a contemporary and a historical prophet, a contemporary and a historical canon, a contemporary and a historical messiah, has always been the difference between excoriation and adoration. So it was that in the early history of Mormonism, at least, it was the context rather than the content, timing rather than tenets, that led inescapably to charges of heresy. For if anything is clear, it is that the targets of scathing denunciation were beliefs absolutely central to Christianity—at least to New Testament Christianity. Scriptural formation, the prophetic calling, heavenly visitations, miracles and spiritual gifts—these were explicitly and repeatedly made the focus of the anti-Mormon crusade.

This is not to say that Mormonism had a monopoly on such unorthodox tendencies or that they alone produced the faith's heretical status. When these same tendencies have been manifest in other religions, they have contributed to their marginalization by American Protestantism as well. Examples would range from Emanuel Swedenborg to Reverend Sun Myung Moon, two of many who have believed that God has revealed himself through special, personal revelations from time to time.[29] In the 1800s, as now, heterodoxies besides Mormonism shared billing as premiere examples in the "Kingdom of the Cults."[30] But when Mormonism's reenactment of Christian origins, its collapse of sacred distance, was combined with a potent, growing, and highly visible presence, the combination proved catastrophic.

From the Reverend Willers's first objections to those of the League for Social Service and beyond, religious protests were directed against early Christian claims and practices occurring "in the age of railways," to use Charles

Dickens's words. Mormonism's radicalism can thus be seen as its refusal to endow its own origins with mythic transcendence, while endowing those origins with universal import since they represent the implementation of the fullest gospel dispensation ever. The *effect* of this unflinching primitivism, its resurrection of original structures and practices, is nothing short of the demystification of Christianity itself. For Mormonism replicates the process of canon formation, prophetic utterance, communion with supernatural entities—all this *without* the veil of intervening history, mythic origins, or tradition. The church is reintegrated into the ongoing flow of human history, origins are concrete and proximate, the process of doctrinal formation is laid bare.

It has been remarked of the Mormons that "they in fact re-enacted in the sociologically conducive conditions of nineteenth-century America the experience of the biblical Hebrews, whom they sought to emulate."[31] But while they were sociologically reenacting Exodus (and much of the Gospels and Acts besides), the whole process struck contemporaries as blasphemous parody rather than mere anachronism. Even the prophet's name seemed calculated to resist any comforting aura of antiquity or exoticism—not Abraham or Hezekiah, but Joe Smith of all things, compounding the insult to religious sensibility! More than one literary character reacts dismissively: "'Smith!' said Miss Priscilla, with a snort. 'That's a fine name for a prophet, isn't it?'"[32] And, as another author's character remarked, Smith didn't even *look* like Isaiah.[33] Having met the prophet, the writer of an Illinois history bristles with similar indignation, the indignation that any attempt to demystify religion elicits: "He is, upon the whole, an ordinary man; and considering his pretensions, a very ordinary man."[34] Another visitor to Nauvoo responded similarly to the disillusion: The prophet was clearly a man of "the nineteenth century, when prophets must get a living and provide for their relations."[35]

The ubiquitous charge of blasphemy in anti-Mormon rhetoric is but another way of acknowledging this feat—the dissolution of that very distance that constitutes the essence of the sacred. Demystification, the devaluing of radical distance as a positive attribute of divinity and its workings, is precisely what critics charged and what Mormons acknowledged.

In one of his religious allegories, C. S. Lewis suggests the enormous psychological investment we have in maintaining the fundamental distinction separating the human and the divine and hints at the crisis their conflation would occasion: "The distinction between natural and supernatural, in fact, broke down; and when it had done so, one realized how great a comfort it had been—how it had eased the burden of intolerable strangeness which this universe imposes on us by dividing it into two halves and encouraging the mind never to think of both in the same context. What price we may have paid for this comfort in the way of false security and accepted confusion of thought is another matter."[36]

In the ancient church, a similar heresy had been known—cosmism, or what Hugh Nibley calls the association of religion with the physical universe in any way, or seeing God as a part, rather than the ultimate source, of reality: "The idea was that anything spiritual or anything divine had nothing to do with the physical world whatever, because God is pure spirit, and matter is vile." In this view, ex nihilo creation is a necessary premise to avoid this taint of cosmism, the idea that God actually participates in this physical realm as an artisan or shaper of materiality.[37] Nibley goes so far as to suggest that Smith's essential work was the revival of this heresy. Accordingly, the hostility directed at him was a response to "the crude literalism of his religion—not only talking with angels like regular people, but giving God the aspect attributed to him by the primitive prophets of Israel."[38]

In his classic study of Mormonism as a theological system, Sterling McMurrin finds this cosmist view aligns Mormonism more nearly with Greek naturalism than with typical Christian thought. In fact, he argues, "this is a radical departure from the position of traditional theism, whether Christian, Jewish, or Islamic." His elaboration of this "somewhat distinctive quality of Mormon theology" is worth quoting at some length:

> The naturalistic disposition of Mormonism is found in the denial of the traditional conception of the supernatural. It is typical of Mormon writers to insist that even God is natural rather than supernatural, in that there is not a divine order of reality that contrasts essentially with the mundane physical universe of ordinary experience known to us through sensory data, which is the object of scientific investigation and is described by natural law. The naturalistic facet of Mormon thought is indicated by the Mormon denial of miracles in the traditional sense of an intrusion of the supernatural that suspends the natural processes. The typical Mormon conception of a miracle is that the miraculous event, though entirely natural, is simply not understood because of deficiencies in human knowledge. From the perspective of God there are no miracles.
>
> The denial of the supernatural is not simply a terminological issue in Mormonism, for reality is described qualitatively as a single continuum.[39]

Joseph Smith's teachings and writings certainly amounted to a rematerializing of Christianity. But his work went beyond this to a rehistoricizing of Christianity as well. By serving as the conduit for a putative restoration of Christianity, he reenacted its origins. The authenticity of his call is almost beside the point. Not to believers, certainly. But to a Christian world generally, the genie cannot be put back into the bottle. Detractors could fume and shout and label him impostor and charlatan, but the unavoidable features of religion-making themselves were there for everyone to see, and *they* became the source of ridicule and fury. Time and again, the brute scope of his claims has served to obscure the contents; the forms, the modes of revealing and constructing his system, far overshadow any question of inherent value pertaining to the particulars constituting that system.

To put Joseph Smith's "canon-making originality" on a par with the Old Testament writer's "creation" of Yahweh, Mark's "invention" of Jesus, and Mohammed's revelation of Allah, as Harold Bloom does, may seem extravagant.[40] But Bloom's lack of any personal religious engagement with Joseph Smith's message at least makes it possible for him to admire as grand daring that which is so blasphemous from any orthodox perspective. Thus, Orson Pratt's sardonic observation: "For men a few centuries ago to hunt up a few scattered manuscripts and compile them into a Bible was considered a very laudable undertaking, but for any man to find a sacred book since that time is considered the highest blasphemy."[41] And, in Oliver Cowdery's words, "to talk of heavenly communications, angels' visits, and the inspiration of the Holy Spirit, *now* since the apostles have fallen asleep, . . . is a novel thing among the wise, and a piece of blasphemy."[42]

Indeed, the very first recorded reaction to the Book of Mormon (even before its publication) was a headline in the *Rochester Daily Advertiser:* "Blasphemy—Book of Mormon, Alias the Golden Bible."[43] And one who dared to teach such things, as the missionary Theodore Curtis did in England, was guilty of the only appropriate charge: He spent five days in prison in Gloucester on a charge of "blasphemy."[44]

A series of editorials in the Baptist *Religious Herald* is especially revealing. The 9 April issue for 1840 has an editorial under the heading "The Mormons": "A correspondent requests information as to the peculiar tenets of this modern sect. We have never seen a copy of the book of Mormon, nor any abstract of their creed upon which we could fully rely, as a fair exposition of their opinions." This frank admission does not, however, preclude a summary verdict: "The book of Mormon is a bungling and stupid production. . . . It contains some trite, moral maxims, but the phraseology . . . frequently violates every principle and rule of grammar. We have no hesitation in saying the whole system is erroneous."[45]

Clearly, it is not *necessary* to see the contents of the new revelation. In fact, those contents would invariably prove disappointing as evidence in any heresy trial. As one religious scholar remarks, "the Book of Mormon, first published in 1830, may not have added enough doctrinal novelty to the Christian tradition to have made Mormonism more than a Protestant sect."[46] That doesn't matter; the new revelation is itself taken as proof of the fraud. This unblushing indifference to the book's *content*, the sanguine a priori condemnation of the text, suggests that the Book of Mormon functions for the orthodox as an empty sign, intimating a divine origin but devoid of any substance that might be internally persuasive one way or the other. Points of doctrinal disagreement are obviously quite beside the point. But Christian editorialists who would vehemently condemn Mormons, Seekers, and other canon-breakers were in something of a quandary. To repudiate divine revelation as a principle would be to undermine the basis of Christianity itself. So the ostensible grounds for the rejection become the most tangible but inconsequential of criteria now imputed to this textual vacuum—bad "grammar" and awkward "phraseology."

When a reader of the *Herald* complains that the editorial writer has unduly compared Mormonism to the Campbellites, the paper responds with its list of definitive and distinctive proofs of Mormonism's heresy, again intimating a peculiar antipathy to Christian origins. It cites "belief in the book of Mormon [i.e., canon development], and in the power of working miracles, and the establishment of a separate community of saints on earth"[47] (which system the editors had already compared to "the primitive disciples and modern Shakers"[48]). Many other contemporary accounts could be cited, such as the 1835 guidebook for Ohio immigrants, warning the English against this "wildest fanaticism" called Mormonism, which espouses belief in miracles, new revelation, gifts of healing and of prophecy.[49]

Heresy may be a little passé as a term of opprobrium today, but a new one has emerged to take its place: "cult." Not surprisingly, defining the parameters of Christian "cults" becomes as elusive a task as defining heresy; ultimately, it becomes more self-referential than descriptive of the Other.[50] Current popular attempts to define the category have a way of being self-incriminating. As a result of the 1993 David Koresh incident in Waco, Texas, religious experts rushed to provide to the public litmus-test kits for identifying "dangerous cults." One typical example is unblushing in its irony. After claiming that "cults . . . are heretical" in unspecified doctrinal ways, the author goes on to the more easily identifiable hallmarks, listing the "behavioral traits" of destructive cults:

—Preaching the coming of the Apocalypse. . . .
—Attacking churches and synagogues for false teachings and not practicing what they preach.

—Relentlessly proselytizing new members.

—Making demands of followers of absolute commitment of time and money.

—Having an absolute leader whose word is law and who often claims to be a prophet. . . .

—Requiring participation in a continuous system of mind-bending lectures, prayers, chants, speaking in tongues or meditation.

—Exploiting members. . . .

—Having a system of secrecy in which members do not know the real aims of the group.[51]

It can hardly go unobserved that the New Testament portrays a Christ who preached an imminent apocalypse (Matt. 24:15), reproved the scribes and pharisees as hypocrites (Matt. 23:13), commanded the rich young man to give away all he had (Mark 10:21), proclaimed himself the Messiah (Luke 4:21), exhorted his disciples to fast and to pray always (Mark 9:29; Luke 18:1), and so forth. And yet here Christian heresy is defined in those very terms.

Heretics teach doctrine that is heretical, and heretics are just like early Christians, except they aren't. And since they aren't, they are certainly exploitative and deceptive. And, by the way, we know they aren't real Christians because they are exploitative and secretive. With "cult" as with "heresy," the semiotic value of the term has obviously been entirely neutralized, but the term's political value is incalculable.

It is most curious that a "cult's" emulation of early Christian forms is itself taken as prima facie evidence of heresy, rather than as potentially suggestive of authority. Certainly one could argue that the singularity of the church's existence consigns all other manifestations to ecclesiastical limbo—there can be only one inauguration of Christianity, as there was only one Incarnation. But as the history, not to say diversity, of Christianity amply demonstrates, movement *beyond* those original forms has long been legitimized. Indeed, such development is sanctioned by virtue of a paradigm that sees Christianity as an unfolding of the original deposit of faith. What John Henry Cardinal Newman calls the "want of accord between the early and late aspects of Christianity" is precisely the problem that he attempts to theorize in his famous *Essay on the Development of Christian Doctrine.*[52]

The intrinsic merits of Mormonism's claims seldom surface as a debatable issue, however. Not because there is no case, but because these claims are themselves taken as a sign of heresy. As the Mormons learned to their surprise, the content of the Book of Mormon was irrelevant. The record seldom elicited serious discussion because its claim to divine authorship was its own condemnation.

Strangely enough, then, it would appear that it is not deviation from origins, but disclosure of those origins—the re-presentation of sacred beginnings—that may effectively constitute the transgression of orthodoxy, at least in the increasingly secularized world of nineteenth- and twentieth-century America. This state of affairs may be explained if we consider prevailing modes of religious faith to be a condition made possible by the various forms of obscurantism that tradition leaves in its wake. Indeed, religions seem to carry as part of their own self-conceiving the means of obscuring germinal moments of their history, thereby creating an opening for the divine, the transcendent, the eternal, to intervene and create the rupture with historical reality that is the root of the sense of the sacred. Like Christ's empty tomb or Moses' mysterious burial, mystification, as the precondition for religious faith, must provide a metaphor pregnant with all the possibilities of true mystery. The weight of centuries, the poetry of creeds, and the rhythm of ritual create of themselves a sense of timelessness and sanctity that further dematerializes such founding ruptures. The immediacy and nakedness of Mormonism's foundations—like those of any contemporary religious movement—make possible a condition that critics call gullibility. What separates orthodox faith from heretical credulousness are the layers—historical, conceptual, or psychological—that intervene between institutional origins and the call to discipleship. That the *objects* of belief are essentially the same in both cases is not a comfortable thought.

In this context, Christian orthodoxy emerges as a category defined not so much by articles of faith, as by the conditions that make faith possible. The heterodoxy of Mormonism and other "cults" challenged the construction of religious belief more than the value of its particulars. Of course, certain core beliefs are essential to any conception of Christian orthodoxy: the Bible as inspired scripture, God as creator, and Christ as divine redeemer of humankind. But neither Mormonism nor other heterodox movements challenged these fundamental tenets. More to the point, as we have seen, Mormonism was not attacked for its departures, but for its retrogressions. What Mormonism and similar heresies did challenge—implicitly—was the fantasy that religious belief can circumvent its own historical conceiving: the notion that God spoke to a man, but never in an actual moment in time or to a man who was anyone's contemporary; the notion that the canon records God's word, but God never spoke a precanonical utterance.

This insistence on maintaining the illusion of religion as timeless self-givenness is implicit in Christian allusions to "the canon" as if it were the same for Catholics and Protestants, while forgetting Saint Gregory's rejection of Revelation, Luther's repudiation of James, and the arguments of some contemporary scholars that the Gospel of Thomas should be added.[53] When a group of seventy liberal religious scholars, the "Jesus Seminar" at the Westar Institute in Sonoma, California, completed work on a radical revision of the Gospels, they came under fire not just for their conclusions but also, perhaps even more so, for their reminder to us that all canons are necessarily the product of historical process. As Norman Hjelm, director of Faith and Order for the National Council of Churches, put it: Christian resistance to revisionism like that of the "Jesus Seminar" results from the tendency of most denominations to see the canon as "a given in history."[54] Popular Christian thought seldom encompasses the notion that the apostles were Christian (that is, disciples of Christ) before there were councils, creeds, or even a New Testament.

This Christian frame of mind is not merely incidental, but is essentially and inescapably related to Paul Tillich's claim that "the intention to speak unsymbolically of religion is irreligious."[55] Symbolic language is certainly lacking in Mormonism's self-presentation. Indeed, Joseph Smith's whole language was startling—and unapologetic—in its hostility to the tradition of religious discourse. Given the language of Smith's spiritual autobiography, one must doubt the comment of the otherwise accurate writer on Mormon history, William Mulder. Referring to Smith, he sympathized that "his was the perennial despair of visionaries striving how to say the unsayable." Mulder goes on to describe him and his peers (Jonathan Edwards, Ralph Waldo Emerson) as "nearly blinded by God's waylaying light, [turning] to analogy and metaphor, finding in nature 'images and shadows of divine things.'"[56] Here Mulder has missed the essential core of the Mormon heresy. For it was precisely the ease and brazenness with which Smith appropriated heavenly matters to his simple, direct discourse that got him—and the church—into trouble to begin with.

When the visionary William Blake described celestial realms, he was keenly aware of the poverty of secular language and material eyes to describe them: "'What,' it will be questioned, 'When the Sun rises do you not see a round Disk of fire somewhat like a Guinea?' O no no, I see an Innumerable company of the Heavenly host crying 'Holy Holy Holy is the Lord God Almighty.'"[57] Not so Joseph Smith. True enough, of his encounter with the angel Moroni, he would write that the angel's countenance was "truly like lightning." But such a description is no more than common metaphor, given the description that precedes it: "His hands were naked and his arms also, a little above the wrist, so, also were his feet naked, as were his legs, a little above the ankles. His head and neck were also bare. I could discover that he had no other clothing on but this robe, as it was open, so that I could see into his bosom."[58] Neither Smith's gaze nor his language scrupled to invade celestial space with artless spontaneity. Contrast his description with Otto's pronouncement: "A spirit or soul that has been conceived and comprehended no longer prompts to 'shuddering' . . . [and] thereby ceases to be of interest for the psychology of religion."[59]

Smith's unrelenting anthropomorphosizing; the chronological and geographical specificity of his encounters with the divine; his commitment of heavenly revelation to the process of transcription, publication, and marketing; his enactment of prophetic restoration through the medium of legal incorporation—these and related aspects of Smith's work rendered religious allegorizing of his message impossible. The stone cut out of the mountain without hands and seen by Daniel might have been an allegory, but its fulfillment was not: It occurred "one thousand eight hundred and thirty years since the coming of our Lord and Savior Jesus Christ in the flesh" (to the day) when the Kingdom of God was "regularly organized and established agreeable to the laws of our country" (and the state of New York).[60] When God commanded Hosea to take a harlot as a wife, the act presumably symbolized something about spiritual apostasy and devotion (Hos. 1:2). But when God commanded Joseph Smith to have Sidney Gilbert "establish a store, that he [might] sell goods," it was fruitless to search for other levels of moral significance.[61] More than one critic noted disapprovingly the prophet's rootedness in this-worldliness. Josiah Quincy was one of many to visit the prophet at Nauvoo, but one of few who refrained from "advancing any theory respecting this extraordinary man." But he could not resist the comment that "no association with the sacred phrases of Scripture could keep the inspirations of this man from getting down upon the hard pan of practical affairs."[62]

Smith's language could be lofty and sublime at times as well (portions of Doctrine and Covenants sections 76 and 88, for example). But it was the unorthodox Mormon mingling of things spiritual and worldly that generally attracted notice, including that of the editor of the *New York Herald*. As persecution heated up in Nauvoo in the summer of 1842, James Gordon Bennett reported with amusement: "Jo goes on prophecying, preaching, and building the temple, and regulating his empire, as if nothing had happened. They are busy all the time establishing factories to make saints and crockery ware, also prophets and white paint."[63]

Moroni's golden plates may have vanished from history as surely as the tablets of Moses. But just at that moment when Mormonism's empty tomb could have invited hearty skepticism, and therefore the possibility of faith, just at that moment when Smith could have nudged material foundations into mystical indeterminacy, he moved decisively in the other direction. Smith's inclusion in the preface to the Book of Mormon of affidavits signed by eleven witnesses to those plates reaffirmed his stubborn insistence on a facticity behind his religion-making that was material, palpable. "We did handle [the leaves] with our hands," report eight of the men, thus defying those within or without the faith who would seek to spiritualize the earthy solidity of the new religion's bases (while at the same time invoking the tactile testimony of the first-generation apostle Thomas).

Similarly, the angel with whom Smith conversed and who delivered to him the plates was not enshrouded in the anonymity of heavenly hosts or drawn from the sanctioned ranks of Israel's murky past, as were so many of William Blake's contacts. Instead, Moroni turns out to be a historical figure from the American continent itself, whose story is told in the Book of Mormon, and who thus serves as yet one more agent by which heavenly manifestations and divine dealings are grounded in a fixed moment and place in history—upstate New York, A.D. 421. Sacred text blurs into local, secular history; divine personages acquire military biographies—the collapsing of such categories could not go without comment among the contemporary audience. Remarked one sarcastic author of an Illinois gazetteer in 1834:

> Those who are particularly desirous of information concerning the millions of warriors, and the bloody battles in which more were slain than ever fell in all the wars of Alexander, Caesar, or Napoleon, with a particular description of their military works, would do well to read the "*Book of Mormon*," made out of the "golden plates" of that distinguished antiquarian Joe Smith! It is far superior to some modern productions on western antiquities, because it furnishes us with the names and biography of the principal men who were concerned in these enterprises, with many of the particulars of their wars for several centuries. But seriously . . .[64]

"Names," "biography," "particulars"—in such words of reproach Mormonism's critics vividly highlight the religious taboos Smith violated.

Even as Smith wrote, preached, and testified of the reintegration of things heavenly and earthly, the notion that heaven had ever been correctly envisioned as a realm exempt from rational law was increasingly vulnerable. The rise of geology in the mid-nineteenth century tended to discredit creationism. As John Ruskin complained: "If only the Geologists would leave me alone, I could do very well, but those dreadful hammers! I hear the clink of them at the end of every cadence of the Bible verses."[65] Charles Lyell published his revolutionary *Principles of Geology* in 1830, which was the first work, as one scholar has noted, "to treat the origin and history of the Earth on the assumption that all its phenomena could be explained naturally and discussed scientifically."[66] Higher Criticism filtered the biblical text through the sieve of scientific credibility, reducing sacred revelation to the status of just another literary text. Utilitarianism, scientism, and other contemporary developments and attitudes combined to make incredible a supernatural paradigm imposed on the present *or* the past.

One ingenious rebuttal to the growing scientism came from Thomas Carlyle. In true Romantic fashion, he argued that not only was the miraculous valid as a category of religious experience but that the miraculous pervaded the very fabric of daily experience as well. The problem is that "Custom" and "Time," the "grand anti-magician, and universal wonder-hider," persuade us that "the Miraculous, by simple repetition, ceases to be Miraculous."[67] From icicles to tollbooths, the right perspective illuminated a hidden wonder and showed up the insufficiencies of a mechanical rationalism as the master key by which to understand the cosmos: "Through every grass-blade . . . the glory of a present God still beams."[68]

But while Carlyle was alerting humankind to the divinity behind the mundane, "the wonder everywhere lying close on us,"[69] Smith was busy insisting on the terrestrial origins of the divine. At every turn, but increasingly toward the end of his life, it seemed he was intent on demystifying traditional categories of the sacred, on deconstructing the other-worldly into its this-worldly bases. There seems to be little other motive behind his claim that "there are no angels who minister to this earth but those who do belong or have belonged to it."[70] The fullest implications of this "heresy" were not unfolded until the spring of his last year, at which point he was publicly teaching that God himself "was once as we are now, and is an exalted man, and sits enthroned in yonder heavens! That is the great secret."[71]

Smith's worldview was the obverse of Carlyle's "natural supernaturalism." It was not that the world was always ablaze with the glory of God and science had merely overlooked this truth; that, in M. H. Abrams's words, "an unassisted transaction between the ordinary object and the dishabituated eye effects authentic miracles."[72] Rather, Smith alleged that the divine had always been more immediately accessible to human understanding and experience than apostate Christianity had acknowledged. Priestcraft had conspired to conceal this fact. The divine, in other words, was not characterized by the radical otherness that religious tradition equated with the sacred. For this reason, his religious innovation was more the naturalizing of the supernatural than the other way around.

Astonishingly, then, Mormonism's response to the secularist impulse seen in the growth of uniformitarianism, materialism, and positivism is not to challenge or defy these critiques of supernaturalism, to insist on a cosmic dualism, but to produce a religious system consonant with a monistic worldview. In one of the last revelations published by the prophet, he would affirm: "There is no such thing as immaterial matter. All spirit is matter, but it is more fine or pure, and can only be discerned by purer eyes; We cannot see it; but when our bodies are purified we shall see that it is all matter."[73]

The protest against Mormonism turns out to be, in the final analysis, much the same as the Enlightenment's protest against Christianity itself. As Gotthold Ephraim Lessing phrased it, "accidental truths of history can never become the proof of necessary truths of reason."[74] The historical situatedness of any church's birth is no small proof against its claim to universal validity. But Mormonism did not merely insert itself conspicuously into historical time; it resisted any attempt to allegorize its origins, its forms, its scriptural canon, or its claims to spiritual gifts and offices.

Why should this tendency be so universally construed as crossing the divide separating heterodoxy from heresy? Clearly, Mormonism's tendencies denied the very basis and conditions of traditional Christian belief, the experience of the sacred as the *mysterium tremendum et fascinosum*. But in addition, one could say that heresy in its simplest terms must be understood as a condition that is not merely repugnant or incomprehensible to orthodoxy, but threatening as well. This threat, in the case of Mormonism, appears to take the form of reflecting back upon Christianity itself in a particularly disconcerting way. Brigham Young's observation on the life of Joseph Smith might therefore not be as simplistic or self-serving as it at first appears: "Again, why was he persecuted? Because he revealed to all mankind a religion so plain and easily understood, consistent with the Bible, and so true. It is now as it was in the days of the Savior."[75] With all the enthusiasm a disinterested sociologist can muster, Rodney Stark lends emphatic agreement to this assessment, while completely bracketing the particular religious truth-claims involved: "It is possible today to study that incredibly rare event: the rise of a new world religion."[76] So whether it is seen by outraged skeptics as sacrilegious parody, as a reenactment of Christian origins that is a sociologist's dream, or as the divine restoration heralded by the faithful, Mormonism stands as a defiant reminder that, much as it tries to, orthodoxy cannot escape the fact of its own construction.

Notes

1. The four were Marmaduke Stevenson, William Robinson, Mary Dyer, and William Leddra. Charles II put an end to such executions in 1661. See David S. Lovejoy, *Religious Enthusiasm in the New World: Heresy to Revolution* (Cambridge, Mass.: Harvard University Press, 1985), 127–29.

2. Ruth Alden Doan, *The Miller Heresy, Millennialism, and American Culture* (Philadelphia: Temple University Press, 1987), 127.

3. Isaac Haight, "Biographical Sketch of Isaac C. Haight," typescript, Special Collections, Brigham Young University Library, 3.

4. Joseph Smith, *History of the Church of Jesus Christ of Latter-day Saints,* ed. B. H. Roberts, 2d ed. (Salt Lake City: Deseret News, 1973), 5:166. In addition, see the references to other excommunications of Mormons during the period 1835 to 1844 in Doan, *Miller Heresy,* 257–58.

5. Robert W. Beers, *The Mormon Puzzle and How to Solve It* (New York: Funk and Wagnalls, 1887), 141.

6. It could be argued, as Jan Shipps has suggested in her study of Mormonism, that "a long tradition of the study of religion in society has produced a body of well-developed and fully articulated theory which makes useful distinctions among these four terms [church, denomination, sect, and cult]." See *Mormonism: The Story of a New Religious Tradition* (Urbana: University of Illinois Press, 1985), 47. I agree with Shipps. However, there are two distinct discursive contexts in which this term has been used. The first is that alluded to by Shipps—usage by sociologists, theologians, and historians of religion. It is in that context she refers to Mormonism as a "cultic movement" that has now evolved into a "full-scale religious tradition" (50).

The second context is the one more relevant to my discussion—the term's popular usage as a label on certain "religious" bookstores' shelves to identify followers of "antichrists" and as an undeniably pejorative term hurled from pulpit and newsroom alike. Martin Marty's observation is the definitive one in this context: The term *cult* is ultimately invalid as a label, he says, since "it has come to be too easily applied to anybody whose religion we don't like." See interview, "All Things Considered," National Public Radio, 8 Mar. 1993. I am therefore interested in the popular legitimization of a term whose *function,* like that of *heresy,* is to establish the transgressive status of a group.

7. Rodney Stark and Charles Y. Glock, *American Piety: The Nature of Religious Commitment* (Berkeley: University of California Press, 1968), 22.

8. Ibid., 58–59.

9. David Steinmetz, "Christian Unity: A Sermon by David Steinmetz," *News and Notes* 5.6 (Apr. 1990), quoted in Stephen Robinson, *Are Mormons Christian?* (Salt Lake City: Bookcraft, 1991), 36–37.

10. Robinson, *Are Mormons Christian?* viii–ix.

11. Ibid., 60–61.

12. Truman G. Madsen, "Are Christians Mormon?" *Brigham Young University Studies* 15.1 (Autumn 1975): 259–80.

13. R. L. Richard, "Trinity, Holy," *New Catholic Encyclopedia,* ed. Editorial staff at the Catholic University of America (New York: McGraw-Hill, 1967), 14:299; Paul J. Achtemeier, ed., *Harper's Bible Dictionary* (San Francisco: Harper and Row, 1985), 1099. Both sources are cited in a fuller discussion of the subject by Robinson, *Are Mormons Christian?* 71–89.

14. Frederick Sontag, "New Minority Religions as Heresies," *International Journal for Philosophy of Religion* 14.3 (1983): 159.

15. Rodney Stark, "The Rise of a New World Faith," *Review of Religious Research* 26.1 (Sept. 1984): 25.

16. Marty, interview, "All Things Considered."

17. Peggy Fletcher Stack, "Some Keep a Close Eye on Mormonism," *Salt Lake Tribune*, 10 June 1995. Another 200 groups, Melton adds, target Mormons along with Jehovah's Witnesses. According to Keith E. Tolbert and Eric Pement, 174 agencies and individuals were targeting Latter-day Saints as of 1993. See their *1993 Directory of Cult Research Organizations: A Worldwide Listing of 729 Agencies and Individuals* (Trenton, Mich.: American Religious Center, 1993), 51–53.

18. James Coates, *In Mormon Circles: Gentiles, Jack Mormons, and Latter-day Saints* (Reading, Mass.: Addison-Wesley, 1991), 198.

19. Stark, "New World Faith," 27.

20. Ibid., 19.

21. *Journal of Discourses* (Liverpool: F. D. and S. W. Richards, 1854–86; reprint, Salt Lake City: N.p., 1967), 16:346.

22. Ibid., 14:169.

23. In Harold Bloom's formulation, "Mormons, if they are at all faithful to the most crucial teachings of Joseph Smith and Brigham Young, no more believe in American democracy than they do in historical Christianity." See *The American Religion: The Emergence of the Post-Christian Nation* (New York: Simon and Schuster, 1992), 91. I take his second point, but not his first.

24. The LDS theologian/prophet Joseph Fielding Smith defined *Gentile* as "one not a Mormon." See *Answers to Gospel Questions* (Salt Lake City: Deseret Book, 1957), 1:138. Though he added that Jews are not Gentiles "in the strict sense of the word," that popular usage persists, and the Mormon apostle Bruce R. McConkie has lent it his considerable authority: "Even Jews are Gentiles when they believe not the truth." See *The Mortal Messiah* (Salt Lake City: Deseret Book, 1978), 1:93. The Mormon scholar Daniel Ludlow concurs, while noting that "this usage is very difficult for many nonmembers to understand inasmuch as the word *gentile* as used by Latter-day Saints could include people who are Jews, Israelites, and Hebrews." See *A Companion to Your Study of the Doctrine and Covenants*, vol. 2 (Salt Lake City: Deseret Book, 1978), appendix A.

25. Rudolf Otto, *The Idea of the Holy,* trans. J. W. Harvey, 2d ed. (London: Oxford University Press, 1950), 12, 13–28, 146.

26. Emil Brunner, *Our Faith* (New York: Scribner's Sons, 1954), 11–12.

27. Elizabeth A. Johnson, *She Who Is: The Mystery of God in Feminist Theological Discourse* (New York: Crossroad, 1992), 7. Her citations are Augustine, *Sermo* 52, c. 6, n. 16 (*PL* 38.360); Anselm, *Proslogium,* chaps. 2–3, *Saint Anselm: Basic Writings,* trans. S. N. Deane (LaSalle, Ill.: Open Court, 1974); Hildegard of Bingen, *Scivias,* trans. Mother Columba Hart and Jane Bishop (New York: Paulist, 1990), bk. 1, vision 1, ST I, q. 3, preface; Luther, theses 19 and 20, "The Heidelberg Disputation," *Luther: Early Theo-*

logical Works, trans. and ed. James Atkinson (Philadelphia: Westminster, 1962); Simone Weil, *Waiting for God*, trans. Emma Craufurd (New York: Harper and Row, 1973), 32; and Sallie McFague, *Models of God: Theology for an Ecological, Nuclear Age* (Philadelphia: Fortress, 1987), 35 and passim.

28. His actual words were "the Son of God died; it is necessarily to be believed, because it is absurd [*ineptum*]. And he was buried, and rose again; it is certain because it is impossible [*certum est quia impossibile est*]" (*De Carne Christi* 5).

29. Mary Bednarowski, for one, notes that both Mormonism and the Unification Church "maintain that special revelation did not end with the Bible." See *New Religions and the Theological Imagination in America* (Bloomington: Indiana University Press, 1989), 7.

30. This is the name of a popular book that discusses several "cults," Mormonism among others. Written by Walter Martin, *Kingdom of the Cults* is used as a text at some fundamentalist colleges (Minneapolis: Bethany House, 1985).

31. Thomas F. O'Dea and Janet O'Dea Aviad, *The Sociology of Religion*, 2d ed. (Englewood Cliffs, N.J.: Prentice Hall, 1983), 86.

32. Charles Pidgin, *House of Shame* (New York: Cosmopolitan, 1912), 90.

33. Robert Richards [pseud.], *The Californian Crusoe; or, The Lost Treasure Found; A Tale of Mormonism* (London: Parker, 1854), 60–61.

34. Henry Brown, *The History of Illinois, from Its First Discovery and Settlement to the Present Time* (New York: Winchester, 1844), 403.

35. Josiah Quincy, *Figures of the Past* (Boston: Little, Brown, 1926), 326.

36. C. S. Lewis, *Perelandra* (New York: Macmillan, 1965), 11.

37. Hugh Nibley, "Unrolling the Scrolls," *Old Testament and Related Studies*, ed. John W. Welch, Gary P. Gillum, and Don E. Norton, vol. 1 of *The Collected Works of Hugh Nibley* (Salt Lake City: Deseret Book and Foundation for Ancient Research and Mormon Studies, 1989), 122–23. Nibley attributes the term *cosmism* to the nineteenth-century scholar Carl Schmidt (122).

38. Hugh Nibley, "Treasures in the Heavens," *Old Testament*, 171. Nibley discusses the cosmist heresy in several of his works, but see especially 122–24, 187–88, and 212 of the above volume.

39. Sterling McMurrin, *The Theological Foundations of the Mormon Religion* (Salt Lake City: University of Utah Press, 1965), 2. Again, Madsen notes the irony of a shift on the part of contemporary theologians toward this same position that "the old dualism must go." He quotes the Quaker Rufus Jones, to give one example, as insisting that "the two world theory has become impossible to those who think in the terms of this generation." See Rufus Jones, *The Radiant Life* (New York: Macmillan, 1944), 150, quoted in Madsen, "Are Christians Mormon?" 262.

40. Harold Bloom, *The Western Canon* (New York: Harcourt Brace, 1994), 6.

41. Orson Pratt, *Divine Authenticity of the Book of Mormon* (Liverpool: R. James, 1850), 1:4.

42. Oliver Cowdery quoted in *Latter Day Saints Messenger and Advocate* 1.6 (Mar. 1835): 95.

43. Francis W. Kirkham, *A New Witness for Christ in America: The Book of Mormon* (Independence, Mo.: Press of Zion's Printing and Publishing, 1942), 1:267.

44. Smith, *History*, 4:380.

45. *Religious Herald*, 9 Apr. 1840.

46. Stark, "New World Faith," 19.

47. *Religious Herald*, 31 May 1840.

48. *Religious Herald*, 9 Apr. 1840.

49. D. Griffiths Jr., *Two Years in the New Settlements of Ohio* (London, 1835; reprint, Ann Arbor: University Microfilms, 1966), 132–40.

50. See Marty, interview, "All Things Considered."

51. *Dictionary of Bible and Religion*, quoted in Ed Briggs, "Traits Are Listed That Make Religious Cults Destructive," *Richmond Times Dispatch*, 5 Mar. 1993, A8.

52. John Henry Cardinal Newman, *An Essay on the Development of Christian Doctrine* (London: Longmans, Green, 1909), 20. Cardinal Newman's book added momentum to a vigorous and ongoing debate. As an example of a more contemporary examination of "the problem of whether Christian doctrine has changed, and if it has why it has, and which changes are legitimate, if any are, and which are not," see R. P. C. Hanson, *The Continuity of Christian Doctrine* (New York: Seabury, 1981), 22. Hanson critiques Newman's work and outlines alternative models of development.

53. The new edition of the Gospels produced by the "Jesus Seminar" was published as *The Five Gospels: The Search for the Authentic Words of Jesus* (New York: Macmillan, 1993). This version casts large doses of skepticism upon the material traditionally attributed to Jesus and adds Thomas to the canon. The seminar members' contempt for canonical ossification is shown by their provocative dedication to "Thomas Jefferson, who took scissors and paste to the gospels" (v).

54. Norman Hjelm quoted in Jeffrey L. Sheler, "Cutting Loose the Holy Canon," *U.S. News and World Report*, 8 Nov. 1993, 75.

55. Paul Tillich, *Christianity and the Encounter of the World Religions* (New York: Columbia University Press, 1961), 71.

56. William Mulder, "'Essential Gestures': Craft and Calling in Contemporary Mormon Letters," *Weber Studies* 10.3 (Fall 1993): 7.

57. William Blake, "A Vision of the Last Judgement," *The Poetry and Prose of William Blake*, ed. David V. Erdman (Garden City, N.Y.: Doubleday, 1965), 555.

58. Smith, *History*, 1:11.

59. Otto, *Idea of the Holy*, 27n.

60. Doctrine and Covenants 20:1. The prophecy is from 2 Dan.

61. Doctrine and Covenants 57:8.

62. Quincy, *Figures of the Past*, 326.

63. *New York Herald*, 4 Aug. 1842.

64. J. M. Peck, *A Gazetteer of Illinois* (Jacksonville, Ill.: Goudy, 1834), 53–54.

65. John Ruskin quoted in *The Norton Anthology of English Literature,* ed. M. H. Abrams, 6th ed. (New York: Norton, 1993), 2:897.

66. Paul Johnson, *The Birth of the Modern: 1815–1830* (New York: HarperCollins, 1991), 562.

67. Thomas Carlyle, *Sartor Resartus: The Life and Opinions of Herr Teufelsdröckh* (London: Walter Scott, 1873), 237, 233.

68. Ibid., 238.

69. Ibid., 237.

70. Doctrine and Covenants 130:5.

71. Smith, *History,* 6:305.

72. M. H. Abrams, *Natural Supernaturalism: Tradition and Revolution in Romantic Literature* (New York: Norton, 1971), 384.

73. Doctrine and Covenants 131:7–8.

74. Gotthold Ephraim Lessing quoted in Klaus J. Hansen, *Quest for Empire: The Political Kingdom of God and the Council of Fifty in Mormon History* (East Lansing: Michigan State University Press, 1967), 12.

75. *Journal of Discourses,* 18:231.

76. Stark, "New World Faith," 18.

5

The Populist Vision of Joseph Smith

Nathan O. Hatch

The young Joseph Smith Jr. had every reason in the world to know keen alienation from mainstream values. In a land of democratic promise and burgeoning capitalist expectation, Smith was born into a family in 1805 that never was able to break the grip of poverty, wearisome toil, and chronic dislocation. His parents, Joseph and Lucy Smith, were habitually destitute despite an ample measure of economic ambition, steady habits, and serious religious faith. To make matters worse, the family once had stood on the brink of modest prosperity. Three years before the birth of Joseph Jr., in fact, his parents owned a farm in rural Tunbridge, Vermont, and ran a store in neighboring Randolph. From that base, they launched a venture in petty capitalism to sell a shipment of the Vermont root ginseng to the China market. Instead of reaping a handsome return on their investment, however, the Smiths were cheated out of their profit entirely and financially destroyed. Resulting debts forced the family into the ranks of the propertyless, a fate that led to seven moves in the following fourteen years. Typhoid ravaged the family in 1812, leaving seven-year-old Joseph in bed or on crutches for the next three years. From 1814 to 1816 consecutive barren harvests forced the destitute family of eleven to abandon their extended family in Vermont in order to try their luck in central New York. But even there, as Joseph Smith Jr. came into manhood, a bitter turn thwarted the family's struggle to make ends meet. In 1825, a conniving land agent evicted his parents—now in their fifties—from the farm in Palmyra, shattering their last hope of regaining a foothold of land.[1]

In the face of such wretched luck, the Smith family looked in vain for solace from the institutional church. The church was not absent from their lives; in fact, it was all too present—but in shrill and competing forms. The experience of this intensely religious family is evidence that the proliferation of religious options in the first two decades of the nineteenth century only compounded the crisis of religious authority already so prevalent in popular

culture. The swift retreat of religious coercion that Jefferson's election symbolized promised a purer and more powerful church, one that would strip away
the centuries of human invention and restore primitive power and simplicity.
Instead, people like the Smiths found their hopes for experiencing the divine
confused by a cacophony of voices. Like his mother, Lucy, who had sampled
an array of denominations while doubting the efficacy of them all, Joseph was
dismayed by sectarianism, particularly that which followed the supposed bliss
of the revivals sweeping New York:

> For, notwithstanding the great love which the converts to these different faiths
> expressed at the time of their conversion, and the great zeal manifested by the
> respective clergy . . . it was seen that the seemingly good feelings of both the priests
> and the converts were more pretended than real; for a scene of great confusion
> and bad feelings ensued; priest contending against priest, and convert against
> convert; so that all their good feelings one for another, if they ever had any, were
> entirely lost in a strife of words and a contest about opinions.[2]

Smith's bleak conclusion was that this "war of words" destroyed all hope for
an authoritative religious voice. Like Roger Williams, his own quest for divine
reality led him to the conclusion that God had withdrawn his presence from
churches in the modern world, all of them having "apostatised from the true
and liveing faith . . . that built upon the Gospel of Jesus Christ as recorded in
the new testament."[3]

This severe skepticism about external institutions did not deter Joseph's own
intense search for salvation but turned it inward, toward a firmer reliance on
religious dreams and visions that were typical of the Smith family. By 1820, he
was convinced that only a new outpouring of divine revelation could pierce
the spiritual darkness and confusion that gripped his own soul and that of the
modern church. He was quite willing to stay away from the orthodox Christianity of his day and to search for truth in unorthodox places, including various forms of folk magic and occult sciences.[4] Smith evinced clearly his skill
as a charismatic seer, a spiritual gift he and his family hoped would lead to the
discovery of treasure as well as to more important spiritual insight. His growing reputation as a youth with unusual spiritual powers put him at the center
of several treasure-seeking escapades, one of them in South Bainbridge, New
York, where he was arrested by a justice of the peace on the charge that his
"glasslooking" disturbed the peace. At his trial, Smith testified that when he
looked at the seer stone he "discovered that time, place and distance were an-
nihilated; that all the intervening obstacles were removed, and that he possessed
one of the attributes of Deity, an All-Seeing Eye."[5]

By 1827, this twenty-two-year-old prophet began to claim that he had gained possession of a cache of gold plates and the Urim and Thummim, an Old Testament seer-stone-like instrument that gave him access to a long-lost story about God's wonder-working providence in America. In 1830, Smith published his translation of these gold plates as a six-hundred-page tome, the Book of Mormon. A work in biblical prose, it retold the entire sweep of salvation history, underscoring America's role in the scheme of redemption through a fifth, or "American," gospel. This "gospel" was a radically reconstituted history of the New World, a drama indicting America's churches as lifeless shells, blind and deaf to the real meaning of their own history and to the divine intent for the latter days, which were swiftly approaching.[6]

For all the attention given to the study of Mormonism, surprisingly little has been devoted to the Book of Mormon itself. What are the patterns deep in the grain of this extraordinary work and what do they reveal about the perceptions and intentions of the Prophet Joseph Smith?[7] Mormon historians, of course, have been more interested in pointing out the ways in which the book transcends the provincial opinions of the man Joseph Smith, thus establishing its uniquely biblical and revelatory character. Mormon detractors, in contrast, have attempted to reduce the book to an inert mirror of the popular culture of New York during the 1820s, thus overlooking elements that are unique and original.[8] More problematic, however, is sheer neglect due to the work's unusual complexity and presumed dullness—following Mark Twain's quip that it was "chloroform in print." Scholars have not taken seriously Joseph Smith's original rationale about the nature of his prophetic mission. The pivotal document of the Mormon church, "an extraordinary work of popular imagination," still receives scant attention from cultural historians, while scholars rush to explore more exotic themes, such as the influence upon Joseph Smith of magic, alchemy, and the occult.[9] As Jan Shipps has argued, historians need to return to the centrality of the "gold bible," Joseph Smith's original testament to the world, which certified the prophet's leadership and first attracted adherents to the movement.[10]

Interpretations of the Book of Mormon have emphasized its rationality in contrast to the religious enthusiasm of American revivalism, its calm millennial hope in contrast to Millerite enthusiasm, its progressive optimism in contrast to Calvinist determinism, and its quest for order in contrast to romanticism.[11] Unfortunately, these interpretations miss the animating spirit of the book. They view it as one intellectual document among others, as if Joseph Smith were sipping tea in a drawing room, engaged in polite theological debate with Nathaniel William Taylor and William Ellery Channing. These interpretations fail to see that the Book of Mormon is a document of profound social protest, an impassioned manifesto by a hostile outsider against the smug complacency of those in power and the reality of social distinctions based on wealth, class, and education. In attempting to define his alienation from the world around him, Smith resorted to a biblical frame of reference rather than to one of conventional politics, a point that Richard Bushman has emphasized. Yet in constructing a grand and complex narrative account of the ancient world, he chose to employ a distinct set of biblical themes: divine judgment upon proud oppressors, blindness to those wise in their own eyes, mercy for the humble, and spiritual authority to the unlearned. This book is a stern and sober depiction of reality.[12]

Like the biblical prophets whose message it champions, the work abounds in divine mercy for an upright remnant. But it also presents a God who is both good and terrible. Surging through its pages are unmistakable undercurrents of divine rage: destruction, famine, pestilence, thunder, earthquakes, tempests, melting elements, flames of devouring fire, and chains from which there is no deliverance. In 1828, the prophet wrote a letter to his cousin declaring that "the sword of vengeance of the Almighty hung over this generation and except they repent and obeyed the Gospel, and turned from their wicked ways, humbling themselves before the Lord, it would fall upon the wicked, and sweep them from the earth as with the beacon of destruction."[13] In the Book of Mormon, Smith chose to quote extensively from Old Testament prophets Isaiah and Malachi, both standing on the brink of cultural desolation and calling a few to repent before the onslaught of brutal judgment. "For behold, the day cometh that shall burn as an oven," says Malachi in 3 Nephi 25:1, "and all the proud, yea, and all that do wickedly, shall be stubble; and the day that cometh shall burn them up, saith the Lord of Hosts, that it shall leave them neither root nor branch."[14] The godly prophet Mormon, a lonely voice to God's people in the New World in the fourth century A.D., found his own Nephite civilization on the same brink of destruction. And from that vantage point, he prophesied that shortly before the final judgment the people of God would know a similar divine winnowing. To those who rejected Christ's latter-day messengers came this warning: "And it would be better for them if they had not been born. For do ye suppose that ye can get rid of the justice of an offended God, who hath been trampled under feet of men, that thereby salvation might come?"[15] The danger of an offended God clearly troubled Joseph Smith no less than it had Jonathan Edwards. What is significant is the way the Book of Mormon depicts the occasion of divine wrath.

The single most striking theme in the Book of Mormon is that it is the rich, the proud, and the learned who find themselves in the hands of an angry God. Throughout the book, evil is most often depicted as the result of pride and worldliness that comes from economic success and results in oppression of the poor. The message of Jacob is clear to the pre-Columbian Hebrews in the sixth century B.C. "But wo unto the rich, who are rich as to the things of the world. For because they are rich they despise the poor, and they persecute the meek, and their hearts are upon their treasures; wherefore, their treasure is their God. And behold, their treasure shall perish with them also."[16] The prophet Nephi makes the same indictment of churches that will appear in the latter day:

> Because of pride, and because of false teachers, and false doctrine, their churches have become corrupted, and their churches are lifted up; because of pride they are puffed up.

> They rob the poor because of their fine sanctuaries; they rob the poor because of their fine clothing; and they persecute the meek and the poor in heart, because in their pride they are puffed up.

> They wear stiff necks and high heads; yea, and because of pride, and wickedness, and abominations, and whoredoms, they have all gone astray save it be a few, who are the humble followers of Christ; nevertheless, they are led, that in many instances they do err because they are taught by the precepts of men.

> O the wise, and the learned, and the rich, that are puffed up in the pride of their hearts, and all those who preach false doctrines, and all those who commit whoredoms, and pervert the right way of the Lord, wo, wo, wo be unto them, saith the Lord God Almighty, for they shall be thrust down to hell![17]

In two other striking ways, the author of the Book of Mormon portrays apocalyptic judgment as the lot of the rich and the proud. In the fourth book of Nephi, the resurrected Christ appears in the New World and establishes a two-hundred-year reign of apostolic power and bliss. But the prophet Mormon explains the reasons for a rapid apostasy and decline after this time:

> And now in this two hundred and first year there began to be among them those who were lifted up in pride, such as the wearing of costly apparel, and all manner of fine pearls, and of the fine things of the world.

> And from that time forth they did have their goods and their substance no more common among them.

> And they began to be divided into classes; and they began to build up churches unto themselves to get gain, and began to deny the true church of Christ.

> And it came to pass that when two hundred and ten years had passed away there

were many churches in the land; yea, there were many churches which professed to know the Christ, and yet they did deny the more parts of his gospel, insomuch that they did receive all manner of wickedness, and did administer that which was sacred unto him to whom it had been forbidden because of unworthiness.[18]

Equally striking is the choice to employ the prophet Isaiah (chapters 2–14) as the one lengthy portion of Scripture used verbatim in the Book of Mormon (2 Nephi 12–24).[19] These chapters include some of holy writ's most appealing prophecies of the end times: that the mountain of the Lord's house will be exalted, that swords will be beat into plowshares, that the wolf shall lie down with the lamb, and that the earth will be full of the knowledge of the Lord, as the waters cover the sea. Yet these blissful scenes constitute a last and merciful chapter to a story that centers on the swift and sure destruction that awaits the oppressive and unjust society of Judah.

The prophet Isaiah indicts God's wayward people on two counts: their arrogant pretension and their oppression of the poor. The prophet thunders against a society of self-importance:

The lofty looks of man shall be humbled, and the haughtiness of men shall be bowed down, and the Lord alone shall be exalted in that day.

For the day of the Lord of Hosts soon cometh upon all nations, yea, upon every one; yea, upon the proud and lofty, and upon every one who is lifted up, and he shall be brought low. . . .

And the loftiness of man shall be bowed down, and the haughtiness of men shall be made low; and the Lord alone shall be exalted in that day.[20]

Isaiah takes particular note of the way people use fine apparel to distance themselves from others, and he warns that the Lord will replace jewelry, rings, headbands, bonnets, bracelets, fine linen, veils, and perfume with sackcloth, baldness, burning, and stench.[21]

The reason for this severity is God's identification with the poor and downtrodden. "What mean ye?" the Lord demands of the wealthy. "Ye beat my people to pieces, and grind the faces of the poor." God condemns the rich for accumulating houses while oppressing the poor, preying on widows, and robbing the fatherless.[22] The interlocking themes of pride, wealth, learning, fine clothing, and oppression of the poor reappear throughout the Book of Mormon as the principal objects of divine displeasure.[23] And it is clergymen and their priestcraft which are said to be the chief sources of these sins.[24] What compounds the foolishness of these clergymen is their smug denial that a God of the miraculous is still powerfully at work.

In one of the most moving passages in the book, the prophet Moroni, the single remaining survivor of a godly civilization, predicts that these accumulated evils will characterize the end times—when a new prophet will discover the golden plates hidden in the Hill Cumorah and proclaim the reopening of the brazen heavens. "Search the prophecies of Isaiah," Moroni counsels that latter-day generation that is drunk with pride and callous religiosity. He proclaims that a flame of unquenchable fire will be kindled in that day because church leaders will have risen in the pride of their hearts, built churches for material gain, denied the reality of God's miraculous power, and loved to adorn themselves and their churches more than to care for the poor and needy:

> Why do ye adorn yourselves with that which hath no life, and yet suffer the hungry, and the needy, and the naked, and the sick and the afflicted to pass by you, and notice them not?

> Why do ye build up your secret abominations to get gain, and cause that widows should mourn before the Lord, and also orphans to mourn before the Lord, and also the blood of their fathers and their husbands to cry unto the Lord from the ground, for vengeance upon your heads?

> Behold, the sword of vengeance hangeth over you; and the time soon cometh that he avengeth the blood of the saints upon you, for he will not suffer their cries any longer.[25]

The final element in this litany of judgment refers to the pervasive naturalism of the end times, the orthodox teaching that the age of miraculous wonders has long since passed away and that there will no longer be "revelations, nor prophecies, nor gifts, nor healing, nor speaking with tongues, and the interpretation of tongues." Other churches and other reformers will deny the religion of the Bible because they are callous to the inspiration, revelation, and apostolic gifts that accompany genuine divine presence. "And if there were miracles wrought then," the prophet Moroni asks, "why had God ceased to be a God of miracles and yet be an unchangeable Being?"[26] His conclusion, like that of Old Testament prophets after the annihilation of the temple, is simply that the glory of God's presence will depart.[27]

The vision of Joseph Smith is intensely populist in its rejection of the religious conventions of his day and in its hostility to the orthodox clergy, its distrust of reason as an exclusive guide, and its rage at the oppression of the poor. In a more positive vein, Smith also projects a distinctly populist vision that suggests how God will restore the ancient order of things. He is violently anticlerical but confident that God will reconstitute the church according to popular norms. The Book of Mormon has its own preferential option for the poor, not as persons to be pitied, but as those whom God has chosen to empower. The book of Alma, chapter 32, contains an extended account of how "the poor class of people" are cast out of the synagogues for wearing coarse apparel. Instead of despising them as the priests did, the prophet Alma blesses them because their physical poverty and the burden of being ostracized has taught them poverty of spirit. Such lowliness of heart puts them in the enviable position of learning true wisdom. In the same spirit, the prophet Nephi says that in the latter days all churches will be given over to abominations and whoredoms except "a few, who are the humble followers of Christ." In the latter days, God would again choose plain and ordinary instruments.[28]

In the most dramatic example of God using the weak things of the world to confound the wise, Nephi predicts the opening of a new word of revelation. The sealed book is first offered to a man of learning, whose efforts are thwarted by greed and ambition. The Lord then turns to an unlearned man to reveal the book to the world, declaring that "a God of miracles" would not be bound by human conventions: "Therefore, I will proceed to do a marvelous work among this people, yea a work and a wonder, for the wisdom of their wise and learned shall perish, and the understanding of their prudent shall be hid."[29] Like the unschooled prophet who revealed that book to America in 1830, Nephi declares, "I glory in plainness."[30] The Book of Mormon anticipated a restored church that would maintain "an equality among all men," calling preachers to work with their hands and earn their bread like everyone else.[31]

Upon the publication of the Book of Mormon, Joseph Smith and a tiny band of followers went forth with the compelling message that God was restoring the one true fold, the ancient order of things. By revealing an up-to-date Bible and insisting upon God's active supernatural presence, Smith gave authoritative answers to many seeking secure moorings.[32] More striking is the evidence that Smith's overall vision also had a distinct class bias. It conveyed the unmistakable claim that common people had the right to shape their own faith and to take charge of their own religious destiny.

These populist themes resonated powerfully with Smith's earliest disciples, young men who were characteristically poor, uprooted, unschooled, and unsophisticated like himself.[33] Brigham and Lorenzo Dow Young were raised in such desperate poverty that their family was broken up when their mother died of tuberculosis in 1815. They were fourteen and eight years old at the time. Denied the opportunity of formal schooling and occasions to cultivate the social graces, Brigham Young retained deep resentment against the social distinctions of the churches of his youth.[34] Orson and Parley Pratt, both in Smith's original group of Twelve Apostles, also grew up in a family trying to break a cycle of poverty and wandering. As teenagers, both were boarded out to other farmers after the family flax farm had failed when a water-powered carding mill nearby made their efforts unprofitable.[35] Parley later reflected on his experience as a wage earner: "The next spring found me in the employment of a wealthy farmer, by the name of Eliphet Bristol. . . . I was then but a lad— being only seventeen years of age—and stood in need of fatherly and motherly care and comfort. But they treated a laborer as a machine; not as a human being, possessed of feelings and sympathies in common with his species. *Work!* WORK! WORK! you are hired to work. . . . I was glad when the time expired; I felt like one released from prison."[36]

Heber C. Kimball, Joseph Smith's greatest missionary, grew up in equally humble and insecure circumstances. The Kimball family had moved to Ontario County, New York, after their farm failed in Vermont in 1809. But their financial reverses continued, and Heber's father, Solomon, who worked as a blacksmith, went to jail for debts in 1815. After 1820, Heber suffered his own financial woes as an unemployed blacksmith "cast abroad upon the world, without a friend to console my grief." He was working as a potter, making simple kitchen and table implements, when he met Brigham Young.[37]

Likewise, the legendary preacher Jedediah Morgan Grant, who came to be known as "Mormon Thunder," was one of twelve children of dirt-poor farmers and shinglemakers who had been forced to pull up stakes on several occasions. In 1833, Mormon elders shared the blessings of the restored gospel with the Grant family in their farmhouse in Erie, Pennsylvania, and successfully applied healing hands to Jedediah's mother, who was bedridden with rheumatism. Jedediah was baptized that year at seventeen; two years later he was selected as one of the First Quorum of Seventy and sent forth preaching in this select cadre of missionaries. Thomas B. Marsh, the first president of the Council of the Twelve Apostles, had been a waiter in a public house, a groomsman, and an unsuccessful grocer. He had withdrawn from the Methodists when that church did not seem to correspond with the Bible and when a spirit of prophecy led him to anticipate the rise of a new church.[38]

None of these seven young men cut an impressive figure in a culture that deferred to wealth and idealized upward mobility. When they heard the call of the Prophet Joseph Smith, these semiliterate young men—a painter and glazier, two blacksmiths, a potter, a farm hand, a shinglemaker, and a waiter— had virtually no stake in society. Their formative years gave them every reason to forego worldly ambition and throw their considerable energy into building a spiritual kingdom in opposition to the competitive and capitalist mores of Jacksonian America. All remained unconvinced by the fervor of emotional revivals and nursed deep resentments against orthodox modes of Christianity. According to Heber C. Kimball, soon to be Brigham Young's closest friend, the members of the Young family "were in low circumstances and seemed to be an afflicted people in consequence of having a great deal of sickness and sorrow to pass through; and of course were looked down upon by the flourishing church where we lived."[39]

Kimball, Young, and their colleagues, ranging in age from nineteen to thirty, jumped at the opportunity to follow a prophet who spoke with authority and not like the scribes. They gladly assumed the roles of full-time saint and missionary and, in time, of apostle and patriarch, high priest and president. They exulted in a gospel whose cornerstone the builders had rejected and that promised to use the weak things of the world to confound the mighty. Severing ties of place and, when necessary, of family, they pursued relentlessly the cause of a church that had returned power—as in apostolic days—to illiterate men such as themselves.

Notes

1. On Joseph Smith, see Richard L. Bushman, *Joseph Smith and the Beginnings of Mormonism* (Urbana: University of Illinois Press, 1984); and Donna Hill, *Joseph Smith, the First Mormon* (Garden City, N.Y.: Doubleday, 1977). The maturing of scholarship on Mormons is evident in these works as well as in two other superb treatments of the movement, Jan Shipps, *Mormonism: The Story of a New Religious Tradition* (Urbana: University of Illinois Press, 1985); and Klaus J. Hansen, *Mormonism and the American Experience* (Chicago: University of Chicago Press, 1981). A subtle and insightful interpretation of the culture that gave rise to Mormonism is Gordon S. Wood, "Evangelical America and Early Mormonism," *New York History* 61 (Oct. 1980): 359–86. On the dynamic and often embattled state of Mormon historical scholarship, see David Brion Davis, "Secrets of the Mormons," *New York Review of Books*, 15 Aug. 1985, 15–19.

2. Joseph Smith, *History of the Church of Jesus Christ of Latter-day Saints*, ed. B. H. Roberts (Salt Lake City: Deseret News, 1932–51), 1:3, quoted in Bushman, *Joseph Smith*, 54.

3. Joseph Smith, "A History of the Life of Joseph Smith, Jr.," reprinted in Milton V. Backman Jr., *Joseph Smith's First Vision: The First Vision in Its Historical Context* (Salt Lake City: Bookcraft, 1971), 156, quoted in Bushman, *Joseph Smith*, 55.

4. Shipps, *Mormonism*, 10. On Joseph Smith's extensive reliance on folk magic, see D. Michael Quinn, *Early Mormonism and the Magic World View* (Salt Lake City: Signature Books, 1987).

5. Alan Taylor, "The Early Republic's Supernatural Economy: Treasure Seeking in the American Northeast, 1780–1830," *American Quarterly* 38 (1986): 24–25.

6. Lucy Smith reported to her brother in 1831 that the lessons she learned from reading the Book of Mormon were "that the eyes of the whole world are blinded; that the churches have all become corrupt, yea every church upon the face of the earth; that the Gospel of Christ is nowhere preached." See Lucy Smith to Solomon Mack, 6 Jan. 1831, Library-Archives, Historical Department, Church of Jesus Christ of Latter-day Saints, Salt Lake City, quoted in Bushman, *Joseph Smith,* 140.

7. Two very suggestive treatments of the Book of Mormon are Richard L. Bushman, "The Book of Mormon and the American Revolution," *Brigham Young University Studies* 17 (Autumn 1976): 3–20; and Timothy L. Smith, "The Book of Mormon in a Biblical Culture," *Journal of Mormon History* 7 (1980): 3–21. A helpful overview of the content of the Book of Mormon is found in Thomas F. O'Dea, *The Mormons* (Chicago: University of Chicago Press, 1957), 22–40.

8. Typical of this approach is Fawn M. Brodie, who suggests that the Book of Mormon "can best be explained, not by Joseph's ignorance nor by his delusions, but by his responsiveness to the provincial opinions of his time." See Fawn M. Brodie, *No Man Knows My History: The Life of Joseph Smith,* 2d ed., rev. and enl. (New York: Knopf, 1971), 69.

9. Gordon S. Wood has suggested that efforts to understand the Book of Mormon have floundered because of a limited and elitist understanding of early nineteenth-century popular culture. See Wood, "Evangelical America and Early Mormonism." My point is not to dismiss the well-documented use of folk magic by Joseph Smith but to suggest that such beliefs and practices must be understood in the context of an overall ideological system, the structure of which still remains elusive. Smith's beliefs were clearly a synthesis which grew out of the Judeo-Christian Scriptures, magic and the occult arts, and his experience with dreams and visions. More than anything else, Smith yearned for everyday life to recover the kind of miraculous power described in the New Testament.

10. Shipps, *Mormonism,* 32–33.

11. The first two interpretations are made by O'Dea, *The Mormons,* 31, 35; the second two are made by Hansen, *Mormonism and the American Experience,* 68–83.

12. Bushman has shown conclusively that the Book of Mormon was not a conventional American book reflecting the ordinary political sentiments of its time ("Book of Mormon"). Bushman has also suggested that in their radical critique of American civilization, the Latter-day Saints showed more affinity for premillennialist disillusionment with society than for American optimism and romantic nationalism (*Joseph Smith,* 139).

13. George Albert Smith, "History," LDS Library-Archives, quoted in Hill, *Joseph Smith,* 83–84.

14. This passage in Nephi is quoted from Malachi 4:1.

15. 3 Nephi 28:35.

16. 2 Nephi 9:30.

17. 2 Nephi 28:12–15.

18. 4 Nephi 1:24–27.

19. The third book of Nephi also quotes extensively from the Sermon on the Mount, Matt. 5–7. In view of Joseph Smith's basic concerns, the themes in that material are also illuminating: blessings upon the poor, the mourning, the meek, and the persecuted; denunciations of hypocrites who give alms and pray in public; admonitions to seek first the kingdom rather than food and raiment; and warnings about false prophets who are ravening wolves in sheep's clothing.

20. 2 Nephi 12:11–17 (Isa. 2:11–17).

21. 2 Nephi 13:16–26 (Isa. 3:16–26).

22. 2 Nephi 13:15, 15:7–8, 20:1–2 (Isa. 3:15, 5:7–8, 10:1–2).

23. A good example of these related themes is found in Alma:

> And it came to pass in the eighth year of the reign of the judges, that the people of the church began to wax proud, because of their exceeding riches, and their fine silks, and their fine-twined linen, and because of their many flocks and herds, and their gold and their silver, and all manner of precious things, which they obtained by their industry; and in all these things were they lifted up in the pride of their eyes, for they began to wear very costly apparel. . . .

> Yea, he [Alma] saw great inequality among the people, some lifting themselves up with their pride, despising others, turning their backs upon the needy and the naked and those who were hungry, and those who were athirst, and those who were sick and afflicted. (4:6–12)

Book 2 of Nephi (26:20) relates pride, learning, despising God's miracles, and grinding the faces of the poor. Alma 5:53–55 threatens unquenchable fire for those who are proud, wear costly apparel, seek riches, persecute the humble, and turn their backs on the poor and needy.

24. "For behold, ye do love money, and your substance, and your fine apparel, and the adorning of your churches, more than ye love the poor and the needy, the sick and the afflicted" (Mormon 8:37). A major theme in the book is the clergy's quest for financial gain. "O ye wicked and perverse and stiffnecked people, why have ye built up churches unto yourselves to get gain?" (Mormon 8:33). For attacks on priestcraft, see 2 Nephi 26:29, 3 Nephi 16:10, and 3 Nephi 30:2.

25. Mormon 8:39–41.

26. Mormon 9:7–11, 15–20. The model saint for the prophet Mormon is one who knows the reality of supernatural gifts: "And he knoweth their faith, for in his name could they remove mountains; and in his name could they cause the earth to shake; and by the power of his word did they cause prisons to tumble to the earth; yea, even the fiery furnace could not harm them, neither wild beasts nor poisonous serpents, because of the power of his word" (Mormon 8:24).

27. "Yea, wo unto him that shall deny the revelations of the Lord, and that shall say the Lord no longer worketh by revelation, or by prophecy, or by gifts, or by tongues, or by healings, or by the power of the Holy Ghost!" (3 Nephi 29:6). On this theme, see

also 2 Nephi 27:23, 28:4–5, 29:3–10, and the Mormon paper from Kirtland, Ohio, *Evening and Morning Star* 2, no. 20 (May 1834): 305–7.

28. 2 Nephi 28:14. The book of Mosiah also gives an excellent illustration of identification with the downtrodden. The injunction is given to generosity with those in need: "Ye will not suffer that the beggar putteth up his petition to you in vain, and turn him out to perish." A strong indictment is also made of those who blame the poor for their plight, withholding assistance because "the man has brought upon himself his misery" and "his punishments are just." "For behold, are we not all beggars?" (Mosiah 4:16–19). The prophet Alma also indicates that it was contrary to the commands of God "that there should be a law which should bring men on to unequal grounds" (Alma 30:7). This theme is also prominent in Doctrine and Covenants 124:1, 133:57–59.

29. 2 Nephi 27:26.

30. 2 Nephi 33:6. The theme of plainness in communication is replete in the Book of Mormon. See 1 Nephi 13:24, 14:23, 25:4, 32:7; Ether 12:23; Jacob 4:13.

31. Mosiah 27:3–5.

32. Mario S. De Pillis, "The Quest for Religious Authority and the Rise of Mormonism," *Dialogue* 1 (Mar. 1966): 68–88.

33. Using Davis Bitton's *Guide to Mormon Diaries and Autobiographies* (Provo: Brigham Young University Press, 1977), Marvin S. Hill has estimated that 92 percent of those converted before 1846 whose birth and conversion dates are given (211 of 229) were under 40 at the time of baptism. The median age was between 20 and 25; more than 80 percent (182) were 30 or under. See Hill, "The Rise of Mormonism in the Burned-Over District: Another View," *New York History* 61 (1980): 411–30.

> 34. I have seen deacons, Baptists, Presbyterians, members of the Methodist church, with long, solid, sturdy faces and a poor brother would come along and say to one of them, "Brother, such-a-one, I have come to see if I could get a bushel of wheat, rye or corn of you. I have no money, but I will come and work for you in harvest," and their faces would be drawn down so mournful, and they would say, "I have none to spare." "Well, deacon, if you can let me have one bushel, I understand you have considerable, I will come and work for you just as long as you say, until you are satisfied, in your harvest field, or haying or anything you want done."
>
> After much talk this longfaced character would get it out, "If you will come and work for me two days in harvest, I do not know but I will spare you a bushel of rye."
>
> When the harvest time comes the man could have got two bushels of rye for one day's work; but the deacon sticks him to his bargain, and makes him work two days for a bushel of wheat or rye. . . . I could not swallow such things.

Journal of Discourses (Liverpool: F. D. and S. W. Richards, 1854–86; reprint, Salt Lake City: N.p., 1967), 15:164–65, quoted in Leonard J. Arrington, *Brigham Young: American Moses* (New York: Knopf, 1985), 26. See also Rebecca Cornwall and Richard F. Palmer, "The Religious and Family Background of Brigham Young," *Brigham Young University Studies* 18 (1978): 286–310.

35. Breck England, *The Life and Thought of Orson Pratt* (Salt Lake City: University of Utah Press, 1985), 8–13.

36. Parley P. Pratt, *The Autobiography of Parley Parker Pratt, One of the Twelve Apostles of the Church of Jesus Christ of Latter-Day Saints,* ed. Parley Parker Pratt (Chicago: Law, King, and Law, 1888), 20–21.

37. Stanley B. Kimball, *Heber C. Kimball: Mormon Patriarch and Pioneer* (Urbana: University of Illinois Press, 1981), 1–24, quote on 10.

38. Gene A. Sessions, *Mormon Thunder: A Documentary History of Jedediah Morgan Grant* (Urbana: University of Illinois Press, 1982), 3–23. On Thomas B. Marsh, see Andrew Jenson, *Latter-day Saint Biographical Encyclopedia,* 4 vols. (Salt Lake City: Andrew Jenson History Company, 1901), 1:74–76.

39. Heber C. Kimball, "History," manuscript, book 94-B, Heber C. Kimball Papers, LDS Library-Archives, quoted in Arrington, *Brigham Young,* 16.

6

Modern Heaven . . . and a Theology

Colleen McDannell and Bernhard Lang

The modern perspective on heaven—emphasizing the nearness and similarity of the other world to our own and arguing for the eternal nature of love, family, progress, and work—finds its greatest proponent in Latter-day Saint (LDS) understanding of the afterlife. While most contemporary Christian groups neglect afterlife beliefs, what happens to people after they die is crucial to LDS teachings and rituals. Heavenly theology is the result not of mere speculation, but of revelation given to past and present church leaders. Although the number of Latter-day Saints certainly cannot compare with the worldwide membership of the Roman Catholic church or many Protestant denominations, its rapid growth and the level of commitment it demands from its members make it an integral part of the contemporary Christian world.[1]

According to Latter-day Saint belief, Jesus established a church on earth called the Church of Jesus Christ, whose members are called Saints. After Jesus' resurrection, he visited the people of the Americas and established his church there as well. Once Jesus had left the earth, persecution, the death of the early church leaders, and the evil character of the people caused the Church of Jesus Christ to be taken from the earth, resulting in a period called the "Great Apostasy." The Savior, however, promised that he would restore his church. In 1820 Joseph Smith (1805–44), a young man from upstate New York, received a vision from God and Jesus Christ telling him not to join any of the existing Christian churches since the true church was not yet on earth. Over the next decade, Joseph Smith received a series of revelations which marked him as the first prophet of the restored church, the Church of Jesus Christ of Latter-day Saints. The ancient golden plates which Joseph Smith discovered and translated, known as the Book of Mormon, set forth LDS sacred history and beliefs. The Bible, the Book of Mormon, and further revelations given by God to Joseph Smith and later prophets comprise their teachings and beliefs. The Latter-day Saints believe that God is a real person with a tangible body of flesh and bones, that all people existed in a premortal life as spirit children of God, and that a lay priest-hood should provide spiritual leadership. They deny the existence of original sin, and they believe that family relations can be made eternal.

Latter-day Saints reject the notion that death destroys either the personali-ty or the soul. "Actually there is no such thing as the dead," wrote Theodore M. Burton (born 1907) in 1977, "unless one refers to the mortal body, which returns again to the earth. The spirit lives on, and in the resurrection all of us will be made alive again as each body and spirit unite to form an immortal whole." Life on this earth is merely one act in a long drama spanning several worlds and existences. Before being born to earthly parents, people live as spirit children with their Heavenly Mother and Father. In order to be tested and to receive the "ordinances" (sacred rites and ceremonies that are necessary for eternal progression), spirit children enter into earthly bodies and are born into this world. Everything which occurred in "premortal" existence is forgotten at birth so that the new person may freely choose the proper religion and path of life.[2]

At death, the soul leaves the body and enters the spirit world, where a new stage of life begins. The spirit world is not heaven but only another place where the soul develops until the resurrection. Following Brigham Young (1801–77), who insisted that the spirit world was contiguous with the earth, Apostle Ezra Taft Benson assured the Saints in 1971 that "sometimes the veil between this life and the life beyond becomes very thin. Our loved ones who have passed on are not far from us." Tendencies and predispositions developed on earth continue in the spirit world. Those who have led an evil life are separated from the righteous, live with like-minded spirits, and experience the torments orig-inating from guilt, fear, failure, lustful desires, and enslavement of their wills to Satan. The righteous, particularly those who have followed the teachings of the LDS Church, find themselves in a paradise which contains lakes, forests, brilliant flowers, and remarkable buildings. There is no death, no confusion, and no suffering. Family members meet and greet each other. Spirits, accord-ing to the authors in *The Life Beyond* (1986), are "free to think and act with a renewed capacity and with the vigor and enthusiasms which characterized one in his prime." Babies and children who have died become adults immediate-ly, although they can revert to their earlier stages in order to be recognized by new entrants into the spirit realm.[3]

Since there is no judgment at death, evil spirits and those ignorant of the truth are not condemned to eternal suffering. They are given the chance in the spirit world to exercise their free will and decide whether or not to believe in the LDS revelation. Departed Latter-day Saints help those unfamiliar with LDS principles and teach—to whatever extent they can—those who were unbeliev-ers on earth. Church president Wilford Woodruff (1807–98) reported that in one of his visions he saw the Prophet Joseph Smith at the door of the temple in heaven, but Smith refused to speak with him because he was in a hurry. Several other "brethren who held high positions on earth" also rushed by. Finally, Woodruff asked the prophet why he was in such a hurry. "I [Woodruff] have been in a hurry all my life; but I expected my hurry would be over when I got into the kingdom of heaven, if I ever did." Smith replied that here there is "so much work . . . to be done, and we need to be in a hurry in order to ac-complish it." Latter-day Saints who have been active members in the LDS society continue to teach, do missionary work, and guide other members in the spirit world.[4]

The family, crucial for the promotion of the gospel on earth, continues to be an important teaching institution in the spirit world. Husbands and wives assume the responsibility to "search out their own progenitors and teach them the gospel." It is partly through their selfless service in the spirit world that the Saints progress and are made perfect. Not only do the activities of the Saints continue there but the church organization itself is maintained. According to some contemporary LDS writers, whatever must be accomplished in the spirit world is under the direction of the LDS priesthood and the priesthood is un-der the direction of the church presidency. Consequently, emphasized the authors of *The Life Beyond,* "we do not speak of such things as harps, and clouds, and angels with wings. We speak of servants of God, each faithfully laboring according to assignment, each standing in his own office, laboring in his own calling." Work and spiritual progress are an integral part of life after death. While paradise, where the righteous live, is free from cares and sorrows of earthly existence, "it is not a place of idleness; it is the spirit's Sabbath." Just as the earthly sabbath is a time not only of prayer but also of service—visit-ing the sick, doing genealogical work, sharing time with family—activities in the spirit world include both religious deeds and thoughts.[5]

Although the Saints in the spirit world spend most of their time teaching other spirits, on special occasions they may also seek to help those still on earth. In her book *Angel Children,* which underwent its sixth printing in 1983, Mary V. Hill described the comforting contact that she received from her dead son. In 1971 Stephen Hill, the fifth child of Mary and Keith Hill and barely four months old, died of a congenital heart defect. To help others understand the meaning of child death, Mary Hill wrote a short book on the Latter-day Saint perspective on infant mortality. Quoting extensively from earlier LDS works, Mary Hill discussed how infants become full-grown adults in the spirit world but during the millennium return to being babies. In the spirit world, Stephen would work as an adult teaching the gospel but, if Mary lived a righteous life, she would be able to rear her child during the thousand years before the final resurrection. Mary's loss would be over when she met her grown son in the spirit world and could enjoy mothering him during the millennium.

While her faith was helpful during the crisis, it was not until she went into labor with her next child that she realized her inner resistance: "My mind said aloud that it was alright that Heavenly Father called Stephen into the spirit world, but my subconscious grieved and mourned." She feared that the baby about to be born would also die. Shortly after her new son's birth, as she lay in the recovery room, she saw Stephen, "not with my physical eyes, but in a manner very real to me." Stephen had become a young man, dressed in softly draped white clothes. "His hair was sandy colored," she recalled, "with a soft wave in it, and his jaw square and muscular." Stephen showed great love, compassion, and sympathy for his mother, telling her, "Well, Mother, now you have your baby, and there's no more need to grieve for me. We'll have *our* time in the resurrection, and now I'm free to do my work in the spirit world." From Mary Hill's perspective, God had allowed Stephen to come to reassure his mother and show her that "somehow my grief prevented him from being truly free to do his work in the spirit world." Stephen had his duties to perform in the spirit world and one of them was to comfort his earthly mother. The experience of Mary Hill is not an isolated incident, but part of a long tradition in LDS history of spirits contacting earthly relatives and friends.[6]

The world of the spirits and the world of the living are linked together not only by love. A much tighter bond unites the two spheres. According to LDS teachings, the ministering Saints in the next world can teach and preach, but they cannot administer earthly ordinances, which are crucial for continued spiritual progress. For each being who has heard the gospel in the spirit world and is willing to accept LDS beliefs, a specific action must be accomplished on earth. Without vicarious rituals, such as marriages or baptisms, converted souls will be limited in their spiritual growth. Members are asked to do the historical footwork needed to learn the names and dates of ancestors who died and to submit their names so the appropriate ordinances may be performed in Mormon temples. Genealogical research and rituals performed for the dead comprise a major aspect of church life. Remembering the dead is not merely a pious sentiment, but an integral part of the religious activities of church members. "It takes as much work and effort to save a dead person," writes Theodore Burton, "as it does to save a living person."[7]

The performance of ordinances on earth for those who cannot perform them in the spirit world enables the dead to look forward to the next stages of eternity. The Latter-day Saints believe in the Second Coming of Christ when Jesus will usher in his thousand-year reign on earth. This will be accomplished by great physical transformations of the planet. Valleys will be raised, mountains will be leveled, and the continents will be joined together. The wicked will be destroyed and will have to wait in the spirit world until the end of the millennium, when they will be resurrected, judged, and assigned to a place in eternity. The righteous, both members of the church and others who have lived virtuous lives, will be resurrected and their spirits will join their renewed bodies. They then will live on an earth transformed into a Garden of Eden with a perfect climate. Satan will be bound and have no power to tempt the people, who will live in peace and harmony together. Children will be born, grow up, marry, advance to old age, and pass through the equivalent of death—but without pain or disease.

The millennium will be a time of tremendous activity and busyness. On a practical level, "crops will be planted, harvested, and eaten; industries will be expanded, cities built, and education fostered." The work being conducted for the benefit of the dead will be finished during the millennium. During this time, temples will be built in order to conduct the ordinances. Marriages will be arranged and "sealed" in the temple for those who were either single on earth or died young. New genealogical information will be assembled and corrections will be made to any faulty research compiled earlier. During the millennium, all the virtuous who have been resurrected will be converted to the church, requiring that missionary activity continue with great vigor. "It can well be said," concluded Gordon T. Allred, "that the resurrection and millennium, among other things, will be a fine time for the genealogist and temple worker—the finale and crescendo to the whole symphony of vicarious work."[8]

All this activity—on earth, in the spirit world, and in the millennium—enables those who so choose to experience the highest order of perfection and thus to become gods. After the thousand-year reign of Christ on earth and a short period when Satan will be permitted to tempt the righteous ("a little season"), the final judgment will take place. All who have ever lived will be reunited with their bodies and assigned either to one of three stages of glory or to an endless hell. The renewed earth—a sea of glass mingled with fire—will be inhabited by those who merit the highest heaven, the celestial glory. Like the lower two divisions of heaven, the celestial glory will be divided into various levels or degrees. Only those who experience the highest degree of the celestial glory will achieve "exaltation" and become like gods. Those who merit exaltation have not merely succeeded in "going to heaven" or "living in the presence of God";

they have accomplished the higher challenge of personal perfection and god-hood. All knowledge, truth, virtue, power, and wisdom may be possessed by those who have reached the highest heaven and become gods. Through exaltation the Saint will display for all eternity the powers and dominion of a god.[9]

Exaltation occurs only if the individual has moved through the appropriate stages of belief and ritual and has led a righteous life. Among the ritual actions which the Saint must accomplish in order to be permitted to enter the highest degree of heaven is to be married for "time and all eternity." LDS theology delineates two distinct types of marriage rites. Marriage performed by civil and most religious authorities joins couples together "until death do us part." At death, the married couple have no rights or responsibilities toward each other; nothing binds them together eternally. A second type of marriage (the one necessary for exaltation) is marriage which endures eternally. This is a special marriage which must be performed in a temple. According to LDS theology only those worthy may enter the temple, and so the couple must be Latter-day Saints in good standing. During this wedding ceremony, the couple kneels at the altar in the temple, where they are joined together for time and all eternity under the direction of the priesthood. This marriage ceremony is called "sealing." Any children born after this special marriage are automatically sealed to their parents. Children born prior to their parents' temple marriage may later be sealed to them in a similar ceremony. It is this sealing power of the "New and Everlasting Covenant of Marriage" which enables the family to exist for eternity in heaven. Without the sealing, nothing keeps the families together after death.

For the members of the church, eternal marriage does not contradict Jesus' reflection that in the resurrection there is no marriage. They take this New Testament passage to refer to those people who were married only for their lives on earth. People who married merely according to the laws of the world will serve as ministering angels to those married for eternity. Single people can become only angels in heaven, never gods. "There is marrying and giving of marriage in heaven," insisted Theodore Burton, "only for those who are willing to accept and live the fullness of God's law." The biblical woman who had been married to seven husbands would find herself married to none of them in heaven—as Jesus stated. Only what is joined by God, through the LDS priesthood, can exist forever.[10]

The family not only serves as the basic unit of life on earth but is the foundation of the celestial heaven. Couples who have been married in the temple for all eternity, and who meet the other requirements for celestial glory, are not only able to join their families after death but can also increase those families. One of the distinct privileges of those in the celestial glory is the power of eternal procreation. "Exalted beings," summarized Duane Crowther, "will enjoy the power of procreation and will continue the process of bearing children which they began on earth during mortality." While the details of this eternal reproduction are not known, it is suspected that the residents of the celestial heaven reproduce "after the same manner that we are here" but without sorrow, pain, or distress. Since the Latter-day Saints believe that God has a body and is not spirit, it makes sense that the gods reproduce in a human manner. A woman achieves her sense of godhood by participating in her husband's eternal priesthood. Because of this, she is permitted to "bear the souls of men, to people other worlds," and to "reign for ever and ever as the queen mother of . . . numerous and still increasing offspring." Those women who have been unable to reproduce on earth, but have been faithful and received the proper ordinances, will make up for the temporary lack of offspring by mothering countless spirit children.[11]

The offspring of exalted husbands and wives are the "spirit children" who eventually enter bodies and populate other worlds. "Just as men were first born as spirit children to their Eternal Father and His companion," Crowther clarified, "the children born to resurrected beings are spirit beings and must be sent in their turn to another earth to pass through the trials of mortality and obtain a physical body." Thus, while the residents of the celestial heaven have achieved full perfection in knowledge, power, and glory, they constantly progress through their eternal reproduction. The essential activity of eternal life of the highest order is to be like God—to populate and rule over countless worlds inhabited by spirit children who have assumed bodies. God does not only grow by learning new laws and discovering new facts but "His never-ending joy and glory is in the immortality and eternal life of His children, and the increase of His dominion is His progression throughout eternity." This is the aim of human progression on earth, in the spirit world, and in the millennium. "The secret of the ages has been made known—God is an exalted man," exclaimed the authors of *The Life Beyond;* "let none in the household of faith be guilty of reducing these exalted verities to myth or metaphor."[12]

The understanding of life after death in the LDS Church is the clearest example of the continuation of the modern heaven into the twentieth century. Since the church rejects the dualism between spirit and matter and insists that "spirit" is only refined and purified matter, a fluidity exists between the two spheres. The belief that the spirit world is on or near the earth emphasizes the closeness of the two worlds. Reports of visits of the spirits to earth or of LDS members to the spirit world make the dividing veil even thinner. The notion of the family—both on earth and in the spirit world—is a controlling theme which dominates the LDS outlook. Collecting historical data on ancestors, to be used for vicarious baptisms and sealings, serves as an everyday reminder that the dead need the help of the living. The two worlds are bound together. Even the notion that human beings have the possibility of becoming gods reduces the distinction between the human and divine realms. God, the angels, and the spirits were all at one time human creatures subject to the vicissitudes of life on earth or in another world. Like the heaven of many nineteenth-century writers, the LDS spirit world remains precariously close to our own.

What continues in the spirit world is not the lives of individuals but the life of the church. Unlike earlier visionaries—novelists, spiritualists, ministers—who described many secular occupations in the other world, the activities of those in the LDS spirit world are entirely religious. Diverging from other Christians, Latter-day Saints place more importance on individual personalities in the continuation of the structure and authority of the church. Not only does a general concern for service and teaching continue but so does the specific rules (e.g., ordinances) and hierarchy (e.g., priesthood) of the church. If writers in the eighteenth and nineteenth centuries tended to eliminate denominational differences in heaven, then LDS teachings promote the reverse. Like the people on earth, the spirits in the other world need specific church ordinances in order to progress spiritually. The LDS afterlife is distinctively sectarian.

In the same manner, the continuation of the family is determined by religious considerations. While other defenders of the survival of love, marriage, and family life after death assume that all who love will be reunited regardless of religious belief, the church plays a much stronger role in LDS family reunions. It is not love by itself which merits eternal life, or even love expressed by devoted Christians, but love sanctioned and made everlasting by the special temple ordinances of the church. Without the specific involvement of the LDS church, no family can hope to be reunited for eternity. They might meet again in the spirit world, but unless the couple and children are sealed together they cannot survive as a family. So, while love, marriage, and family life are essential to the LDS understanding of the afterlife, they will not achieve anything everlasting in their own right. The key to eternal marriage and everlasting love comes through the specific beliefs and activities of the church, not through the human institutions of marriage and family.

Likewise, other advocates of the modern heaven would reject the notion that heavenly love between men and women results in birth. Latter-day Saints hold this as a critical part of their theology because it explains how we arrived on the earth. Over and over again in LDS literature the emphasis is not on the celestial family's eternal love but on its ability to reproduce. It is not only the continuation of human love which is important from the LDS perspective; it is the reproduction of spirit beings. The establishment of an eternal patriarchal order based on rule and reproduction is a stark divergence from much of the nineteenth-century heavenly literature which predicted the continuation of intimate, couple-based family life.[13]

While LDS theologians world probably reject the idea that their beliefs have much in common with liberal Protestantism, they do share a confidence in postmortem salvation with many late nineteenth-century theologians. Both would agree that earthly life, although of great significance in the plan of salvation, is not the final step. Consequently, life in the spirit world will be busy. Latter-day Saints believe they will progress through selfless service and that non-Saints will grow in knowledge of the truth of the gospel. Growth and progress will continue during the millennium through preaching and administration of the temple ordinances. While even nineteenth-century spiritualists were reluctant to predict that spiritual growth in the other world could eventually end with human deification, LDS theology took spiritual progress after death to its logical conclusion. The possibility of people evolving into gods is a Latter-day Saint tenet. Even after the person becomes a god and experiences perfect power, knowledge, and righteousness, eternal reproduction allows for continual growth.

In the nineteenth century, the Latter-day Saints bent to the will of the U.S. government and stopped the practice of polygamy. Revelations have changed the earlier prohibition of blacks from receiving the priesthood. There has been, however, no alteration of the LDS understanding of the afterlife since its articulation by Joseph Smith. If anything, the Latter-day Saints in the twentieth century have become even bolder in their assertion of the importance of their heavenly theology. The number of books on eternal life increases yearly, Mormon information centers throughout the world dramatize the story of salvation for the nonbelieving public, and contemporary LDS writers feel comfortable in quoting extensively from nineteenth-century visionary accounts. In the light of what they perceive as a Christian world which has given up belief in heaven, many Latter-day Saints feel even more of a responsibility to define the meaning of death and eternal life.

Notes

1. The Church of Jesus Christ of Latter-day Saints acquired its first million members in 1946. It took another seventeen years, until 1963, to gain a second million. Af-

ter the sixties, however, the number of members increased sharply. In 1971 the membership had climbed to three million, in 1978 to four million, and by 1986 the membership was six million. While over four million of those members live in North America, the church's active missionary work has made converts in over ninety-five different countries. The church takes pride in explaining that every two minutes a new convert is made.

I would like to thank Harald Frome for loaning me hard-to-come-by Mormon materials and for patiently explaining to me the LDS afterlife.

2. Theodore M. Burton, *God's Greatest Gift* (Salt Lake City: Deseret Book, 1977), 175.

3. Ezra T. Benson quoted in *Official Report of the Annual General Conference of the Church of Jesus Christ of Latter-day Saints* (Salt Lake City: Church of Jesus Christ of Latter-day Saints, 1971), 18; Robert L. Millet and Joseph F. McConkie, eds., *The Life Beyond* (Salt Lake City: Bookcraft, 1986), 18.

4. Wilford Woodruff quoted in Millet and McConkie, *The Life Beyond*, 64.

5. Millet and McConkie, *The Life Beyond*, 54 (first quote), 64 (second and third quotes); for the priesthood and presidency persisting in the next life, see 53.

6. Mary V. Hill, *Angel Children* (Bountiful, Utah: Horizon, 1975), 40–41.

7. Burton, *God's Greatest Gift*, 237.

8. Bruce R. McConkie, *Mormon Doctrine* (Salt Lake City: Bookcraft, 1958), 497; Gordon T. Allred, *If a Man Die* (Salt Lake City: Bookcraft, 1964), 174.

9. Exaltation is described in Doctrine and Covenants section 132, especially verse 20: "Then shall they be gods, because they have no end; therefore shall they be from everlasting to everlasting, because they continue; then shall they be above all, because all things are subject unto them. Then shall they be gods, because they have all power, and the angels are subject unto them." See also Duane S. Crowther, *Life Everlasting* (Salt Lake City: Bookcraft, 1971), 333–34.

10. Burton, *God's Greatest Gift*, 20. On eternal and temporal marriages, see Doctrine and Covenants 132:15–19. The best scholarly discussion of the evolution of Mormon marriage practice is Lawrence Foster, *Religion and Sexuality: The Shakers, the Mormons, and the Oneida Community* (Urbana: University of Illinois Press, 1981), 123–80.

11. Crowther, *Life Everlasting*, 339 (first quote), 341 (second quote, citing Orson Pratt), 339 (fourth quote, citing Parley P. Pratt); N. B. Lundwall, ed., *The Vision or the Degrees of Glory* (Salt Lake City: Bookcraft, n.d.), 147 (third quote).

12. Crowther, *Life Everlasting*, 340; Lynn A. McKinlay, *Life Eternal* (Salt Lake City: Deseret Book, 1950), 164; Millet and McConkie, *The Life Beyond*, 143. Like many of his nineteenth-century contemporaries, Joseph Smith believed in a plurality of worlds in the universe. The earth is not the only planet inhabited by intelligent beings: see Michael J. Crowe, *The Extraterrestrial Life Debate, 1750–1900* (Cambridge: Cambridge University Press, 1986), 241–46.

13. The importance of rule and reproduction is emphasized in Crowther, *Life Everlasting*, 340.

7

Beyond the Stereotypes: Mormon and Non-Mormon Communities in Twentieth-Century Mormondom

Jan Shipps

The story of modern Mormonism and its relationship to the non-Mormon world is often misunderstood because there is a tendency for persons with a superficial understanding of Mormonism to view the Latter-day Saints collectively, seeing them as a people subject to an ecclesiastical hierarchy whose control over their thoughts and actions is by and large absolute. Despite much negative publicity about the Saints that has been and is being purveyed in the *Godmakers* books and films and in other publications produced by militant anti-Mormons, it is likely that the prevailing Mormon image is still the stereotypical picture of persons who drink neither alcoholic beverages nor coffee and tea, who do not smoke, so they are very healthy, who, despite strange beliefs, are very nice people who "take care of their own."[1] They work very hard and by really trying often succeed in show business or "real" business (especially if their names happen to be Osmond or Marriott). Yet in the stereotypical portrait of the Saints, such successes are not regarded so much as personal triumphs as results of a certain "Mormonness," a commitment to an LDS lifestyle that includes acceptance of a powerful work ethic as well as involvement in church activity. Within the stereotype, the LDS Church itself is seen as a monolithic institution whose authority Latter-day Saints rarely, if ever, question.[2]

In the popular mind, this prevailing misperception of Latter-day Saints is usually accompanied by a stereotypical image of the Gentiles (persons who are not Mormon) who reside in Utah and other geographical areas where significant numbers of Saints live. Probably originally drawn from fictional accounts of Mormon-Gentile struggle, this composite pictures non-Mormons as persons engaged in a perpetually adversarial relationship with the Saints. This is a misperception quite as divorced from reality as is the image of a monolithic LDS community and LDS culture. In reality, the world that the Mormons and non-Mormons have been inhabiting together since the 1850s has rarely, if ever, been a world as neatly divided as the popular press and many historical works about the Latter-day Saints have intimated.

If these stereotypes are to be stripped away, some means has to be found to make distinctions *within* the Mormon and non-Mormon communities. Here the census helps. But not much. Even though census takers at the turn of the century treated religion as a variable, their data reveal little aside from relative numbers of Latter-day Saints and Gentiles, and statistical information concerning the numbers of "Utah Mormons," as opposed to members of the Reorganized Church of Jesus Christ of Latter Day Saints, and marginally useful denominational breakdowns among the non-Mormon population.

As related in *Special Reports [on] Religious Bodies* (a Bureau of the Census publication from 1910), at the turn of the century the population of Utah (where the great bulk of the Saints then lived) was 276,749. Of this number, 172,814 (a little over 62 percent) were reported as communicants of some religious body. If 62 percent of Utah's children under five years of age is added to this number, and if 62 percent of Utah's children ages five and six is likewise added, the total number of Utahns who might be described as religious communicants is 208,218, or a little over 75 percent of the state's population. Thus slightly less than a quarter of Utah's residents were not active enough in any church, whether an LDS church or some other, to have been counted as communicants. Utah citizens who fit into this category can appropriately be described as "unchurched."[3]

Not surprisingly, of the Utah residents who at the turn of the century were communicants of some church, more than 87 percent were Latter-day Saints. Communicants in various Protestant bodies made up 4.7 percent of the Utah citizens who fit in the "churched" category. A slightly higher percentage (4.8 percent) were Roman Catholics, while the remainder of those who counted themselves as communicants of religious bodies were Greek Orthodox or Jewish.[4] (About 0.2 percent of the Utah population, 550 persons, were included in a very small category described as "all other bodies.")

A number of historians have used such census data to work up valuable religious profiles of other geographical areas in the United States.[5] For purposes of such analyses, however, historians of American Protestantism usually make distinctions between so-called liturgical groups, such as Lutherans and Episcopalians, and evangelical groups, such as Methodists and Baptists. This conventional distinction did not really operate in Utah in the early part of the twentieth century, however. Not enough Lutherans lived there to merit a separate category in the census report, while the Episcopalians (one-fifth of all Utah Protestants) often cooperated so closely with Utah Baptists, Methodists,

Congregationalists, and Presbyterians that this liturgical/evangelical difference that discriminated so nicely elsewhere had little significance in the Great Basin kingdom. Moreover, from time to time, especially in the Utah political arena, the importance of the division between Mormons and non-Mormons was great enough to lead Roman Catholics and Protestants to make common cause together, a circumstance obtained nowhere else in the nation in 1900. In addition to allowing a dichotomous division of the Utah population into "churched" and "unchurched" categories, census data reveal that relative proportions of Utah's "churched" and "unchurched" people were not evenly distributed throughout the state. On the one hand, for example, in 1900 in such counties as Beaver (in the southwestern part of the state, close to the Nevada border), 39.5 percent of the residents were unchurched; in Carbon County (including an important coal mining area), 50.7 percent of the population was unchurched; and in Summit County (including the silver mining area around Park City), 35.4 percent of the people were unchurched. On the other hand, in Cache County (a fairly isolated valley area encircled by mountain ranges), originally settled by the Latter-day Saints, the proportion of unchurched was only 4 percent.[6] In Box Elder, Davis, Emery, Weber, and a number of other counties, the number of unchurched was less than 12 percent.

As for making distinctions among Latter-day Saints, elsewhere I have argued that by the end of the nineteenth century Mormon theological claims—in themselves not entirely unique, but put forward within a unique medium—and the experience of those who accepted these claims had created a people, a new ethnic group.[7] But the cohesiveness of this group was being severely strained at the turn of the century because the Latter-day Saints were living through the trauma that wracked the Mormon body in the wake of the dual demise of plural marriage and the LDS political kingdom. Consequently it would be possible to develop a categorical scheme locating Saints on a continuum based on rejection or acceptance of the changes that took place in Mormonism during the ecclesiastical administrations of Wilford Woodruff, Lorenzo Snow, and Joseph F. Smith. As for the non-Mormons, in a curious way it would also be possible to develop a continuum reflecting their attitudes about whether the Mormons had, or had not, accepted the changes they had been forced to make in the late nineteenth century.[8]

But here, categorizing both the Mormons and the Gentiles in a different manner is called for. With regard to the latter, categories need to be established that will separate non-Mormons according to whether any concerns they had about the Saints were mainly religious or primarily political and economic. As necessarily inexact as such a division must be, rough categories can be established by making an assumption that those non-Mormons whose concerns about the Latter-day Saints were primarily religious are likely to have affiliated with one of the Protestant, Roman Catholic, or—much less likely—Jewish congregations in Utah.[9]

No matter how carefully the statistics gathered by the Census Bureau are examined and manipulated, however, they cannot reveal the relative numbers among the "unchurched" of those persons who had no particular interest in religious matters and might be described as truly secular and those persons who came to Utah as Mormon converts or the children of Latter-day Saints who, for one reason or another, were no longer officially counted as Latter-day Saints. In view of this lack of information, the safest strategy is to divide Utah citizens over seven years of age who fit into the unchurched category equally between the LDS and Gentile groups. If this is done, 23,416 non-Mormons (8.4 percent of the state's population at the turn of the century) were located in the "unchurched Gentile" category, while 21,782 persons (7.9 percent of the state's population) were located in the "churched" non-Mormon category. Even without a hard and fast determination of exactly which members of the non-Mormon community fit into these categories, this strategy allows the identification of two non-Mormon groups whose populations were basically equal: those who were essentially secular in their orientation and a group of what might be called "religious" non-Mormons, many of whom had sentiments about the Saints not unlike those of the Protestant missionaries who, at the turn of the century, conceived of their task as the converting of Latter-day Saints away from "the heathen, pagan, 'Mohammedan-ish' heresy foisted onto the world by the so-called Mormon prophet."[10] Utah's Roman Catholics and Jews were never as hostile to the Saints as were the Protestants, and as the years of the twentieth century have passed, the division between liturgical and evangelical Protestants has asserted itself in the state. Such denominations as the Episcopalians and, to some extent, the Presbyterians and Methodists have settled into a much less adversarial relationship with the Latter-day Saints than is the case with most Baptist groups and other evangelical and fundamentalist Protestant organizations.[11]

Among the Saints, contrary to the perennially popular notion that Mormonism is, and has ever been, a monolithic movement in which internal conformity is rigorously enforced, diversity has never been entirely alien. During the pioneer period, the practicalities of the Mormon experience made universal suppression of dissident behavior and unconventional belief so difficult that, despite all the overblown stories of the refusal of LDS leaders to countenance dissent and notwithstanding all the fictionalized accounts of the terrible fate awaiting apostates, a surprising degree of multiformity was tolerated in the early years within the LDS Church itself. Moreover, there were yet other Mormons in the Utah LDS community who were not a part of the church over which Brigham Young presided. The claims of the "Brighamites," as the Saints who followed Young were sometimes called, were contested firsthand in Utah Territory by the "Josephites," members of the Reorganized Church of Jesus Christ of Latter Day Saints led by the Prophet's eldest son, Joseph Smith III.[12] And there were other Mormons, too, Saints who had first moved into and then back out of the church without following up their ecclesiastical exits (which were often, though not always, voluntary) with physical removal from the society of their former faithmates. Some of the persons in this interesting former Mormon category stayed in Utah for economic reasons.[13]

Others who, for one reason or another, were bitter toward the church seem to have functioned in the Mormon community mainly as thorns in the side of the "almighty hierarchy."[14] But many former Mormons stayed in the LDS community because, even as they rejected the legitimacy of the church organization and the authority of its leaders, or as they were rejected by the church, they continued in their own ways to affirm the truth of the LDS gospel.[15]

Disagreement about matters of faith was, then, not a novelty first making its appearance in the LDS community after that community was no longer effectively set apart from the larger world. Still, while intra-Mormon diversity was not new in the early twentieth century, developments across the years since 1890 have allowed that diversity to become more intense. Before 1890, even as they had occupied the same geographical space, Utah's Mormon and non-Mormon populations had lived in communities separated from each other psychologically. Each community had developed its own structures of internal governance and its own means of enforcing internal cohesion. Serving to counterpoise one another, each community had set limits on the degree of diversity tolerable in the other. But with the coming of statehood in 1896, interpenetration of the two communities occurred, and as the Gentile barrier around the LDS community grew progressively weaker, the latent diversity within the Mormon world began to make itself known.

Obvious differences in ethnic background had encouraged variety in the LDS population long before the pioneer era came to an end.[16] Lineage had made a difference historically, too. Distinctions between Latter-day Saints whose families had been long in the church and LDS converts new to the faith had been possible for decades, and distinctions between the members of the families of the Mormon elite, whose main business from the beginning had been running the church, and the members of ordinary, everyday Mormon families had likewise been felt for years.[17] But in the twentieth century, a different form of diversity started to cut across these more or less traditional LDS population categories. Perhaps it would be an overstatement to say that many LDS subcultures came into being during the first decades of the new century. Yet simply making distinctions between "true believers" and "cultural Mormons," as some students of modern Mormonism are prone to do, does not yield categories elegant enough to clarify the connections and relationship between what might be termed "modern Mormonism" and the secular establishment.

The general character of Mormondom became increasingly varied and complex after 1890, but because personal LDS behavioral patterns were not as set in the early years as they are now—and because behavioral patterns are notoriously difficult to tease out of the historical record in any event—a useful means of examining the variegated and catholic nature of the world of modern Mormonism is noting how Latter-day Saints are situated along an orthodoxy continuum, on the one hand, and, on the other, a dimension along which is measured levels of church activity and attitudes toward it.

Without making any effort at this juncture to determine the relative proportions of the LDS populations who fall into the various categories located along this belief-behavior continuum at various chronological points—a task that would be even more difficult than determining the relative number of non-Mormons in the secular and religious categories described above—the continuum itself can be described as follows:

1. At one extreme are those persons who regard themselves as the only true Mormons, but who are not recognized as Mormons by most Latter-day Saints, i.e., the Mormon "fundamentalists." In a sense, their beliefs are more than orthodox, in that they accept the Book of Mormon as a historical document, believing that this basic LDS Scripture is precisely what it claims to be; they accept the LDS doctrinal formulations that were established during the lifetimes of Joseph Smith and Brigham Young, but reject the 1890 Manifesto proscribing plural marriage on the basis of its having been promulgated outside a "Thus saith the Lord" context, and they "live the gospel" as fully as they can by joining with like-minded Saints in isolated communities. In other words, at one of the continuum's extremities one finds, to use Eric Hoffer's term, the truest of true believers—the Saints who continue to practice plural marriage.

2. A second, less extreme category next to this "fundamentalist" one is the one in which is found active, almost superorthodox Saints. These are the persons who seem to be certain that the Book of Mormon is historically accurate and who do not question the versions of LDS history long since canonized by

the church. Saints in this category exhibit a very high level of church activity, not only in attendance at worship, but also in fulfilling church callings.

3. In a third category along this orthodox/active dimension are found Latter-day Saints who accept the truth of the LDS gospel, but concede that it might be held in "earthen vessels." These are persons who are not very worried about whether the Book of Mormon is history in the ordinary understanding of that term, as long as the book's narrative captures and represents truth in some abstract sense. They understand the principle of canonization and are inclined, as opposed to those in the very extreme categories, not to be threatened by academic approaches to the study of the past. They are generally active, not only in worship and in carrying out church callings, but also in quasi-official LDS organizations such as the Mormon History Association or the various Sunstone symposia.

4. Then there is a Mormon group that fits in the central category in this classification scheme. Their thought patterns were formed by their immersion in Mormon doctrine, but for one reason or another they do not themselves take much of a role in church activities, although they may send their children to Sunday school and sacrament meeting. They are not hostile to the institution or to other Saints. This category includes "cultural" and/or "ethnic" Mormons, large numbers of whom do not reside in Utah.

5. Moving further from the center is a category that might be described as mildly anti-Mormon. Popularly known as "Jack Mormons," such Saints are located between the category that includes "cultural" or "ethnic" Mormons and a category that includes Saints hostile to the LDS Church and contemptuous toward its active members. This is a fairly heavily populated category that embraces inactive Mormons of many stripes, including those who are more amused than threatened by the actions of the members of the LDS ecclesiastical hierarchy.

6. A second "Jack Mormon" category includes Latter-day Saints whose level of hostility toward the church as an institution is fairly high, who deny that in LDS Scriptures might be repositories of truth, and whose attitude toward active and committed Mormons is generally one of contempt. This category often includes persons who have been disfellowshipped or even excommunicated, but who have not rejected their Mormon ethnicity.

7. Finally, at the opposite extreme from the Mormon fundamentalists is a category in which are found former Mormons who are extremely antagonistic not only toward the LDS Church hierarchy but also toward anything Mormon. Truly anti-Mormon, the persons in this category believe that Mormonism is so dangerous that they expend an enormous amount of energy deprecating

Mormon theology and opposing the LDS Church and its authority in the community.

Except for the subtle connotations that are sometimes attached to the terms *Gentile* and *non-Mormon,* with the latter sometimes referring to persons unfriendly to the Saints, not many attempts have been made to identify and clarify distinctions within the non-Mormon community. But this present one is by no means the only effort that has been made to describe the variation within the Mormon community.[18] Whether these particular classification schemes or different ones are used to describe the structure of the "human landscape" in the world that Mormons and non-Mormons have been inhabiting together for more than a hundred years, discriminating descriptions of the two communities beyond the prevailing stereotypes point to the immense complexity of the history of Mormonism in the twentieth century. Such descriptions reveal, in fact, an intricate historical fabric that can be properly characterized only if the multiple strands in the pattern of the fabric are separated and considered in isolation, as well as together. While there are many fine threads in this fabric, three interwoven strands form the principal pattern. By identifying these, we can now begin to appreciate the relationship between the Mormon and the non-Mormon establishments. The first of these basic strands is the internal history of the Mormon community, the history of how Saints related to other Saints, and how the community as a whole managed to negotiate the troubled times in which traditional LDS social, political, and economic arrangements were given up and new social, political, and economic arrangements instituted.[19] That story can never be fully and properly told, however, without paying attention to a second strand in the fabric of twentieth-century Mormon history, the strand that deals with the relationship between modern Mormonism and evangelical (later in the century, fundamentalist) Protestantism. Quite as clearly as the story of conflicts that can often be found within the Mormon community, this is a story of religious conflict in which the deeply held convictions of one group are more or less constantly challenged by the members of the other group.

The third prominent strand in the design of this historical fabric is the story of the Saints and the essentially secular Gentiles, those who, after the demise of plural marriage and the Mormon political kingdom, were far less concerned about Mormon religious beliefs than about the willingness of the Saints to permit Gentiles to participate fully in the creation of a modern society in the Intermountain West. To an amazing degree, as is shown in the history of Salt Lake City by Thomas G. Alexander and James B. Allen, this is not a story of unending conflict, but of surprising cooperation.[20] To be sure, a narrative of this strand of the Mormon-Utah story is by no means without conflict, but it generally includes accounts of healthy rather than destructive challenges. Often Latter-day Saints and Gentiles struggled together, not against each other. An unusually significant part of this strand covers the development of institutions that facilitated and continue to facilitate Mormon–non-Mormon interaction—the Alta Club, the Commercial Club, Rotary, the Salt Lake Kindergarten Association, the Ladies Literary Club, the Art Institute and Utah Symphony boards, and so on.[21]

Looking briefly at three historical examples will illustrate the value of separating the various strands in the Mormon story. One of these examples is drawn from the early years of the twentieth century, one is from the post–World War II years, and one is very current.

Edward Leo Lyman and Henry J. Wolfinger, who have made close studies of the coming of Utah statehood, have described the deliberations that led up to the striking of an unwritten bargain between the Latter-day Saints and the national government in 1890. In return for Utah statehood, the Saints would give up the practice of plural marriage and enter into politics in the manner of other American citizens, dividing the LDS body politic, as it were, into national political parties.[22] As the new state came into existence, a second unwritten understanding was reached: Utah's congressional delegation would, as far as possible, be evenly divided between Saints and Gentiles, with the state's two senators always representing the two components of the Utah population.[23]

Nevertheless, after Reed Smoot, a member of the Quorum of the Twelve Apostles and prominent Utah Republican, was elected to the Senate in 1903, his right to hold the seat to which he had been elected was also challenged. In view of the fact that, with the blessing of the LDS Church hierarchy, the non-Mormon Thomas Kearns was Utah's other senator at the time, this was a somewhat surprising turn of events, especially since the challenge was not based on any illegal act committed by Smoot.[24] It rested instead on the fact that he held a position of ecclesiastical authority in the LDS Church. Although the political situation in Utah was exceedingly complicated during this transition period and although the subtle partitioning that would separate non-Mormons into those primarily concerned about religious issues and those primarily concerned about secular matters was just beginning to occur, the challenge mounted against Smoot and the LDS Church is easier to comprehend if the story of the bitter adversarial relationship that existed between Mormonism and the non-Mormons concerned about religious issues is separated from the story of Mormonism's relationship with the secular establishment. Otherwise, the Smoot challenge, which upset the bargain that had been so carefully hammered out to ensure fair play in the national political arena, appears to have been counterproductive for the challengers.[25]

A clearer picture of the complicated situation emerges if the role played in this drama by the Salt Lake Ministerial Association is kept in focus. The challenge to Smoot's right to occupy a seat in the U.S. Senate was penned by the Reverend W. M. Paden, pastor of the First Presbyterian Church of Salt Lake City; unsubstantiated charges about Smoot's having been a polygamist were added by the Reverend J. M. Leilich, superintendent of the Utah missions of the Methodist Episcopal Church; and a huge proportion of the petitions (that are supposed to have included four million signatures) against Smoot's being seated contained signatures gathered in evangelical Protestant congregations throughout the nation. Adding this dimension to our understanding of what happened lets us see that the Smoot investigation was one of the catalysts that helped to precipitate divisions *within* the non-Mormon community. This approach also clarifies the final outcome of the investigation, for it was, finally, the support of Theodore Roosevelt, probably the most prominent member of the secular establishment of the day, that led to the Utah senator's being allowed to take his seat.

The Smoot investigation was an early example of cooperation between particular segments of the Mormon and the non-Mormon communities, i.e., between Gentiles, whose primary concerns about the Saints were/are religious concerns, and former Mormons, those prior members of the LDS community who fit into the category that includes persons extremely antagonistic to the LDS Church and to everything Mormon.[26] Apostates in the eyes of the LDS Church, such individuals have made common cause with the Saints' evangelical Protestant opponents across the years. By the time of the Smoot investigation, Frank J. Cannon, one of the sons of LDS apostle George Q. Cannon, was such a person. He provided information and even the wording for the initial attacks questioning the motives of the LDS Church and questioning the right of Reed Smoot to hold a Senate seat, and throughout the hearing he worked behind the scenes in opposition to Smoot. Wayne Stout, who wrote and (at his own expense) published a highly partisan multivolume history of Utah, portrays Julius Caesar Burrows, the senator from Michigan who chaired the Committee on Privileges and Elections, as another link between former Mormons and the non-Mormon antagonists of Senator Smoot and the LDS Church. Whether Stout was correct about Senator Burrows having been "a nephew of the notorious apostate Sylvester Smith, who brainwashed Julius into a vehement Mormon hater," the public record shows the Smoot investigation to have been an early instance of cooperation between former Mormons and evangelical Protestants in fighting the LDS Church.[27]

Turning from cooperation among the opponents of Mormonism, a prime example of cooperation between the Latter-day Saints and the Utah secular establishment was the activities of an unusual "extra-political triumvirate" composed of Gustave P. Backman, John Fitzgerald, and David O. McKay, who, as Backman recalled, met together every Tuesday morning in the coffee shop of the Hotel Utah to decide what needed to be done in Salt Lake City.[28] Composed of an inactive Mormon, one who would have fit nicely in the benign Jack Mormon category, a Gentile, whose primary concerns about the Saints (at least in his later years) had to do with finding ways to work together with them for the common good, and a very active LDS Church authority, this triad of unelected yet extremely powerful Salt Lake City leaders had started working together when they were all members of the Executive Committee of the Utah Centennial Commission, which had been charged with planning the state centennial observance in 1947. For nearly a decade afterward, they continued meeting to consider social, political, economic, and religious issues that were of common concern to Utah's citizens—and particularly to Salt Lake City residents—and afterward communicated their ideas and tentative decisions informally to the business community and elected officials of the city, county, and state.

Persons who are suspicious of the secular power of the LDS Church would probably regard these weekly meetings of Backman, who was the executive secretary of the Salt Lake City Chamber of Commerce, Fitzgerald, who was the editor of the *Salt Lake Tribune,* and McKay, who was the president of the LDS Church, as evidence of the church's power and its desire for total control over Salt Lake City and the State of Utah. But Backman's informal memoirs suggest otherwise. These meetings seem, instead, to represent the visible working out of a pattern of cooperation between non-Mormons and Latter-day Saints (many of whom were/are very active and devoted to the LDS Church and many others who were/are inactive) which has functioned reasonably consistently all across the twentieth century. Keeping the historical strands separate, making it easy to differentiate between the cooperative relationship the Saints have maintained with the non-Mormon secular establishment and the adversarial relationship between the Saints and non-Mormons who are concerned about the LDS religious claims, makes a conspiratorial interpretation of the Backman, Fitzgerald, McKay meetings far less likely.[29]

In the religious arena, the Church of Jesus Christ of Latter-day Saints has never stopped dedicating its energies to proselytizing. Moreover, during the ecclesiastical administration of Spencer W. Kimball (1973–86), the church renewed its commitment to taking the message of the LDS gospel across the nation and throughout the world.[30] Appreciating the distinctions among Gentiles and keeping the exclusive nature of the LDS religious claims in mind helps to clarify the current success in evangelical and fundamentalist Protestant congregations of the *Godmakers* campaign in which, through professionally produced films and books, the LDS Church is being portrayed as a menace to the health of families and society, as well as a demonic threat to the salvation of humanity. Otherwise, this vocal anti-Mormon movement, being conducted against the LDS Church by an alliance of former Mormons violently antagonistic to Mormonism and some very conservative Protestants, appears to fly in the face of the current existence of unusually cordial social, political, and economic relationships between Mormonism and the secular establishment in Washington, D.C., as well as in Salt Lake City and elsewhere. As curiously out of phase and out of place as this virulent campaign may appear to be, it has historical roots in the nineteenth century when bitter former Mormons joined forces with persons from Protestant and Roman Catholic churches across the country in a futile effort to deliver a death blow to the LDS Church.

As always, when one is dealing with the web of history, things are not as simple as the foregoing analysis would seem to make them. The multiple strands in the pattern of the LDS historical fabric cannot merely be identified in Utah, or even simply in the Mormon culture region in the Intermountain West. A separate and somewhat different story of twentieth-century Mormonism must be recounted for California, and for all the other areas in the United States that Saints in Indiana, Illinois, Georgia, and elsewhere often describe as "the mission field." And still other twentieth-century Mormon stories abound, in Europe, in Latin America, in Asia, and in all the places where the Saints have carried the LDS gospel and established outposts of "the Kingdom."

Yet if all these separate stories differ one from another, much about them is continuous from one place to another. As the Mormon gospel takes root in different cultures, it takes on different forms. Always, however, there is the church and "the world," the Saints and the Gentiles. Wherever the LDS story plays itself out, its chroniclers and its interpreters would do well to remember that neither group is made up of ideal types.

Notes

1. Currently Saints Alive, which was formerly known as Ex-Mormons for Jesus, is the most vocal and visible anti-Mormon group. The Saints Alive leader Ed Decker is the producer of the *Godmakers* films, which the group distributes, and is coauthor with Dave Hunt of *The Godmakers* (New York: Harvest House, 1984). A number of militant anti-Mormons are associated with the Modern Microfilm Company in Salt Lake City. Operated by Jerald and Sandra Tanner, this company produces a large number of publications that call LDS historical and theological claims into question. *Mormonism: Shadow or Reality,* one of the most elaborate of the Modern Microfilm publications, is distributed nationally by the Moody Press in Chicago. The *Utah Evangel,* a newsprint periodical, is distributed by the Reverend John Smith, who served as the minister of a Utah Baptist congregation for more than fifteen years before moving to Texas to establish a ministry primarily devoted to converting Mormons away from Mormonism.

2. This description of the Mormon image is drawn from an examination of all the periodical articles on the Mormons and Mormonism indexed in *Poole's Index* and *Readers' Guide* between 1860 and 1960 as well as from impressionistic evidence developed from paying close attention to the treatment Mormons and Mormonism have received in both print and electronic media since 1960.

3. Adding in those who were too young to be counted as communicants in order to develop a reasonably accurate religious profile of Utah called for a certain amount of guesswork. Counted in the total state population of 276,749 were 41,852 children under the age of five. Also, 38,128 children between the ages of five and nine were included in the census count. As no means exists to determine how many of these children were actually under age seven—the age when many churches start counting children as communicants—it seemed best simply to assume an equal number of children in each age category from five through nine—i.e., to divide by five and add two-fifths of the total (15,251) to the number of children under five to get a general notion of the number of children in Utah under seven years of age. This strategy was used to obtain a percentage of the Utah population under the age of seven and this percentage (20.6) was uniformly added to the numbers of communicants reported by the census takers whenever percentages were calculated throughout this essay.

4. At the turn of the century, the Reorganized LDS Church had 493 members in Utah. They were divided among five congregations. Exact numbers of Jews in Utah cannot be determined from the census data since only heads of households were reported.

5. See, for example, Linda Pritchard, "Another Look at Religion in Texas, 1845–1900," paper presented at the meeting of the American Society of Church History, Ft. Worth, Texas, 5 Apr. 1986. Both Paul Kleppner and Richard Jensen have used such religious profiles to explicate political behavior in the Midwest: Paul Kleppner, *Cross of Culture* (New York: Free Press, 1970); Richard Jensen, *Winning of the Midwest* (New Haven: Yale University Press, 1967).

6. Since more than 99 percent of the churched population was LDS, this was a significant number.

7. This contention is crucial to the argument I made in *Mormonism: The Story of a New Religious Tradition* (Urbana: University of Illinois Press, 1985).

8. In a presentation made to clergy in the Idaho–Eastern Washington Conference of the United Methodist Church, such a scheme proved extremely helpful in clarifying where the LDS "fundamentalists," i.e., those Saints who continue to practice plural marriage, stand in relation to other Latter-day Saints. See Jan Shipps, "The Mormon Human Landscape," lecture presented to the Methodist Circuit Rider Seminar, Boise, Apr. 1982; an extensive report of this lecture was published in *Sunstone Review*.

9. This is not an unreasonable assumption since, in such an environment, personal identity was (and often still is) very much tied to religious affiliation. Because many non-Mormon children who grew up in Utah without some definite religious affiliation often moved over into the LDS camp, the members of non-Mormon family units generally identified themselves with some non-Mormon religious group.

10. This description is a composite taken from the published reports of Methodist, Baptist, Presbyterian, and Episcopal missionaries to Utah. See Jan Shipps, "From Satyr to Saint: American Attitudes toward the Mormons, 1860–1960," paper presented at the annual meeting of the Organization of American Historians, Chicago, Apr. 1973. For the most complete description available of Protestant missionary efforts to convert Mormons away from Mormonism, see T. Edgar Lyon, "Evangelical Protestant Missionary Activities in Mormon Dominated Areas, 1865–1900," Ph.D. diss., University of Utah, 1962.

11. This observation is based on personal discussions I have had with members of various Protestant groups in Utah. To some degree the difference seems to be theological, reflecting a division among Protestants into so-called liberal and conservative camps. See also the editorials published in the *Utah Evangel*.

12. Altogether the RLDS Church had 40,851 members in 1900; they were concentrated in the upper Midwest, but, as indicated, there were five congregations in Utah.

13. Most of the Latter-day Saints who were involved in the "New Move" (the Godbeite movement), which was regarded as heresy, stayed in Utah following their excommunication from the church. However, as Ronald W. Walker indicates in his study of the careers of T. B. H. and Fanny Stenhouse, apostates sometimes had difficulty collecting due bills in the LDS community. For that reason, former Mormons who stayed in Utah for business reasons were more likely to be Saints who simply became less than fully involved in LDS endeavors, adopting a position somewhat analogous to that of inactive Mormons today. See Ronald W. Walker, "The Stenhouses and the Making of a Mormon Image," *Journal of Mormon History* 1 (1974): 51–72.

14. The most prominent former Mormon in the early years of the twentieth century was probably Frank J. Cannon, the author of *Under the Prophet in Utah: The National Menace of a Political Priestcraft* and many other exposes, who had once served as a U.S. senator from Utah.

15. The Godbeite "heresy" was presented as a form of *true* Mormonism. Other forms of Mormonism that existed alongside normative Mormonism are described in Russell R. Rich, *Those Who Would Be Leaders: Offshoots of Mormonism* (Provo: Brigham Young University Extension Publications, 1968).

16. In addition to large-scale emigration from England and Scandinavia, the LDS community included a significant German-speaking sector. The native Mormon population not only included Saints from all across the United States and Canada but also American Indians.

17. An analysis of the leadership of the LDS Church as a social elite is found in D. Michael Quinn, "The Mormon Hierarchy, 1832–1932: An American Elite," Ph.D. diss., Yale University, 1976.

18. Such schemes are found in Robert Gottlieb and Peter Wiley, *America's Saints: The Rise of Mormon Power* (New York: Putnam's, 1984), and in James L. Clayton, "On the Different World of Utah," a presentation made 31 October 1985 at the National Collegiate Honors Council's Twentieth Annual Conference in Salt Lake City and printed in *Vital Speeches of the Day* (1 Jan. 1986): 186–92.

19. The internal dynamics characterizing the relationships among those situated in various categories along the LDS belief-behavior continuum is a fascinating history in and of itself. Two works deal with this topic: Richard Cowan, *History of the LDS Church in the Twentieth Century* (Salt Lake City: Bookcraft, 1985), and Thomas G. Alexander, *Mormonism in Transition: A History of the Latter-day Saints, 1890–1930* (Urbana: University of Illinois Press, 1986).

20. Thomas G. Alexander and James B. Allen, *Mormons and Gentiles: A History of Salt Lake City* (Boulder: Pruett, 1984).

21. The records of most of these groups are housed in the Special Collections sections of the Marriott Library at the University of Utah. As an example of how these organizations worked to create arenas for Mormon and non-Mormon political, social, and economic intercourse, see especially the proposition of one of the founders of the Commercial Club, C. N. Strevell, who asked that the club be "a non-sectarian, non-political organization where Mormon, Jew, and Gentile could meet together." This club was organized in 1887 and, despite the need to guard against the development of cliques, it became, in the words of a Mr. Armstrong (whose sentiments were recorded in the minutes of the Commercial Club Board for 19 January 1914), "the one place in Utah where open forum exists and where all men, regardless of race, color, creed, or previous condition of servitude can meet and be heard." See O. N. Malmquist, *The Alta Club: 1883–1974* (Salt Lake City: N.p., n.d.). See also Leonard J. Arrington, *Service over Self: A History of Salt Lake City Rotary Club No. 24* (Salt Lake City: Rotary Club, 1981).

Indeed, this is a story that cannot yet be fully told, for at this point there are more questions than answers. For example, while there was a high level of cooperation between certain Mormons and certain non-Mormons in Salt Lake City, what level of cooperation existed in Utah's small towns where the Latter-day Saints outnumbered the non-Mormons by fifteen or twenty to one? If such institutional avenues as the

Commercial Club and the Federation of Women's Clubs existed to facilitate cooperative action in the public arena, did those institutional networks spill over into private
arenas, so that pure socializing in which Mormons and non-Mormons came together
simply for the pleasure of enjoying each other's company became commonplace? Economics and politics, and such particular areas as that represented by the Irrigation
Congresses, all brought Mormons and non-Mormons into productive working relationships. Did such working relationships extend to the national level, or are such close
working arrangements as that which developed between Senator Reed Smoot and
President Warren Harding to be accounted for as personal friendships that might well
have developed even if the overall relationship between Mormonism and the secular
establishment had been primarily negative, rather than positive?

22. Edward Leo Lyman, *Political Deliverance: The Mormon Quest for Utah Statehood*
(Urbana: University of Illinois Press, 1986); Henry J. Wolfinger, "A Re-Examination of
the Woodruff Manifesto in the Light of Utah Constitutional History," *Utah Historical
Quarterly* 39 (Fall 1971): 328–49.

23. Jan Shipps, "Utah Comes of Age Politically: A Study of the State's Politics in the
Early Years of the Twentieth Century," *Utah Historical Quarterly* 35 (Spring 1967): 94.

24. An earlier challenge to the right of a Latter-day Saint to hold a seat in the national congress had been based on that person's open defiance of the law forbidding
polygamous cohabitation. Brigham H. Roberts, an assistant to the LDS church historian and a prominent Utah Democrat, was elected to Congress in 1900, but his right
to occupy the seat to which he was elected was challenged and the challenge was up-
held by the House of Representatives.

25. The official record of the Smoot investigation is contained in *Proceedings before
the Committee on Privileges and Elections of the United States Senate in the Matter of
the Protest against the Right of Hon. Reed Smoot, a Senator from the State of Utah, to
Hold His Seat,* 4 vols. (Washington, D.C.: Government Printing Office, 1904–6). The
best description of the Smoot election and investigation is found in Alexander, *Mormonism in Transition.*

26. Such people fit in one of the extreme categories (category 7) in the classification
scheme previously devised to describe the "Mormon human landscape."

27. Wayne Stout, *History of Utah* (Salt Lake City: N.p., 1967–71), 2:250.

28. Gustave P. Backman, unpublished memoirs in the files of the Salt Lake City
Chamber of Commerce, Special Collections, Marriott Library, University of Utah. The
characterization of these three as an "extra-political triumvirate" comes from Alexander and Allen, *Mormons and Gentiles,* 263.

29. In fact, a wider recognition of this part of the design in the Mormon historical
fabric on the part of those who study the topic might make less likely the publication
by respected presses of such broad conspiratorial interpretations of modern Mormonism as Ray Hinerman and Anson Shups, *The Mormon Corporate Empire* (Boston: Beacon Press, 1986).

30. The decision made by the highest LDS Church authorities to agree not to carry out a proselytizing program in Jerusalem is important to understanding the development of Mormonism as a new religious tradition, since it indicates an implicit recognition of the limits of LDS expansion. But the assurances given to Israel should not be interpreted as an indication that Mormonism may be blunting its missionary thrust. Conference talks continue to emphasize the importance of missionary activity and young Latter-day Saint men and, increasingly, young Latter-day Saint women are still encouraged to accept missionary calls.

8

Utah and the Mormons:
A Symbiotic Relationship

Richard D. Poll

For all but the first seventeen of its 150 plus years the Church of Jesus Christ of Latter-day Saints has been based in Utah. The harried Mormon refugees from Kirtland, Far West, and Nauvoo soon felt at home "in Deseret's sweet, peaceful land," and their heirs by blood and adoption still sing:

High on the mountain top
A banner is unfurled. . . .

For God remembers still
His promise made of old
That he on Zion's hill
Truth's standard would unfold! . . .

His house shall there be reared
His glory to display. . . .

For there we shall be taught
The law that will go forth,
With truth and wisdom fraught,
To govern all the earth.[1]

For its entire history as a political entity, Utah has been Mormon country. Not only have most of its inhabitants been members of the "Church" but this is the single fact most likely to be known by non-Utahns. People who have never heard of Alta, Bingham, or Canyonlands know about the Tabernacle Choir and "This Is the Place." Neophytes in LDS congregations hundreds of miles from the Wasatch Front still feel at a status disadvantage if they have no forebears who crossed the plains for the gospel's sake.

Symbiosis, however, is more than geographic coexistence or association in the popular mind. It is, by one dictionary, "the intimate living together of two dissimilar organisms in a mutually beneficial relationship."[2] The fig wasp that inhabits and fertilizes the fig tree is a classic example. The tickbird on the rhino is another. Other definitions encompass interaction in which the benefits are disproportionate or one-sided—the cuckoo's egg in the robin's nest or the flea on the dog.

That the association between Utah and the Mormons is a symbiotic relationship in the mutually interactive sense seems clear. Utah and the Mormons are what they are because their lives have been so intertwined—so interactive. Without the Mormons, Utah would be just another Wyoming or Nevada. And without its Utah experience Mormonism would be just another small denomination in American Protestantism.[3]

The symbiosis falls into four stages, each characterized by the nature and scope of Mormon initiative vis-à-vis Utah and the reciprocal effect of Utah on the church and its people.

Period 1 extends from 1847 to 1890—from the Mormon arrival in the Great Basin until the Woodruff Manifesto. Utah was at least temporarily Zion, refuge for the gathered and beleaguered Saints, and its location and resources helped to shape the culture of the kingdom. Church participation in the affairs of the territory was aggressive and comprehensive.

Period 2 covers the years 1890 to 1945—from Utah's acceptance of the conditions for statehood until World War II. Utah became "home" for most of the Saints as expectations of a return to Jackson County receded into the future. Intent on improving its image to facilitate peaceful coexistence with "the world," the church interacted with the state on a selective and primarily defensive basis.

Period 3 extends from 1945 to the present—the era of Mormonism's transformation from a regional to a national and then a world religion. An improving church image has remained linked to Utah's sheltering valleys, both in the perceptions of those who view from afar and in the perspectives of those sons and daughters of the pioneers who have gone beyond the mountains to preach and prosper in Babylon. The church behind the image, more confidently dominant in Utah than during Period 2, has exerted its influence selectively but aggressively.

Period 4 begins with the present. Since history and prophecy are separate callings—perceived by some, alas, to be at odds with each other—I shall deal only tentatively and briefly with the shape of things to come. The image and substance of Mormonism will, I believe, be less and less influenced by Utah-based events and attitudes. The influence of the church on the state will still be pervasive, but attention will be focused on the defense and enhancement of Mormonism's worldwide concerns.

The most studied aspects of this symbiotic relationship are from period 1, when most Mormons were Utahns and most Utahns were Mormons. The theocratic communitarian commitments of the Saints interacted with the physiographic realities of the Great Basin and Colorado Plateau to shape Utah Territory. An underdeveloped economy, embattled politics, and psychological isolation reflected both terrestrial distance and celestial aspirations. Even the Gentiles who came to Utah for the same reasons that brought miners to Montana and ranchers to Wyoming found their lives affected by the fact that they were in Mormon country.

It is arguable that the two most valuable contributions that Utah made to Mormonism in the nineteenth century were isolation and insufficient rainfall. They made it possible and necessary for the Saints to apply cooperative concepts received in the East successfully enough to become something more than a beleaguered community of followers of a charismatic leader.

The Mormon subculture took shape, not in New York, Ohio, Missouri, or Illinois, but in Utah, described in pioneer times as "a thousand miles from anywhere." Isolation was not complete, and Leonard Arrington pointed out years ago that the Gentile intrusions had their beneficial windfall aspects. But the preoccupations with building and defending Zion reinforced a doctrinally based "we-they" image of the world, and that perception has persisted among the descendants of the first Utah Mormons to the present day.

The "Americanization" of the tens of thousands of European converts who came to territorial Utah was hardly typical of the larger nineteenth-century assimilation process in the United States. A minority of the Mormon immigrants tarried long enough to sample life in New Orleans, St. Louis, Philadelphia, or New York, but most of the converts were shepherded straight through to the Great Basin. Never having voted in England, Scandinavia, or Germany, they cast their first ballots for church-nominated candidates in generally uncontested elections. They learned to venerate the American Constitution as a symbol, but they sometimes heard presidents and congressmen denounced as rascals and the government as a corrupt institution destined soon to fall. The "melting pot" for these newcomers was described in 1852 by Apostle Erastus Snow: "put all these parties through the furnace and run out a party of Saints for the Kingdom of God."[4] Helen Papanikolas notes that while there was some resistance to acculturation, "the logic of submerging national origins, languages, and customs to give strength to the new Church, reverence for English as the language in which the Book of Mormon had been translated, and the wholehearted acceptance of Utah's Zion as the immigrants' permanent home kept resistance low."[5]

In a paper on the demography of the Utah church, Dean L. May observes that the immigrants who comprised a large part of the adult population of many pioneer settlements had as role models the "Deseret Mormons" who had converted them and led them to their new world.[6] The consequences are still discernible. Trace elements of Old World culture like Sanpete's Scandinavian stories have foreign accents but 100 percent Mormon Utah content.

Erastus Snow's furnace might have produced Saints of a different mettle if the Mormon country had not been so dry. Mark P. Leone has emphasized what others had earlier noted—that pioneer irrigation required an uncommon degree of cooperation and obedience to leadership, both reinforced by church sanctions. Building and rebuilding dams, cleaning ditches, and adjudicating water claims were acts of devotion to God. As Leone puts it: "Success happened by making economic and political decisions, which were often difficult and trying, calling them religious necessity, and defining the resultant material success as religious experience."[7]

If one sees in the Nauvoo period evidence that Joseph Smith had lost some of his enthusiasm for innovative economic schemes, then Mormonism's migration to Utah was critical for the survival of communitarian economics. "It was inevitable," according to Leone, "that the problem of learning how to farm a desert was handled through rituals."[8] Not everyone will be convinced by the interpretive superstructure which Leone builds on his evidence, but who will deny that the cooperative and authoritarian aspects of Mormonism were reinforced in meeting the Utah challenge?

Utah, of course, has always had non-Mormon minorities. In the territorial period their status was to a considerable extent a function of how they chose to relate to the majority. The Lamanite factor in LDS ideology had some impact upon the Indian story. The Native Americans who begged or bargained were accommodated by a policy that it was "better to feed them than to fight them." Those who chose to fight were met, as Howard A. Christy has persuasively argued, with a strategy of defense and conciliation.[9] In the end the outcome for the Indians was not radically different from what came to pass in other parts of the American West.

Catholics and Jews, themselves subject to discrimination in nineteenth-century America, got along more or less amiably with the Mormons. Simon Bamberger would not later have become the second Jewish governor of an American state if Utah had not been comparatively free from anti-Semitism. On the other hand, Protestants and politicians who were more or less identified with the anti-Mormon crusade found minds and doors closed to them. The first women's club in Provo was formed by Gentile women as a response to social ostracism.[10]

Papanikolas and other students of Utah's ethnic minorities have shown that even the people who settled in towns and jobs outside the Mormon mainstream were involved in the symbiosis. Mormon mores shaped their perceptions of Americanism and local biases kept them at arm's length. The first who came to the mines and railroads prompted some Mormons to say: "If God had dipped them in once more, they'd have come out black."[11] The Joe Hills who came later with labor radicalism in their baggage found that the "right to work" concept had become a corollary of Mormonism. Still, the sons of the Swensons married the daughters of the Deniches and cultural accommodation was in time achieved.

The symbiosis presented different aspects in period 2, the interval from statehood to World War II. Anxiety to escape the old reputation and concern to develop the new Utah led the church to move toward the American mainstream. Millenarian supranationalism gave way to circumspect, conservative, patriotic politics and institutional programs that emphasized gospel impact on individual lives. But it is impossible to understand what happened to Prohibition, progressivism, social services, or Saltair without remembering that Utah was the state of the Mormons.

Between 1890 and 1930, according to Thomas G. Alexander, the church accepted, for the first time, the necessity of finding a way for God's Kingdom "to coexist with Caesar's."[12] The process affected politics and economics in many ways, but the net effect was far from that total separation of church and state that Congress insisted on in the 1890s. Several factors made it more difficult to determine the direction and scope of church influence than before, whether one was a Latter-day Saint looking for signs to follow or an anti-Mormon seeking evidence that nothing had really changed.

One new factor was the transformation of the mechanism of church leadership. Gone was the charismatic, intensely personal leadership of Joseph Smith and Brigham Young, which sufficed for a movement still relatively uninhibited by structures, norms, and precedents. Still in the future was the bureaucratic church, managed by experts and vesting the aura of leadership in the office of "the Prophet" rather than the individual holding that position. Alexander characterizes the interval between as the period of "collegiality." Policies were worked out in councils in which presidents such as Joseph F. Smith and Heber J. Grant were seen by many of their colleagues as merely *primus inter pares.* The concept of "harmony" did not yet preclude the public advocacy of minority opinions.[13]

Illustrations of maverick tendencies are not hard to find, from Moses Thatcher's defiance of the political manifesto of 1896 to John W. Taylor and Matthias F. Cowley's resistance to the second antipolygamy manifesto after 1904. The apostle and editor Charles W. Penrose felt free to oppose compulsory smallpox vaccination in the *Church News* in spite of President Smith's favorable view of the health measure. (A voluntary state program resulted.) Apostle Heber J. Grant clashed openly with Smith on approaches to Prohibition, and Apostle and Senator Reed Smoot later disagreed publicly with Grant over the League of Nations. Alexander notes that in the latter case doctrine as well as politics was involved; Mormon foes of the league tended to see it as futile because of the calamities that their premillennialism saw as imminent, while Saints who saw the achievement of the millennium as partly a human enterprise thought of the league as a useful tool.[14] This ambivalence about coming events has affected Mormon concepts of civic responsibility to the present day.

A second factor complicating the Mormon-Utah relationship in period 2 was the decision that Mormons should identify with the American political party system and the implicit corollary that the church would use the process to protect its interests. Apostle Joseph F. Smith put it pragmatically in an 1891 letter: "We have nothing to look for—nothing to hope for from the Dem's for the next two years. The Repubs. are in power, and *can* help and have helped us. And if we had more Repubs. among us, they would help us still more."[15]

Given this stratagem and the fact that in the early twentieth century the Mormon component in the Utah population dropped below two-thirds for the one interval in history, it is not surprising that the only Gentile U.S. senators and representatives and two of the state's three non-Mormon governors were elected then. Thomas Kearns was the last active anti-Mormon to represent Utah in Congress, however. His successor in 1905, Senator and later Supreme Court justice George Sutherland, was the unique non-Mormon in the first class at Brigham Young Academy; his interpretation of the Constitution has by now achieved semicanonical status among politically conservative Latter-day Saints.

In any event, implementation of the pragmatic policy contributed to the tacit understanding that Utah should have one Mormon and one non-Mormon senator in the years before the Seventeenth Amendment was adopted. It contributed also to the growth of Reed Smoot's Republican machine and then to its derailing by disputes about Prohibition. The same pragmatism made church leaders quite willing to work with Gentile officeholders such as Governors Bamberger and George Dern. (J. Bracken Lee, Utah's most successful non-Mormon politician, expressed the opinion that some LDS leaders preferred working with officials who did not have to worry about appearing to be church puppets. Dennis L. Lythgoe presents evidence that Governor Lee enjoyed a "special relationship" with some church officials until he had the temerity to veto Sunday-closing legislation in 1953.)[16]

It seems clear that Joseph F. Smith's editorial endorsement of William Howard Taft in 1912 had something to do with Utah's being one of only two states to approve a second term for the biggest man who ever occupied the White House. The decisive rejection of President Grant's endorsement of Alfred Landon in 1936, on the other hand, demonstrates that church influence was ineffective when it asked the Saints to go against what they perceived to be their secular interests. Since the same generation of Utahns and their predominantly Mormon legislators also rejected church counsel when they voted to repeal Prohibition, it is arguable that the political *power* of the hierarchy reached its lowest ebb during the Great Depression.

Alexander and others have shown that in the first statehood decades church concern for the family influenced legislative action affecting public health, limiting child labor, and protecting women in the labor market. It also produced a temporarily successful campaign against "moonlight dancing" at Saltair and a short-lived legislative ban on selling cigarettes in Utah. Under the influence of Amy Brown Lyman and Arthur Beeley, the Social Advisory Committee introduced progressive social service concepts into LDS auxiliary programs and generated momentum for the establishment of the Utah State Welfare Commission.[17]

Mormonism's accommodation to American capitalism was another aspect of period 2 that radically affected the Utah connection. Ronald W. Walker's vivid account of Heber J. Grant's going hat in hand from one New York banker to another to avert church bankruptcy in 1893 helps one to understand the subsequent thrust of Mormon policy.[18] As it worked its way out of debt, the church abandoned the effort to shape Utah's economy along the lines of consecration and stewardship. The revitalized tithing program was put on a cash basis, taking bishops' storehouses and tithing labor out of the market picture. Church-owned enterprises ranged from sugar factories to insurance companies and a hotel with a bar. At least as significant was a new posture toward Gentile enterprise; the copper magnate Daniel Jackling, like Bamberger and Dern, was a business friend of the Mormon businessmen who were also church leaders.

This building of bridges helped to dethrone the American party in Salt Lake

City politics and to convert the *Salt Lake Tribune* from what it was to what it has become. It also linked the secular policies of the church to the vicissitudes of regional economic colonialism and national business cycles, eventually giving rise to a new approach to gospel economics—the Church Welfare Plan. It is possible that if Utah had been less agrarian, less dependent, and less severely wracked by the Great Depression, the plan would have been different in emphasis, scope, or timing. Certainly the plan is being reassessed by both leadership and laity as the focus of church programming moves from the Utah heartland.

An important fringe benefit of the welfare plan for Utah and Mormonism was the favorable effect it had on the popular image of both. According to Jan Shipps's analysis, media attitudes toward Mormons moved from negative to "slightly positive" for the first time with the publicity generated by the plan. (The graph trended upward to "extremely positive" in the early 1970s and then dipped a little with the controversy over the ERA.)[19]

The spectacular growth of Mormonism during the post–World War II generation has changed but has not ended the symbiotic relationship. Still Utah-based, with leaders shaped by the pioneer tradition, the church has reflected these conditioning factors in its approach to issues as disparate as the racial revolution and the cold war. Its impact on social policy has extended from minibottles to Westminster College, from women's rights to the revitalization of downtown Salt Lake City. Its influence on the quality of life can be measured in the pedestrian traffic on Sunday mornings and in the vital statistics— birth and death rates—that put the state in a class by itself. Roots and retirement plans have produced a new kind of geriatric gathering, and as legions of missionaries have presented the gospel message in the accents of American Fork and Ephraim, Saints and sinners around the world have continued to think of Utah as Mormon country.

The political interaction between church and state in period 3 has been at two levels. At the grass roots the fact that the Mormon component of the population has grown past 70 percent means almost inevitably that most of the candidates for public office have been members of the church. In a study of two elections for the legislature, J. Keith Melville expresses the opinion that "the necessity of being a Mormon is probably overrated" but then concludes: "It appears that non-Mormons, women, and ethnic minority candidates may have no more, or possibly even less, chance of being elected today than when Utah first became a state."[20] The public perceptions supporting this conclusion are the same that lead most Mormon candidates to feature church affiliation in their campaign literature. The same perceptions have made statewide office a virtual Mormon monopoly for the last two decades and have produced majorities in excess of 80 percent in the state legislature. Stake presidents, former stake presidents, and former bishops make good candidates and often effective legislators; they "know the territory."

It would be a mistake, however, to identify every political position taken by a Mormon legislator as "the church position." Knowledgeable people in both political parties make these points persuasively:

1. To the extent that the church has an institutional political orientation, it is a nonpartisan conservatism that stands some distance to the left of the John Birch faction of the Republican party. It is more moderate than ten or fifteen years ago, when President Hugh B. Brown used to jest about being the "token Democrat" in the hierarchy. Though most of the leaders are nominally Republican, they are at least as pragmatic as Joseph F. Smith about working with officeholders of both political parties.

2. Church intervention in governmental affairs is selective and infrequent, largely confined to areas of social policy, and as likely to curb or temper legislation as to initiate it. Laws to protect battered wives and to fund bilingual education, for example, have benefited from church support. The impetus for the tax limitation amendment did *not* come from the church.

3. The Special Affairs Committee follows the political scene and may make recommendations to the First Presidency. The committee is the channel through which political communication usually takes place. Legislators concerned about whether there is a "church position" on a pending matter are likely to consult with a committee member or with an executive secretary.

4. On issues that the church leadership defines as moral—such as liquor control, pari-mutuel betting, pornography, and the ERA—the official LDS position is effectively communicated to legislators, and it is almost always decisive.

5. When the institutional church enters the open political arena, as with the "liquor by the drink" referendum in 1967 and the ERA ratification, each congregation is a potential political action committee and the disciplined response is—depending on one's point of view—awesome or fearful.

6. Given its numerical base and authoritarian structure, it is not surprising that the church is often able to secure desired governmental actions—such as the right of eminent domain for Brigham Young University—and almost always able to block unwanted measures. Objections to this power come mostly from two groups—Mormons who object in particular instances and non-Mormons who object in general.[21]

The trapper Miles Goodyear was the first white Gentile who faced the prospect of living in Mormon Utah. He left. For two generations Utah's anti-Mormons tried to get the federal government to change the situation, but in the end what they changed was not the substance of power but the form of its exercise. Alfred Cumming is reported to have said at the close of the Utah War in 1858 that he was now governor of Utah Territory, "but Brigham Young is still governor of the people."[22]

Now, as in the past, non-Mormons have three options—to retreat, to resist, or to relax. The University of Utah—widely perceived among Mormons as a hotbed of resistance—has at least one persuasive spokesman for relaxation. In a delightful essay that circulates in mimeographed form, Noel de Nevers discusses how to cope with a society in which Mormonism is pervasive, active Latter-day Saints are too busy with church work to be social resources for Gentiles, children of the Gentiles are sometimes subject to social pressure at school, and Gentiles "are occasionally the object of the vigorous Mormon proselyting effort." Of de Nevers's several constructive suggestions, which include taking advantage of the cultural and educational opportunities that abound, this is the fourth: "Conscientiously cultivate the attitude of a worldly Mormon-watcher. Anywhere else in the world when there's nothing to talk about one talks about the weather; in Utah . . . one talks about the Mormons. Mormon history, folklore, customs, and practices are extremely interesting and entertaining."[23]

An area of obvious church impact is Salt Lake City itself. According to Neal A. Maxwell, two interrelated considerations have led to an expanding institutional role in metropolitan affairs: the quality of life of the people and the vitality of the capital city of Mormonism. Impressions of these concerns are everywhere. The Salt Palace, Symphony Hall, and the Capitol Theatre would hardly have materialized without church support. When Obert Tanner took the chairmanship of the Ford Foundation challenge campaign on behalf of the Utah Symphony, it was with the understanding that President David O. McKay would give public support. He did. Wendell Ashton's efforts with the orchestra were of both substantive and symbolic value. Other prominent Mormons and church instrumentalities have contributed to the opera and ballet.

That the church has a lot of money worries a lot of people, especially noncontributors. That some of that money has gone into rebuilding downtown Salt Lake City is clear to anyone who remembers where the city was trending a quarter century ago and who knows the functions of agencies like Bonneville Development Corporation, Deseret Management Corporation, and Zion's Securities Corporation. It may be anticipated that the combination of civic concern, image consciousness, business foresight, and seed money that has wrought such changes in the immediate environs of 47 East South Temple will continue to influence metropolitan development.

When federal pressure and financial necessity long ago led the church to abandon the idea of a parochial school system, the consequence was—and is today—a unique educational environment. It is hardly debatable that Mormonism is primarily responsible for the level of support for schools and the large and still increasing school-age population in Utah. (A projection of high school graduates in 1995 showed that the United States as a whole would be down 19 percent while Utah would be up 58 percent.[24])

Frederick Buchanan and Raymond Briscoe have documented the non-Mormon perception that Mormons dominate the public schools and that Mormon values are taught therein.[25] The commonest reported complaint—that the required junior high school course in Utah history is full of the Mormons—is as nonrational as a complaint that Irish history is full of Catholics. But other interrelationships are vulnerable to challenge. Knowing that a primary reference in the seminary class on the Old Testament is the LDS Pearl of Great Price, should anyone have been surprised that an ACLU lawsuit in Logan resulted in denying high school credit for the course?

An illustration of constructive symbiosis in the educational sphere is the role of the church in the late 1970s campaign to meet a financial crisis at Westminster College. When one recalls that the college originated in the nineteenth-century Protestant effort to fight Mormonism with Christian education, the fact that Nathan Eldon Tanner chaired the fund-raising drive is remarkable.

As one who finds demographic history rather tedious but is grateful that others are getting into it, I will close this observation of the period 3 symbiosis with a reminder of what numbers can tell us about Utah and the Mormons.

1. Utah's birthrate has been higher than the United States' for a century. For the state's Latter-day Saints it is now approximately double the national figure.

2. The state death rate is less than two-thirds the national figure and that for Utah Mormons is lower still.

3. Utah has a significantly lower infant mortality rate, a death rate from cancer and heart disease, and a longer life expectancy rate than the United States'. According to University of Utah medical researchers these differentials stem almost entirely from the active Mormon component of the populations.[26]

4. Obesity is a serious health problem, despite Word of Wisdom counsel that is apparently taken less seriously than that to which the favorable medical statistics are commonly attributed.

5. The marriage rate is about 10 percent higher and the divorce rate is almost exactly the same as the U.S. rate.

6. About 70 percent of teenage pregnancies—both in Utah and in the United States—are out of wedlock, and 70 percent of Utah's teenage brides are pregnant at marriage.

7. The rate of induced abortions in Utah is just over one-fourth the U.S. figure, and the rate of illegitimate births is just over one-third.

8. Utah County, where the world's highest concentration of active Mormons is probably to be found on the Brigham Young University campus, has the highest birthrate of any county in America. It has a lower ratio of teenage mothers than the state as a whole. Births out of wedlock are at one-half the state rate and induced abortions are only one-fourth as common.[27]

If they do not exactly prove it, these statistics strongly suggest that Utah is as full as it is of vigorous oldsters, rambunctious youngsters, and hard-working in-betweensters because it is Mormon country.

As one looks back on the years since 1847, it seems clear that the most powerful symbiotic impact of Utah upon the Mormons has been the simple fact that it has been "home." For almost a century—the time span from Fort Sumter to Hiroshima—a majority of the Saints lived in Utah or the immediately contiguous Mormon communities. At its peak around the turn of the century the concentration exceeded 80 percent. The limited carrying capacity of Utah's dependent economy then contributed to the downplaying of the doctrine of gathering, but it did not change the geographic focus of the church. The net out-migration of population between 1900 and 1940 was mostly the surplus youth of Zion, leaving their homes but keeping their roots. They produced little outposts of Utah in California, New York, and Washington, D.C., but did not at first affect the way their kinfolks at home perceived the world beyond the mountains. At the outbreak of World War II there were more Mormons outside Utah than inside, but a generation later the members, leaders, and programs of the church still reflected the psychology of a "gathered" people—isolated and shaped by a historic experience in the valleys of the American West.

Dean May, whose demographic study has already been mentioned, points out that what he calls "Deseret Mormons" still command a numerical and cultural majority in the church, and he believes that their attitudes and values will continue to be imparted to converts around the world for a long time.[28] I believe that he underestimates the forces for change that are operating within Mormonism as it enters its fourth half-century.

From within the church come unmistakable signs that homogenizing converts into Deseret Mormons is not a policy objective. *Mormonism: A Faith for All Cultures*, the product of a 1976 conference at Brigham Young University, is one indication that total deculturizing is seen as neither feasible nor desirable.[29] In the sesquicentennial issue of *Ensign,* April 1980, Lavina Fielding Anderson reported in "The Church's Cross-Cultural Encounters" that increasing effort is being made to separate gospel universals from historical particulars.[30] With missionaries from Utah now comprising less than 25 percent of the total proselytizing force and with the number from outside the United States and Canada approaching 30 percent and rising, the prospects for cultural pluralism improve.

Even doctrinal emphases reflect the trend. "Sesquicentennially, we are a Church of multiple Zions," Neal A. Maxwell noted in the 5 January 1980 issue of *Church News.* There are "no more treks to be made—except one last trek by those assigned to build the temple and establish a central presence in Missouri." Then he projected future growth in terms that clearly illustrate that premillennial expectations are not dictating church planning.[31] Priesthood manuals no longer interpret adoption into the gospel kingdom in ethnic terms, and speculation about what happens to the blood of converts is now largely confined to such people as assign theological significance to the administration of capital punishment by firing squad. The ban on priesthood for blacks possibly lasted as long as it did because traditional Mormons were valley dwellers. The splendid pictorial representation of Mormons from many lands in the April 1980 issue of *Ensign* demonstrated a quick and remarkably painless adjustment to the concept of a polychrome church.

In a 1979 essay in *Sunstone,* Sterling M. McMurrin took favorable note of the trend. After reviewing some of the historic fetters that the church still wears, he said: "Mormonism has been the most successful American religious movement. Now that it is promising to become a world religion, it will encounter new and perhaps greater problems, but it has remarkable vitality and inventiveness and is capable of even radical adaptation and change. The Church has a powerful commitment and loyalty from its members and a strong tradition and habit of facing things head on." McMurrin added a judgment with which I fully concur: "I have nothing but admiration and appreciation for the breakthrough toward universality which the Church has made in the last three decades."[32]

Factors outside the church are likely to accelerate this universalizing trend and further weaken the symbiotic relationship with Utah. Two tendencies are illustrative:

1. That *close* families will continue to be a gospel ideal is much more certain than that *large* families will continue to be so. Dean May argues persuasively that "contemporary Mormon fertility [is] an artifact of their having been a

frontier people and then being prevented by a provincial self-consciousness from dropping frontier values and habits, especially in those areas where doctrine and belief reinforce the frontier condition."[33] On the fragmentary evidence available, converts from other cultures have not—at least so far—assimilated this artifact. The birthrate among European, Japanese, and Korean Mormons is probably one-third less than for their Utah coreligionists. Even in prolific Latin America it is apparently lower than the Utah Mormon rate.[34]

2. That Deseret Mormons will continue to monopolize the church hierarchy is also unlikely, given the demographic realities. Projections of a membership of 11 million by the year 2000 may reflect an optimism born of faith, but the implications of the figures charted in the April 1980 issue of *Ensign* are profound.[35] Thirty-six hundred stakes and 29,000 wards and branches will require and produce legions of leaders from the new converts. Administrative oversight, which has already found expression in area presidencies manned by general authorities, will almost certainly require the bureaucratization of the office of regional representative, and this new level of full-time leaders will likely have a relationship to Salt Lake City somewhat analogous to that between the non-Italian cardinals of Catholicism and Rome. Must one look beyond the next half-century to see the day when Mormonism sustains a president with a name like Karol Wojtila?

As one reflects on the future of the Utah-Mormon symbiosis, it can confidently be predicted that the church—hierarchy and rank-and-file—will continue to influence the development of the state. It is more difficult to foresee how Utah will affect Mormonism as Salt Lake City becomes the center of a truly international church, led by men and women who as children never learned to sing "Land of the pioneers, Utah, we love thee."[36]

Notes

1. Joel H. Johnson, words, and Ebenezer Beesley, music, "High on the Mountain Top," *Hymns of the Church of Jesus Christ of Latter-day Saints* (Salt Lake City: Church of Jesus Christ of Latter-day Saints, 1985), no. 5. At least eleven selections in this Mormon hymnal identify Mormonism with its geographic center.

2. *Webster's Seventh New Collegiate Dictionary* (Springfield, Mass.: G. and C. Merriam Company, 1967), 892.

3. Inferential support for this suggestion may be found in the current circumstances of such nineteenth-century radical groups as the Campbellites and Millerites, as well as the followers of Joseph Smith who did not follow Brigham Young into the West.

4. Erastus Snow quoted in Frederick S. Buchanan and Raymond G. Briscoe, "Public Schools as a Vehicle of Social Accommodation in Utah," in *Social Accommodation*

in Utah, ed. Clark Knowlton, American West Center Occasional Papers (Salt Lake City: University of Utah, 1945), 99.

5. Helen Papanikolas, "Ethnicity in Mormondom: A Comparison of Immigrant and Mormon Cultures," in *"Soul Butter and Hog Wash,"* ed. Thomas G. Alexander, Charles Redd Monographs in Western History, no. 8 (Provo: Brigham Young University Press, 1978), 102.

6. Dean L. May, "A Demographic Portrait of the Mormons: 1830–1980," in *After 150 Years: The Latter-day Saints in Sesquicentennial Perspective,* ed. Thomas G. Alexander and Jessie L. Embry (Provo: Charles Redd Center for Western Studies, 1983), 64–65.

7. Mark P. Leone, *Roots of Modern Mormonism* (Cambridge, Mass.: Harvard University Press, 1979), 85.

8. Ibid., 87.

9. Howard A. Christy, "The Walker War: Defense and Conciliation as Strategy," *Utah Historical Quarterly* 47 (Fall 1979): 395–420.

10. I was so advised when I first talked to Provo's Nineteenth Century Club in the 1950s.

11. Papanikolas, "Ethnicity in Mormondom," 92.

12. Thomas G. Alexander, "'To Maintain Harmony': Adjusting to External and Internal Stress, 1890–1930," *Dialogue* 15 (Winter 1982): 54. See also James B. Allen and Glen M. Leonard, *The Story of the Latter-day Saints* (Salt Lake City: Deseret Book, 1976), 486–88, 512–13.

13. Alexander, "'To Maintain Harmony,'" 44–58.

14. Ibid., 52–53.

15. Joseph F. Smith quoted in J. Keith Melville, "Political Conflict and Accommodation in Utah since Statehood," in *"Soul-Butter and Hog Wash,"* 140.

16. Dennis L. Lythgoe, *Let 'Em Holler: A Political Biography of J. Bracken Lee* (Salt Lake City: Utah State Historical Society, 1982), 91–107.

17. Thomas G. Alexander, "Between Revivalism and the Social Gospel: The Latter-day Saint Social Advisory Committee, 1916–1922," *Brigham Young University Studies* 23 (Winter 1983): 19–39.

18. Ronald W. Walker, "Crisis in Zion: Heber J. Grant and the Panic of 1893," *Sunstone* 5 (Jan.–Feb. 1980): 26–34.

19. Jan Shipps, "Media Attitudes toward Mormons," graph, *Church News,* 5 Jan. 1980, 22.

20. Melville, "Political Conflict and Accommodation," 137, 152.

21. Conversations with many people contributed to these impressions; they include Leonard J. Arrington, Edwin B. Firmage, Willard H. Gardner, Brigham D. Madsen, Neal A. Maxwell, and S. Lyman Tyler.

22. Alfred Cumming quoted in T. B. H. Stenhouse, *The Rocky Mountain Saints* (New York: D. Appleton, 1873), 445n.

23. Noel de Nevers, "Suggestions for Outsiders Moving to Utah," ms., n.d., 1–5.

24. "Changing Numbers in High School Graduating Classes," *Chronicle of Higher Education*, 7 Jan. 1980, 8.

25. This information was given to me by S. Lyman Tyler.

26. Joseph L. Lyon and Steven Nelson, "Mormon Health," *Dialogue* 12 (Fall 1979): 84–96.

27. Statistical observations about contemporary Utah and the LDS Church are derived from information provided in 1980 by the Historical Department, Church of Jesus Christ of Latter-day Saints, Salt Lake City; Utah State Department of Health, Bureau of Health Statistics, *Vital Statistics Summary: Utah, 1978–1979*, 1–4; "Family Planners under Attack in Utah," *Macomb (Ill.) Daily Journal*, 20 Feb. 1980, 28; *1979 Utah Statistical Abstract* (Salt Lake City: Bureau of Economic and Business Research, University of Utah, 1979); and *1983 Utah Statistical Abstract* (Salt Lake City: Bureau of Economic and Business Research, University of Utah, 1983).

28. May, "Demographic Portrait," 65–66.

29. F. LaMond Tullis, ed., *Mormonism: A Faith for All Cultures* (Provo: Brigham Young University Press, 1978).

30. Lavina Fielding Anderson, "The Church's Cross-Cultural Encounters," *Ensign* 10 (Apr. 1980): 44–49.

31. Neal A. Maxwell, "The Church Now Can Be Universal with Priesthood Revelation of 1978," *Church News*, 5 Jan. 1980, 20.

32. Sterling M. McMurrin, "Problems in Universalizing Mormonism," *Sunstone* 4 (Dec. 1979): 17.

33. May, "Demographic Portrait," 56.

34. The birthrates were derived from partial 1979 LDS membership statistics by geographic area.

35. "A Statistical Profile: What Numbers Tell Us about Ourselves," *Ensign* 10 (Apr. 1980): 15.

36. Evan Stephens, "Land of the Mountains High," *Hymns* (Salt Lake City: Church of Jesus Christ of Latter-day Saints, 1948), no. 140. The 1985 LDS hymnal does not include this hymn or O. P. Huish, "Utah, the Star of the West," no. 71 in the 1948 hymnal.

9

Noble Savages

Michael Hicks

The desire to build Zion has energized Mormonism for a century and a half. Brigham Young was perhaps the most erudite in explaining what building Zion entailed, observing that it would be erected on the principle of gathering "truth from any source, wherever we can obtain it." Young taught that the citizens of Zion would acquire truth partly through revelation and prayer and partly through the "arts and sciences," the latter being a catchall phrase that for him included any social grace or refinement, from tempering copper to painting murals, from farming to music theory. And Young believed that some of those refinements might well lie outside of Western culture, that indeed the "arts and sciences in the so-called heathen nations in many respects excel the attainments of the Christian nations."[1]

In its isolated valleys and villages nineteenth-century Mormonism thrived under Young's leadership, evolving into what one sociologist has labeled a "near nation."[2] Their success in building a self-contained community spurred the Mormons to want to build a kingdom of colonies throughout the earth. As they did so, Mormonism's emphasis seemed to shift: rather than importing Zion, or building it for themselves alone, the Saints hoped to export the culture their faith had built. Brigham Young's calls for the Saints to educate themselves and gather to the Great Basin were quietly transformed into a Mormon desire to educate others in Zion's budding glories. This devout imperialism has been neither consistent nor free from ambivalence. One sees its fluctuations in the church's evolving responses to the indigenous musics of Native Americans, Polynesians, and West Africans.

Early American settlers regarded Indians through the eyes of both primitivism and puritanism. Native Americans were at once innocent citizens of the state of nature, devoid of civilization's discontents, and rude, or even diabolical heathens (except when they were consenting to the white man's occupation of the New World). Somewhere between these conflicting views lay the

Book of Mormon's teachings, which described "native" Americans as descendants of Hebrew migrants, once noble but now degraded by apostasy from the true faith. For Mormons, Native Americans represented a sacred kindred to be reclaimed, literal descendants of Israel in need of civilizing.[3] And when they were converted, the Indians would not only be saved, they would become "white and delightsome," divinely readied to possess the continent.[4]

Indian dancing, like most any sort of dancing, troubled early denominational missionaries to the Indians. The music that accompanied it grieved them as well. Missionaries almost universally found its monophony, static melodies, and hypnotic drumming ugly, if not terrifying. They sought to replace it with revival hymns or, in the case of Catholic missionaries, with plainsong. None seems to have made any attempt to adapt Christian worship to the indigenous musics of the natives. This was chiefly because they considered these musics, as one scholar has expressed it, a "persistent phase of heathenism" and indeed not music at all.[5] A revivalist expressed this well when he recalled in 1846 the sound of converted Indians singing the hymns he had taught them, their strains "being made more strikingly sweet by the yelling and whooping of the wild Indians by whom they were surrounded. What a contrast!" he continued, "the woods made vocal on the one hand by Christian music, and startled on the other by the wild yells of the uncivilized! And yet both proceeding from the same race."[6]

Early Mormons expressed their unique empathy for Indians (or "Lamanites," as they called them) by frequently singing the American popular songs "The Indian Hunter" and "The Indian's Lament" as well as their own hymn "The Red Man." This last song spoke clearly of the Mormons' hope that Native Americans would "quit their savage customs," including, one presumes, their ritual music and dancing. Joseph Smith's responses to Native American music are unknown, but he did invite Sac, Fox, and other tribes around Nauvoo to dance for the Saints.[7] One LDS missionary to the Pottawatomies in this period referred to their singing without criticism and even spoke admiringly of their dancing, saying that he had never seen anyone keep such good time.[8] After the death of Joseph Smith, Apostle Parley Pratt issued a proclamation on the Saints' duty to educate the Lamanites in all aspects of culture, including music and "all other things which are calculated in their nature to refine, purify, exalt and glorify them, as the sons and daughters of the royal house of Israel."[9]

During the Mormon trek to the Great Basin, a sympathetic non-Mormon observed the local tribes' curiosity toward the Saints' music on the plains and wrote that the natives had a natural "inability to comprehend the wonderful performances."[10] In at least one instance, the Saints were equally awestruck by an Indian's music. In Nebraska the Indian William McCarey entered the pioneer camp claiming to be a Lamanite prophet and playing a variety of music on crude instruments. Wilford Woodruff, who had heard sophisticated European music during his British missions, wrote in his journal that McCarey was "the most perfect natural musician I ever saw on a flute fife, sauce pan, ratler, whistle, &c. . . . [He] made the most music on several instruments of any man I ever herd."[11]

In Utah, Brigham Young remained firm that the white man's ways were superior to the Indians' and indeed that the Lamanites were looking to the Saints for both spiritual and cultural redemption. But little appears to have been said of Indian music in early Utah because the Saints were too concerned about the squalor in which the natives lived to pay much attention to the question of ceremonial culture. Not only did Mormons find Indians disease-ridden and poverty-stricken but they also discerned serious vices among them: lying, stealing, gambling, idolatry, drunkenness, and bloodthirst, all vices they believed had been propagated among the Lamanites by white settlers. Young manifested the Saints' peculiar mixture of pity and cultural imperialism in this 1854 admonition: "Preach the Gospel to the natives in our midst, teach them the way to live, instruct them in the arts of civilization, and treat them as you would like to be treated, if you through the transgression of your fathers had fallen into the same state of ignorance, degradation, and misery."[12] While Young used the phrase "arts of civilization" primarily to denote technology and hygiene, he also may have intended the refinements of Western music and dancing, as Parley Pratt had written of earlier.

If native dancing was loathsome to some Mormons in this period, it was partly because they associated such dancing with aggression against whites.[13] Certain dances also struck some Saints as unchaste. In at least one instance, Young's solution to such dancing among converted Indians was severe. When the bandleader Dimick Huntington, one of his chief ambassadors to the Indians, complained that some Mormon Indians were dancing what he called a "whore dance," Young is said to have advised him to whip them until they stopped.[14]

Mormon missionaries, like their denominational counterparts, probably agreed with the assessment of one elder, who found in Indian music "the most horrible noises I ever heard."[15] But the longer they lived among Native Americans, and the closer they drew to them, the more fascinated some Mormon missionaries became with Indian musical customs. One Mormon elder, Thomas D. Brown, described at length a Ute Indian "sing," a ritual during which the medicine man seemed to be healing a patient through his singing and gestures.

Brown acknowledged the apparent medicinal powers of the strange singing, writing that it may have helped to induce faith in the sick person or even to cause a "magnetic stream" to pass through the sick person's body with "a mesmeric influence that heals."[16] Perhaps because such approbation of Indian ritual, however cautious, was rare, Mormon successes among Native Americans were slight and short-lived.

Christian missionary societies had tried proselytizing in Polynesia since the eighteenth century. Some denominational missionaries considered the Pacific natives' music and dance, like that of American Indians, symptomatic of their debasement. One wrote that Polynesian drum and flute music was "loud and boisterous, and deficient in every quality that could render it agreeable to one accustomed to harmony."[17] Nevertheless, Christian missionaries generally felt more comfortable with Polynesian music than with Indian music, for it at least had its own form of counterpoint and harmony. Indeed, its nasal melodies and thin harmonies seem to have borne a resemblance to "old way" singing and shape-note psalmody. And the dancing was often relaxed and graceful; some of it was performed sitting down.

During the late 1840s and early 1850s, Mormon leaders began to view Pacific islanders as brothers to the Lamanites. In 1843 Joseph Smith directed Mormon missionaries to begin proselytizing in the Pacific (although it is not clear that he personally considered Polynesians to be Lamanites). These missionaries used the natives' love of music to attract them to Mormon preaching. But like Christians generally, Mormon missionaries felt compelled to reset some of the islanders' songs with Western tunes.[18] As Mormon missions to the islands expanded in the 1850s under the belief that the natives were really Israelites, little was said of the islanders' musical habits, for the Saints regarded their poverty and squalor as the most pressing needs. But the Polynesians' love of religious dancing was something the elders hoped to suppress.

In the fall of 1851, the Mormon elder James Brown visited a Putuhara feast and reported that amid the natives' seminaked dancing "the confusion was so great and turbulent that it looked more like an actual battle of savages than a dance." He went on to say that, in comparison to Native Americans' dancing, "this excelled in confused savage deeds anything I ever beheld before." After making converts in this region, Brown and his colleagues held a massive Mormon conference among the Polynesians. During this conference the natives went into a religious "frenzy" of dancing in the new meetinghouse. Brown rebuked the crowd and ordered dancing be banned from the house, to which the congregation assented.[19]

By the late nineteenth century, the Saints' intense interest in redeeming

Native Americans led to rumors of a conspiracy between Mormons and Indians. Some observers believed that the Saints and the Indians might band together, war against the States, and set up a Mormon-Lamanite dynasty over the American continent. These rumors reached a summit during the intertribal Ghost Dance movement of the 1880s. This movement took its name from the ecstatic dances of the Indians who proclaimed the advent of a new messiah who would liberate them from white oppression. The Ghost Dance garment worn by these Native Americans was said to be impervious to the white settlers' bullets and some Americans linked its magic properties to the similar properties Mormons claimed their temple garments possessed. While evidence is weak that Mormons directly encouraged the Ghost Dance movement, some church leaders spoke approvingly of the Ghost Dance religion and said that they hoped that the Lamanites indeed would rise in power against their oppressors.[20] But their endorsement notwithstanding, many of these same Mormon leaders feared that the church might be linked to the "Messiah craze" and its wild dances. Their fear helped ward them away from Lamanite proselytizing at the close of the century. The church would return actively to reclaiming Native Americans only after it had secured for itself a good reputation in the States—nearly halfway into the twentieth century.

As late as 1876 the standard view of Polynesian music and dance had been expressed in vivid tones in the *Juvenile Instructor:* "The acme of pleasurable excitement to them is a war dance, and if you could see, as I have, their violent exertions, demoniac grimaces and disgusting contortions while going through its performance, you would say it was one of the most laborious and horrid sights you ever beheld."[21] But as the church quietly closed most of its Indian missions and expanded its missionary efforts in the Pacific new attitudes emerged. Several of the most prominent Mormon elders sent to the islands during the 1890s were skilled musicians, and they seem to have found the natives' music enchanting, especially when the natives sang and danced for "joy at seeing the Lord's servants increased in number on the islands."[22] One missionary wrote of the natives' festive responsorial singing that the leader sang "in high treble, while the rest chimed in with a sort of chanting, which was neither alto, tenor nor bass, but withal harmonious and pleasing to the ear."[23] Another missionary described the Samoans' rowing songs similarly, adding that "the most accurate time is kept while they sing, and I must say at times sounds sweet and breaks the manotiny of the Ocean."[24] Only occasionally did a missionary write with deprecation about the native musical groups. One diary entry from Tahiti reads: "What they call the native band . . . consists of about a dozen women sitting around in a circle, one will start in a song and then all the others will join in the chorus, and what a noise they make. I don't see much of a band about it as there was only an accordian and a piccolo. They had a jug of rum which they passed to each other."[25]

Mormon missionaries to Samoa fell under the spell of casual island life and frequently exchanged songs and dances with the natives. The missionaries spent much of their time listening to indigenous hymns and teaching the Samoans the "songs of Zion"—primarily Sunday school songs.[26] The islanders craved Western music, even though they associated it with the colonial domination they had endured for decades. And while few natives spoke English, many had learned to read musical notation from Western sojourners.[27] The Hawaiian and Samoan Saints happily formed brass bands under the direction of Adelbert Beesley (a son of Ebenezer), modeling them upon the royal military bands they could hear at the docks and in the village squares. Several missionaries used handheld instruments such as harmonicas, ocarinas, and guitars to accompany their sabbath hymn singing. Elder Beesley ingeniously constructed a xylophone from timber salvaged from a shipwreck in Apia Bay. His frequent concertizing and hymn-accompanying on this instrument "surprised and pleased" the natives and drew many to hear the elder's message.[28] Once converted, the Saints were summoned to church on sabbath mornings by the drums that on weekdays were played in the native dances.[29]

Mormon missionaries thought most Polynesian dances hauntingly graceful. In turn, the Polynesians hoped to learn dances from their visitors. In one instance, a group of Samoans tried to execute a waltz for the missionaries, one of whom reported "they did not seem to understand much about it." The missionaries showed them how it should be done. But when the natives asked for lessons in the round dance, the elders demurred, no doubt conscience-stricken about corrupting the natives.[30]

To reject native cultures would have proven disastrous for the missionaries in Polynesia. Not only did the missionaries face a constant threat of expulsion, particularly as civil power struggles erupted in the islands from time to time, but they also faced the constant harassment of well-entrenched Protestant groups. Coming to the Pacific in a position of relative weakness, the Mormon missionaries found that only making friends before making converts would ensure their continuance in the islands.

The Polynesian Saints also benefited from a new Mormon attitude toward the "gathering." Throughout most of the nineteenth century Mormon leaders had urged converts to leave their homelands and build up the culture in the Rocky Mountains. But after 1890 the leaders began to soften and even reverse their position. They now taught that Mormonism would not immediately triumph over the world, but would need to establish itself in all nations. This attitude encouraged the systematizing of LDS missionary work and Mormon schooling around the world in the early twentieth century. Although missionary forces dwindled during World War I, the 1920s saw the construction of Mormon schools in the Pacific and several apostolic tours of the missions. David O. McKay led one tour to the Pacific and found several Mormon brass bands there, especially at Sauniatu, the official gathering place of Samoan Saints. The genial apostle joined the natives in their dances and songs, so much so that they named a new band for him.[31] The missionary Matthew Cowley likewise endeared himself to the Maoris of New Zealand, singing and dancing in native style and encouraging the Mormon converts to amuse and recreate themselves freely.[32] Whatever "savagery" still seemed to cling to Polynesian music and dance, most Mormons seem to have regarded them as the quaint expressions of a friendly, open-hearted people.

By this time, pseudo-Indian tunes had become the source of much self-consciously "American" composition. Songs such as Thurlow Lieurance's "Waters of Minnetonka"—a Tabernacle Choir favorite—blanketed the United States. One church musician, William Hanson, emulated the Lieurance style by adapting Ute Indian songs and dances for his two operas, *The Sun Dance* and *The Bear Dance*.[33] But Mormon leaders remained virtually silent about Native American culture. One finds in the official writings and discourses of the early twentieth century only oblique remarks about the "degradation" of Lamanite culture and, conversely, about its merits in comparison with white Gentile culture.[34] However, a number of Mormon hymns perpetuated common ideas of Indian savagery. Hymn texts referred to the "barbarian" of the plains ("by darkness debased") seeking "rude delights," and promised that, while the Indians' "arts of peace shall flourish ne'er to die," their "war-whoop . . . shall cease."[35]

In the meantime, writers and speakers throughout the church and the nation began to attack the new popular music styles, linking them with the primitive and barbaric in world culture. One Mormon author in 1926 pointedly complained that jazz had indeed been "copied from savage tribes."[36] As if to confirm the link between savagery and the new music, the *Salt Lake Tribune* carried an article in 1931 bearing the title "Indians Drop Tom-Tom for Modern Jazz." Implying a natural progression from the one style of music to the other, the article also mused on how powerfully white culture was eroding Indian life.

As denominational missionaries and sectarian schools began to fill the reservations, the Indian homelands became outposts of American mass culture.

At the same time, native customs faded. Generations of Native Americans grew up with the belief that their own traditions were indeed debased and many of them gladly turned to the prevailing American customs of music and dance. Moreover, the radio brought popular music to the reservations. As it did, countless traditional Indian songs passed into oblivion.

Insofar as Mormon missionaries of the 1940s and 1950s tolerated what Native American traditions remained, they seem to have done so for one principal reason: "We feel this is a good way to get next to them & win at least some of them over."[37] But the Mormon elders clearly were impressed by how well the Lamanites were able to adapt to the white man's music. As Indians gradually converted throughout the North- and Southwest, they placed their talents at the service of the faith. Intertribal reservation choirs formed to sing Mormon hymns. One church leader requested that a southern Utah intertribal choir be brought to Salt Lake City to sing in the church's general conference. This would show, he said, how cultivated Lamanite music could be, although he conceded that the choir was "not the best."[38] A mission leader praised a Uintah children's singing group by saying that "their singing was probably better than the singing of white children."[39] As for traditional Indian music, the mission leaders occasionally allowed and even encouraged it in church socials and entertainments, where it could be kept separate from tribal rituals. But many of the Native Americans had already drifted far from their traditional ways. On at least one occasion a local Boy Scout troop had to provide the reservation dancers with some "genuine Indian costumes."[40]

By the early 1950s the church began trying to educate Indians through reservation seminaries, an "Indian Placement Program" (wherein Indian youths were sent to live with white families during school months), and a quota system for Lamanites at Brigham Young University. As early as 1950 a group led by white former missionaries to the Indians organized itself as a tribe on the BYU campus, calling itself the Tribe of Many Feathers, complete with a chief and a tribal council. Among its aims was to "acquaint the student body of this University with some of the cultural contributions of the various Indian tribes."[41]

In Polynesia, wind bands continued to be organized in the 1950s, some of them at the behest of mission presidents. Tabernacle Choir broadcasts continued to be popular in the islands as well.[42] Between the bands and the choir, Polynesian Mormons developed a taste for the musical grandiosity that had filled Great Basin Mormondom in the late nineteenth century. According to one observer, by 1958 over half of the musicians in Samoa had joined the LDS Church and many of these had begun to create a hybrid church-music style, a

pseudo-oratorio tradition in which sacred words were set to band-tune medleys. The people called these medleys hymns, but they were really much more.
One listener described them as four times the length of a typical choral an-
them, "many Overtures merged in one . . . and it was one monotonous tem-
po and rhythm that blasted from the beginning to the end, with no consideration of dynamic whatsoever." The choirs and bands who performed these
"hymns" in church services sometimes even marched into the meetinghouses
in military fashion. For some years such exercises went on more or less unre-
stricted, with only an occasional critique from visiting church musicians.[43]

Meanwhile, plans were underway to create a church-sponsored cultural center in Hawaii that would preserve traditional native music and dancing. With
the Church College of Hawaii drawing students from throughout the Pacific,
local and general church leaders proposed building the center as a tourist attraction that could employ students to perform. Once it was established in 1963,
the Polynesian Cultural Center offered entertainment that had its roots in tribal
styles, yet was mingled with Mormon themes. There were, for example, the
Lakalaka on the Joseph Smith story, and dances in praise of the beauty of the
Mormon temple at Laie, recordings of the music of which appeared on a souvenir phonograph album produced by the center. During the 1960s through
the 1980s, the center drew huge crowds to hear traditional music mingled with
Mormon messages. The cultural center became the core of church public relations in the Pacific.[44] Severed from their old pagan origins, the energetic
music and dancing of Hawaiians, Samoans, Tongans, Fijians, Maoris, and
Tahitians provided a healthy, wholesome image for Mormonism. But for main-
land Lamanites the path to acceptance was not so clear.

As more and more American Indians enrolled at BYU in the late 1950s and
early 1960s, the Tribe of Many Feathers helped keep native dances and medicine-man "sings" alive among them. Some campus advisers to the Indians
counseled them to stop such practices because they violated the laws of the
gospel and, indeed, were demonic. These advisers believed that the students
were preserving Lamanite culture at the expense of their loyalty to Mormonism, that to perpetuate the singing and dancing was to perpetuate the legacy
of the race's ancient decline. The paradoxes of Mormon attitudes during this
period were great. At the same time that school advisers were decrying Native
American customs they were presenting visiting Indian leaders with souvenir
copies of the Polynesian Cultural Center phonograph album, a token of
church-sponsored "Lamanite" culture.

Many Indian students bristled at the suggestion that their music and dance
was satanic. George Lee, president of the Tribe of Many Feathers, insisted that

the traditional social dances, at least, were as graceful as any European dances, while the ritual singing of medicine men was a gift from God to the Lamanite branch of Israel. Indian ways, Lee said, were probably more harmonious with the gospel than European ways because "many of our traditions held close ties to Israelite thought and expression."[45] After a number of private debates on the subject, the university's director of Indian affairs, Paul Felt, asked Apostle Spencer Kimball to speak to the Lamanite students on the subject "Dangers in Placing Unique Emphasis in the Perpetuation of the Indian Culture."[46]

Kimball had sympathized with the American Indian peoples from his early childhood. His father, a former president of the Indian Territory Mission, often sang tribal chants and recounted adventures from the reservation to young Spencer.[47] Called from his home state of Arizona to be a Mormon apostle (1945), Kimball was immediately assigned to Lamanite work. He treated Native Americans kindly and paternally. Throughout his life he spoke of the white Saints as the "nursing fathers and mothers" of the Indians, whom church members "must carry on their shoulders till they can walk straight and tall."[48]

Kimball rarely discussed Indian music directly, although he was known to perform it from time to time in family gatherings. He wrote in 1963 that he hoped that music leaders in the church who were "possessed of much patience" would give free music lessons to the Lamanites until they could lead and accompany church music properly. He occasionally measured spiritual success among the Lamanites in musical terms and once remarked that it pleased him more to hear an Indian child playing a hymn on the piano with one finger than to hear Alexander Schreiner playing the Tabernacle organ. With proper schooling, Kimball hoped, American Indians would be able to compete with whites in the world of the arts.

Felt's invitation to speak at BYU allowed Kimball at last to speak freely and in detail on Lamanite culture. In two addresses given on 5 January 1965, Kimball told the Indians at BYU that their culture was "distorted" and that it was wrong for them to try to maintain a cultural identity apart from that of historic Mormonism. To the surprise of many, he even attacked the fostering of traditional Polynesian culture: "Down in New Zealand I was the recipient of many, many courtesies while I was there. They sang and they danced. They sang their songs, and they rolled their eyes, and they stuck out their tongues. . . . And so we applaud them, you know; and they think that's wonderful to encourage the continuation of that culture. That *isn't* the Lord's culture. What they are doing . . . is perpetuating the paganism that they brought from the other islands." He urged that the islanders stop "digging up the cultures of yesterday that were paganistic. . . . Anything that is associated with paganism or sectarianism or devilism or anything, we eliminate." While he said that "any beautiful ideas not in conflict may be incorporated into the Program [of the church]," he insisted that all questionable practices be discarded by Latter-day Saints. Specifically, he said, Polynesians should give up their war chants, and Indians should stop having medicine-man sings.[49]

Over the next two years Paul Felt and other faculty members and students expanded on Kimball's remarks in memos to the university president and in editorials for the school's Lamanite newspaper, *Indian Crossroads*. Felt explained that, although he agreed that Polynesian dances were inherently as bad as Indian dances, they were more easily separated from their religious origins. (They thus could be performed acceptably by the school's folk-dancing groups.) But Indian dances, he argued, were too deeply rooted in paganism to continue on the campus. Some Indian students accepted the banning of the dances with little regret. Others fought the new policy vigorously. One of them even left the church and began to tour the reservations to urge Indians to reject Mormonism. When campus protests became too great, and the university's executive committee spoke its disapproval of Felt's tactics, Felt compromised, deciding that the students must be left to govern themselves in such matters.[50] But the precedent had been set for more cross-cultural regulation to come.

Denominational churches had wrestled for decades with the problems of internationalism.[51] Whatever debates lingered over how much primitive culture could be tolerated in Christian societies, there remained the separate question of what could be played *in church*. The Church Music Committee briefly discussed this question in 1967, admitting that it was becoming "increasingly acute."[52] The members were well aware that the Catholic church had formally settled the matter during the Vatican councils of 1962–65, with the statement that missionaries should look toward "adapting worship to [the people's] native genius . . . [and] promoting the traditional music of these peoples, both in schools and in sacred services, as far as may be practicable."[53] One member of the committee who endorsed the Catholic position was Alexander Schreiner, who observed that the Old Testament peoples had danced and clapped before the Lord with drums, timbrels, and cymbals: "In view of [this] I would recommend a very liberal and comprehensive allowance for approval of what is used in connection with worship. What I would be inclined to condemn would be for one person to dictate his own preferences in musical matters to others who have other feelings."[54]

As such topics began to be discussed in the mid-1960s, Native American Mormons persuaded the McKay administration to remove the remaining offensive treatments of their people in the hymnal.[55] But within a few years, as the church began proselytizing in West Africa, deeply held views of culture, race, and religion resurfaced when black converts tried to drum and dance in Mormon meetings.

For much of the twentieth century the bush region of West Africa was filled with Anglican and Assemblies of God congregations, who tended to mingle freely their tribal and Western customs of worship. Pentecostalism found especially easy access into the hearts of West African blacks, in part because it allowed for intense physical worship. West African blacks generally considered a blend of New Testament grace theology with Old Testament worship styles the most congenial form of Christianity.

In the 1940s some Nigerians began writing Salt Lake City for Mormon tracts, hoping to found branches of the church in West Africa. Mormonism appealed to these inquirers for at least three reasons. First, it professed to be a restoration of Christ's original church and therefore might be more compatible with their non-Western ways. Second, it emphasized the importance of family and community, compelling virtues in tribal culture. Third, it was widely known once to have sanctioned polygamy, which was commonly practiced among the African blacks. While the church did send tracts to the African inquirers, it declined to send missionaries, chiefly because the church had not yet admitted blacks of African descent into the priesthood.[56]

At the close of the 1950s, David O. McKay considered the matter of opening a formal mission to Nigeria. When a group of missionaries arrived in Africa in 1961 to study the prospects, they found thousands of pseudo-Mormons, who had established their own congregations. These Africans conducted their own services in high Pentecostal style. The services lasted about five hours apiece and consisted mainly of public confession of sins, loud responsorial singing, and dancing to tribal drums. One of the missionaries showed his goodwill by dancing with the natives. But both he and his companion apparently were troubled by such worship and one wrote in his journal that the music was "very apentecostal," adding that "they have a lot to learn" about worship.[57]

The hoped-for mission to Nigeria fell through in 1963. Upon learning that the church proscribed blacks from its priesthood, the Nigerian government refused to issue the missionaries visas. Meanwhile, a charismatic Ghanaian had begun to found unofficial Mormon branches in his homeland after he saw a vision of "angels with trumpets singing songs of praise unto God," a vision in which he was told by Jesus to "take up my work."[58] Church leaders assigned various men to correspond with Africans interested in Mormonism, but abruptly stopped this in 1965. In the early 1970s several Mormons were assigned to inspect conditions among the pseudo-LDS groups in Nigeria and Ghana. One of them described the music in 1975: "Music is by the congregation, almost always in native languages, and introduced first by a song leader or minister, then echoed by the congregation. Hand drums are used to accompany the songs, and a song leader sometimes uses a megaphone. Members stand and add handclaps. Tunes are simple, very repetitive, and easy for young and old to sing. Part-singing consists usually of duets, with an occasional bass line added. It is a happy, lively service, similar in style, but more restrained as far as dancing goes, to the apostolic and pentecostal worship services we have visited."[59] The indigenous pseudo-Mormon groups who worshipped in this way received no support from the church until after the church lifted its priesthood ban on blacks in 1978.

As soon as the priesthood was proffered to faithful Mormon blacks, the church sent missionaries to West Africa. These missionaries were married couples who could serve more or less as spiritual fathers and mothers to the natives. The missionaries quickly baptized hundreds of blacks and organized Salt Lake–approved congregations. Of the natives' boisterous worship style, one of the missionary couples reported that "as you become familiar with it, it was really not that objectionable, because they had nothing else." But this couple, like some others, were disturbed that the Africans "jazzed up" their hymns and sang indigenous sacred songs that, to the Americans, resembled rock music.[60] The missionaries were perplexed by the native worship, but at least one conceded that "they have such good harmony and unity and a sense of singing together that I stopped worrying about the accompaniment. . . . They have a very sophisticated sense of musical composition and keeping together. . . . They're much better than we are."[61]

The mission president responded perhaps the most negatively to the music and dancing in Mormon services, flatly declaring that it was satanic and that it had descended from the culture of Cain himself. He ordered all drumming and dancing in church stopped and the native percussion instruments replaced by cassette tapes of organ music. The missionaries were to teach their converts that God was pleased by quiet reverence especially during the sacrament. But many natives feared that God would think them timid for keeping their peace in worship. Hence, the congregations complied outwardly, but with evident sadness. "It was like asking them to give up their right arm to give up those drums," one missionary explained. "Their countenances would fall. . . . Some even cried. They asked, 'But why? Why do we have to give up our drums?'"[62] Some members, unable to cope with the loss, held services in their old style each Sunday when the missionaries left their areas.

Spencer Kimball, now president of the church, was partially incapacitated in his old age and could not directly deal with the questions raised by the musical worship in West Africa. He did inquire if the blacks were "singing the songs of Zion," to which the mission president replied, "yes, and with gusto"— a reply which was said to have pleased the infirm leader. Feeling assured that Kimball would have encouraged his attempts to "civilize" the Africans, the mission president worked to eradicate indigenous styles from church.[63] In time, hundreds left the church over the restrictions placed on their worship. As the church shrank in the bush areas, it flourished in port cities, urban centers where European- and American-trained blacks could lead the services.

The church's early experiences in West Africa suggest that further conflicts over style will come. So far, Mormon leaders have avoided public discussions of such issues. Some scholars in the church have challenged the continuing cultural imperialism, while others have resigned themselves to it, feeling that the Westernization of alien cultures is inevitable.[64] In the absence of official debate, a quiet synthesis continues. West African blacks have added subtle syncopations into their performance of Sunday school songs. Polynesian choirs have rearranged by ear the standard hymns into their traditional seven- and eight-part harmonies. On some reservations, and among Lamanite performing groups at BYU, Native Americans have synthesized their traditional music and gospel hymnody, bringing sacred chants and ritual percussion instruments into the service of Mormon song.

Perhaps more important than questions of style are the questions that cross-cultural encounters pose about the place of music in human life. Many societies regard music as a magic that invokes the divine in virtually every act that accompanies it. Indeed, in some societies music is so much a part of other activities—marriage, medicine, cooking—that their languages lack a separate word for "music." To them, the meaning of tonal art lies precisely in its use, its power to complete some human action, without which, in turn, the "music" could not fully exist. But for most of the Christian world music has entered churches only through a tradition that tolerates it for its power to indoctrinate and unify. And Christianity remains an anomaly among world religions: a faith with no sacred dance.

Mormons now aspire to penetrate further into the Third World and communist Asia. As they encounter some of the world's most ancient musical traditions, they will grapple with a longstanding dilemma: whether to pry their converts away from those traditions or to preserve the traditions from cultural erosion. And as Zion implants itself in nations whose identities are inseparable from their music, it will find fresh dilemmas about its own music, its own identity.

Notes

1. For the Young quotations see *Journal of Discourses* (Liverpool: F. D. and S. W. Richards, 1854–86; reprint, Salt Lake City: N.p., 1967), 14:197, 8:171. For a further study of this see Michael Hicks, "Notes on Brigham Young's Aesthetics," *Dialogue* 16 (Winter 1983): 124–30.

2. Thomas O'Dea, "Mormonism and the Avoidance of Sectarian Stagnation: A Study of Church, Sect, and Incipient Nationality," *American Journal of Sociology* 60 (Nov. 1954): 285–93.

3. For a general study of American attitudes toward Native Americans, see Robert F. Berkhofer Jr., *The White Man's Indian: Images of the American Indian from Columbus to the Present* (New York: Knopf, 1978), 71–104. On Mormon attitudes, see Leonard J. Arrington, *Brigham Young: American Moses* (New York: Knopf, 1985), 210–22, and that work's bibliography on the subject, 467–68; Leonard J. Arrington and Davis Bitton, *The Mormon Experience* (New York: Knopf, 1983), 145–60; and David J. Whittaker, "Mormons and Native Americans: A Historical and Bibliographical Introduction," *Dialogue* 18 (Winter 1985): 33–64. For a history of Christian missions to Indians, as well as to Polynesians and West Africans, see J. Herbert Kane, *A Global View of Christian Missions from Pentecost to the Present* (Grand Rapids: Baker Book House, 1971).

4. See especially Grant Underwood, "Book of Mormon Usage in Early LDS Theology," *Dialogue* 17 (Autumn 1984): 42–45.

5. Frances Densmore, *The American Indians and Their Music* (New York: Woman's Press, 1926), 59.

6. Thomas L. M'Kenney, *Memoirs, Official and Personal, with Sketches of Travels among the Northern and Southern Indians* (New York: Paine and Burgess, 1846), 83–84, quoted in Charles Hamm, *Music in the New World* (New York: W. W. Norton, 1983), 20. See also Robert M. Stevenson, *Protestant Church Music in America: A Short Survey of Men and Movements from 1564 to the Present* (New York: W. W. Norton, 1966), 3–11; and Leonard Ellinwood, "Religious Music in America," in *Religious Perspectives in American Culture,* ed. James Ward Smith and A. Leland Jamison (Princeton: Princeton University Press, 1961), 289–95.

7. See Joseph Smith, *History of the Church of Jesus Christ of Latter-day Saints,* ed. B. H. Roberts (Salt Lake City: Deseret News, 1932–51), 4:401, 6:402; and Joseph Smith Diary, 22 and 23 May 1844, Library-Archives, Historical Department, Church of Jesus Christ of Latter-day Saints, Salt Lake City.

8. Jonathan Dunham in Smith, *History of the Church,* 5:545–46.

9. *Proclamation of the Twelve Apostles of the Church of Jesus Christ of Latter-day Saints* (Liverpool: Wilford Woodruff, 1845). For more on the evolution of official attitudes toward Indian music, see P. Jane Hafen, "'Great Spirit, Listen': The American Indian in Mormon Music," *Dialogue* 18 (Winter 1985): 133–42.

10. Thomas L. Kane, *The Mormons: A Discourse Delivered before the Historical Society of Pennsylvania: March 26, 1850* (Philadelphia: King and Baird, 1850), 31.

11. Scott G. Kenney, ed., *Wilford Woodruff Journal: 1883–1898* (Midvale, Utah: Signature Books, 1983), 3:139. For more on McCarey, see Newell G. Bringhurst, *Saints, Slaves, and Blacks: The Changing Place of Black People within Mormonism* (Westport, Conn.: Greenwood Press, 1981), 84–85.

12. Brigham Young quoted in James R. Clark, ed., *Messages of the First Presidency of the Church of Jesus Christ of Latter-day Saints, 1833–1964* (Salt Lake City: Bookcraft, 1965–), 2:143.

13. See Daniel W. Jones, *Forty Years among the Indians* (Salt Lake City: Juvenile Instructor Office, 1890), 397; and James S. Brown, *Giant of the Lord: Life of a Pioneer* (Salt Lake City: Bookcraft, 1960), 340–42.

14. Brigham Young Manuscript History, 8 Sept. 1856, 629, LDS Library-Archives, quoted in Arrington, *Brigham Young*, 220–21.

15. Elijah Nicholas Wilson, *Among the Shoshones* (Salt Lake City: Bookcraft, 1969), 26–27.

16. Juanita Brooks, ed., *Journal of the Southern Indian Mission: Diary of Thomas D. Brown* (Logan: Utah State University Press, 1972), 23.

17. *History of the Establishment and Progress of the Christian Religion in the Islands of the South Sea* (Boston: Tappan and Dennet, 1841), 53.

18. Brown, *Giant of the Lord,* 506. Despite such attempts to civilize the Polynesian natives, some Christians attributed Mormon successes in the islands to the natives' attraction to anything degraded. See Rufus Anderson, *History of the Mission of the American Board of Commissioners for Foreign Missions to the Sandwich Islands,* 3d ed. (Boston: Congregational Publishing Board, 1872), 257–58. Much of the general information concerning the Mormon Pacific islands missions may be found in R. Lanier Britsch, *Unto the Islands of the Sea: A History of the Latter-day Saints in the Pacific* (Salt Lake City: Deseret Book, 1986). On Mormon views of the genealogy of Polynesian races, see Russell T. Clement, "Polynesian Origins: More Word on the Mormon Perspective," *Dialogue* 13 (Winter 1980): 88–98.

19. Brown, *Giant of the Lord,* 232, 237–38.

20. The best treatment so far is Lawrence G. Coates, "The Mormons and the Ghost Dance," *Dialogue* 18 (Winter 1985): 89–111.

21. Hugh Knough, "Fun," *Juvenile Instructor* 11 (1 Nov. 1876): 250.

22. "Ejay" [Edward J.] Wood, "My Samoan Experience," *Juvenile Instructor* 28 (15 May 1893): 328.

23. Henry L. Bassett, *Adventures in Samoa* (Los Angeles: Wetzel, 1940), 57.

24. Joseph Quinney Diary, 3 Dec. 1895, holograph in Harold B. Lee Library, Brigham Young University.

25. Eugene M. Cannon, Journal, 21 Mar. 1893, holograph in Harold B. Lee Library.

26. On this period in Samoa, see Britsch, *Unto the Islands of the Sea,* 358–74. On sing-

ing exchanges, see Cannon Journal, 1893. This source, 17 December 1893, also describes one of the Tahitian Protestants' "himene" meetings, a hymn-singing session after sabbath services.

27. William Alfred Moody, *Years in the Sheaf* (Salt Lake City: Granite, 1959), 153.

28. On these musical developments, see Bassett, *Adventures in Samoa,* 52, 55–56, 75; and Joseph Dean Diary, 11 June 1887, 12 Oct. 1888, microfilm of holograph in LDS Library-Archives. The Dean diary entry for 27 October 1888 contains an apparently typical program of a missionary feast. It includes three Sunday school songs sung in English, one song each in Hawaiian and Samoan, three xylophone solos by Beesley, and a duet for violin and guitar by Beesley and Dean. In another episode, a Samoan chief called the elders to come and play harmonicas for him (Quinney Diary, 8 Nov. 1895).

29. Moody, *Years in the Sheaf,* 62.

30. See Quinney Diary, 9 and 21 Oct. 1895; and Moody, *Years in the Sheaf,* 69, 77.

31. See Britsch, *Unto the Islands of the Sea,* 389–90; and Clare Middlemiss, comp., *Cherished Experiences from the Writings of President David O. McKay* (Salt Lake City: Deseret Book, 1970), 66–67, 75. On the expansion of missions during this period, see Thomas G. Alexander, *Mormonism in Transition: A History of the Latter-day Saints, 1890–1930* (Urbana: University of Illinois Press, 1986), 212–38.

32. See Henry A. Smith, *Matthew Cowley: Man of Faith* (Salt Lake City: Bookcraft, 1954), 45, 58, 262.

33. See "Preserving the Music and Legends of the Utes for Future Generations," *Deseret News,* 7 Mar. 1925; and William F. Hanson, *Sun Dance Land* (Salt Lake City: J. Grant Stevenson, 1967).

34. See Joseph Fielding Smith, *The Progress of Man* (Salt Lake City: Deseret News, 1936), 263–65.

35. See Hafen, "'Great Spirit, Listen,'" 134–38.

36. Fred L. W. Bennett, "Why Not Abolish Jazz?" *Improvement Era* 29 (Jan. 1926): 273.

37. Evan Gardner to Golden Buchanan, 19 Oct. 1950, Indian Relations Committee Correspondence, microfilm in LDS Library-Archives.

38. S. Dilworth Young to Spencer W. Kimball, undated report of July 1951 visit to Kanab Stake, Indian Relations Committee Correspondence.

39. Milton R. Hunter to Indian Relations Committee, 15 Aug. 1951, Indian Relations Committee Correspondence.

40. Unsigned report on meeting of Piute Indians of Cedar Stake, 22 Nov. 1950, Indian Relations Committee Correspondence.

41. "The Constitution of the Tribe of Many Feathers," dittoed copy of typescript, and Melvin D. Thom to Will Rogers Jr., 31 Jan. 1961, both in Institute of American Indian Studies Papers, Harold B. Lee Library. For a survey of Indian education in the church, see Ernest L. Wilkinson, ed., *Brigham Young University: The First Hundred Years* (Provo: Brigham Young University Press, 1975), 3:503–35. For a different perspective and critique of Mormon Indian programs, see Robert Gottlieb and Peter Wiley, *America's Saints: The Rise of Mormon Power* (New York: Putnam's, 1984), 157–77.

42. See Britsch, *Unto the Islands of the Sea*, 67, 313.

43. On this "hymn" practice, see Kipeni Suapaia to Harry Dean, 14 Mar. and 23 May 1958, "History of the Revised Edition of the Samoan Hymn Book," manuscript letter collection in Harry Dean Papers, Harold B. Lee Library.

44. For the history of the center, see Britsch, *Unto the Islands of the Sea*, 186–89.

45. George P. Lee, *Silent Courage* (Salt Lake City: Bookcraft, 1987), 273–74; Lacee Harris, "To Be Native American—and Mormon," *Dialogue* 18 (Winter 1985): 148–49. Indeed, some Indians were troubled by the close dancing of males and females at school dances, which violated certain tribal customs. See Helen Sekaquaptewa, *Me and Mine: The Life Story of Helen Sekaquaptewa*, as told to Louise Udall (Tucson: University of Arizona Press, 1969), 117–18.

46. Paul E. Felt to Spencer W. Kimball, 30 Dec. 1964, Institute of American Indian Studies Papers.

47. Edward L. Kimball and Andrew E. Kimball Jr., *Spencer W. Kimball* (Salt Lake City: Bookcraft, 1977), 236–48.

48. For the quotations and information in this and the following paragraph see Spencer Kimball, "The Lamanite," address given at Regional Representatives Seminar, 1 Apr. 1977, reprinted in Jeffrey L. Simons and John R. Maestas, comp., *The Lamanite*, rev. ed. (Provo: Privately distributed, 1981), copy in Harold B. Lee Library; Indian Committee to James Mathews, 15 Oct. 1963, and Spencer Kimball to James Mathews, 19 May 1963, both reprinted in James D. Mathews, "A Study of the Cultural and Religious Behavior of the Navaho Indians Which Caused Animosity, Resistance, or Indifference to the Religious Teachings of the Latter-day Saints," master's thesis, Brigham Young University, 1968; Edward L. Kimball to Michael Hicks, 29 Sept. 1987; and Bryan Espinscheide, telephone interview with Michael Hicks, 19 Aug. 1987.

49. The typescripts of these two addresses are in the Institute of American Indian Studies Papers. Compare the edited version of these remarks in Edward L. Kimball, ed., *The Teachings of Spencer W. Kimball* (Salt Lake City: Bookcraft, 1982), 394.

50. See Paul Felt to Hal Taylor, 26 Apr. 1965, Paul Felt to Ernest Wilkinson, 21 Apr. 1966, Ernest Wilkinson to Paul Felt, 13 May 1966, and Paul Felt to Ernest Wilkinson, 10 Aug. 1966, all in Institute of American Indian Studies Papers; see also the editorials in *Indian Crossroads*, 28 Feb. 1966 and 18 Apr. 1966. For the varied views of some students, see Mathews, "A Study of the Cultural and Religious Behavior," 47–48.

51. See, for example, the discussions of the legitimizing of the American Indian Sun Dance by Christians in the 1940s in Åke Hultkranz, *Belief and Worship in Native North America*, ed. Christopher Vecsey (Syracuse: Syracuse University Press, 1981), 229; of Christian adaptations of Krishna worship in W. K. Lowther Clarke, ed., *Liturgy and Worship: A Companion to the Prayer Books of the Anglican Communion* (London: Society for Promoting Christian Knowledge, 1932), 822; and of syncretism in East Java in Philip van Akkeren, *Sri and Christ: A Study of the Indigenous Church in East Java* (London: Longworth, 1970), 82–87. See also the various chapters in William Smalley, ed., *Readings in Missionary Anthropology* (Tarrytown, N.Y.: Practical Anthropology, 1967).

52. Church Music Committee Minutes, 25 Oct. 1967, LDS Library-Archives.

53. Walter M. Abbott, ed., *The Documents of Vatican II* (New York: Herder and Herder, 1966), 172–73.

54. Alexander Schreiner to Joe L. Spears, reprinted in Alexander Schreiner, Oral History, typescript, 25, LDS Library-Archives.

55. See Joe E. Weight to David O. McKay, 5 Jan. 1965, and Leroy J. Robertson to Alva R. Parry, 16 Apr. 1965, both in Church Music Committee Subject and Correspondence Files, LDS Library-Archives.

56. Many sources have treated this subject. Among the best is Lester Bush, "Mormonism's Negro Doctrine: An Historical Overview," *Dialogue* 8, no. 1 (1973): 11–68.

57. See Lamar S. Williams Diary, quoted in Davis Bitton, *Guide to Mormon Diaries and Autobiographies* (Provo: Brigham Young University Press, 1977), 385; and Marvin Reese Jones Diary, 22 Oct. 1961, microfilm of holograph, LDS Library-Archives. On the general history of the mission and experiences of Mormon missionaries to West Africa, I have relied upon Emanuel Abu Kissi, address to conference on African religions, 22 Oct. 1986, Brigham Young University, notes in my possession; Bryan Espinscheide, conversation with the author, 22 Oct. 1986, and telephone interview with Michael Hicks, 19 Aug. 1987; E. Q. Cannon to Michael Hicks, 2 Oct. 1987; Murray Boren, telephone interview with Michael Hicks, 19 Aug. 1987; Murray Boren, "Worship through Music Nigerian Style," *Sunstone* 10 (May 1985): 64–65; M. Neff Smart, "The Challenge of Africa," *Dialogue* 12 (Summer 1979): 54–57; Janet Brigham, "Nigeria and Ghana: A Miracle Precedes the Messengers," *Ensign* 10 (Feb. 1980): 73–76; and Rendell N. Maybey and Gordon T. Allred, *Brother to Brother: The Story of the Latter-day Saint Missionaries Who Took the Gospel to Black Africa* (Salt Lake City: Bookcraft, 1984), esp. 70–72 (on native worship meetings).

58. See J. W. B. Johnson to First Presidency, 9 Sept. 1978, holographs and photocopies of holographs, Edwin Q. Cannon Papers, LDS Library-Archives.

59. "Summary [of] Mormon Church of Nigeria," a report apparently written by Lorry Rytting, photocopy of typescript, Cannon Papers.

60. LaMar S. Williams and Nyal B. Williams, Oral History, interview with Gordon Irving, May 1981, typescript, 101–3, LDS Library-Archives.

61. Edwin Q. Cannon Jr. and Janath R. Cannon, Oral History, interview with Gordon Irving, 1980, 21, LDS Library-Archives.

62. Williams and Williams, Oral History, 117.

63. Espinscheide conversation. Generally, local cultural expressions among West African blacks appear to have been tolerated in social settings apart from worship services.

64. See Soren F. Cox in Spencer J. Palmer, *The Expanding Church* (Salt Lake City: Deseret Book, 1978), 159–60; and, conversely, Michael Moody, interview with Michael Hicks, 27 May 1987, transcript in my possession. The most erudite exploration of Mormonism and world cultures is F. LaMond Tullis, ed., *Mormonism: A Faith for All*

Cultures (Provo: Brigham Young University Press, 1978). See also Don Hicken, "The Church in Asia," *Dialogue* 3 (Spring 1968): 134–42; Wesley Craig Jr., "The Church in Latin America: Progress and Challenge," *Dialogue* 5 (Autumn 1970): 66–74; John L. Sorenson, "Mormon World View and American Culture," *Dialogue* 8, no. 2 (1973): 17–29; and *Dialogue* 13 (Spring 1980).

10

Mormonism, Millenarianism, and Modernity

Grant Underwood

In popular discourse, millennialism is often reduced to the simple belief that the Millennium (in the sense of a final, glorious conclusion to world history) is near. In reality, even the subset of Christian millennialism is neither simple nor singular. There are millennialism*s* and each presents a distinct and comprehensive way of looking at human history and ultimate salvation. These various types of millennialism "involve a great deal more than the time of Christ's return." The millennial kingdom expected by each is different "not only with respect to the time and manner in which it will be established but also in regard to its nature and the way Christ will exercise control over it."[1]

Originally millennialism was a predominantly Christian outgrowth of Jewish apocalypticism.[2] Reflecting a profound discontent with the status quo and seeing society and its power brokers as evil and antagonistic, apocalypticism promised that the first would be last and the last first. It was the dream of "the great reversal." Such a faith engenders hope. It is consoling to know that no matter how bleak the contemporary scene may appear, God and good will ultimately prevail. What is more, apocalypticism inevitably portrays the transformation as imminent. Apocalypticists not only live in the latter days, but they also live in the last days. Though the present is viewed with a profound pessimism, a period of "tribulation" or "messianic woes," as it has been variously called in Judeo-Christian tradition, it is felt to be a necessary prerequisite to the end. Thus, if the present generation is viewed as "ripe" in iniquity, and especially if the righteous are being persecuted, the faithful are thereby provided with additional assurance that all is proceeding according to plan, that everything is in place for "the great reversal" soon to be effected by the divine deliverer.

The novelty of Christian millennialism was its expectation of a future "golden age" on earth *before* the final, apocalyptic transformation at the end of time. As various versions of the millennial dream developed over the centuries, some retained the vivid and dramatic spirit of their eschatological progenitor, lashing out against contemporary society and promising imminent vindication for the beleaguered faithful. Others drifted toward a more irenic view of the world around them and thought they saw in human progress evidence of either an imminent millennial kingdom or one that was already underway. Reinforced by their experience of sustained and severe persecution, early Mormons developed an eschatology that reflected the former outlook. The early Saints are best characterized as apocalyptic millenarians. Their literature, whether private diaries and letters or public sermons and tracts, is permeated with this perspective. In it one finds a stinging indictment of the contemporary religious world, along with the warning of an imminent visitation in judgment.

A key component in most millenarian eschatologies is dualism. Millenarian apocalypticists divide the world into opposing factions, with "the establishment" and its supporters as the enemy and themselves as the last remnant of righteousness. Added to this sociological dualism is a satisfying soteriological (salvation-related) dualism that ultimately damns the opposition and consigns them to perdition, while "the elect" live on triumphantly in a transformed world. As apocalyptic millenarians, the Mormons did not expect to convert the world, only to warn it. To modify a phrase from Leonard Sweet, the Saints have always believed that they were called to bring to pass the gathering of the elect, not the broad electorate, of humankind. As one early Mormon apostle wrote, "Many are flattering themselves with the expectation that all the world is going to be converted and brought into the ark of safety. Thus the great millennium, in their opinion, is to be established. Vain, delusive expectation! The savior said to his disciples that 'as it was in the days of Noah, so shall it be also in the days of the coming of the Son of Man.' Query. Were all the people converted in the days of Noah, or mostly destroyed?'" The answer was clear, and events "will soon show to this generation that the hour of God's judgment hath come."[3]

Apocalyptic millenarians like the Mormons were also distinguished from other millennialists by the literal hermeneutic with which they approached the interpretation of scripture. Contrary to popular notions of Christ reigning in the hearts of the regenerate, early Latter-day Saints looked forward to the day when the "King of Kings" would physically reign as supreme terrestrial monarch. "Not," remarked a church leader, "as some have said, a spiritual (which might be more properly called imaginary) reign; but literal, and personal, as much so as David's reign over Israel, or the reign of any king on earth."[4] The Lord of Hosts was also the Lamb of God, and the Saints anxiously contemplated the privilege of enjoying a thousand years in his visible presence. Mormons waxed eloquent in their descriptions of an earth renewed to its Edenic state, for this was the ultimate meaning of the "restoration of all things which God hath spoken by the mouth of all his holy prophets since the world began."[5] It would, they reasoned, "materially affect the brutal creation. The lion and the ox are to eat straw together; the bear and the cow to graze the plain in company, and their young ones to lay down in peace: there shall be nothing to hurt or destroy in all the Lord's holy mountain."[6]

Though early Latter-day Saints expected the "great and dreadful day of the Lord" in their own lifetimes, unlike other millenarians, they were not given to prophetic numerology or exact calendrical calculations as to the date of Christ's Advent. Still, as their very name testified, the Latter-day Saints did feel that the divine reestablishment of the church of Christ in their day lifted the curtain on the final act in human history. In the words of their beloved hymn, they believed they were witnessing the "dawning of a brighter day, majestic rises on the world."[7]

In the end, the brighter day majestically rising upon the world was to take longer than enthusiastic Latter-day Saints first expected. Indeed, it has yet to arrive in full splendor. Nonetheless, it is impossible to understand the dynamics of early Mormonism without acknowledging the pervasive way in which eschatology helped the Saints make sense of the world around them and their place in it. Since that time, one of the great themes in religious history has been the confrontation with modernity. Of interest to this exploration of the millenarian world of early Mormonism is how within the LDS community modernity has influenced, and been influenced by, millenarianism.

An important initial distinction is the difference between institutional and intellectual modernization. The former has been described as the "permeation of religious institutions by techniques and procedures developed in other sectors of [modern] society" that seem institutionally advantageous yet intellectually innocuous.[8] From statistical reports and time management to telecommunications and computerization, from the bureaucratic rationalism symbolized by its now insufficient twenty-six-story headquarters building to its public relations typified by Brigham Young University athletics and the Mormon Tabernacle Choir, Mormonism, as an institution, has taken on the coloration of modernity.[9]

When it comes to the world of thought, to beliefs and values, however, modernity has been met with a different mind-set. In important ways, this has been due to the mutually reinforcing persistence of primitivism and millenarianism. Both maintain a similar philosophy of history which, in spirit, is antimodern. The march of time is not upward; history is actually a long downward spiral of spiritual decay. It is the story of apostasy. Not surprisingly, severe judgments are proclaimed against a present considered to be the faint and fallen image of a distant golden age. Both millenarianism and primitivism see resolution only in restoration, by a dramatic return to pristine purity. Primitivism focuses on *what* is to be restored, while millenarianism emphasizes *when* and *how* the former glory will be recovered. The link between primordium and millennium is well illustrated in Mormonism.

The rise of modernism, however, has been antagonistic to such ideals. Two important consequences of this dramatic paradigm shift in Western consciousness are of particular relevance—the creation of secularism and the emergence of "scientific" history. "Modernization is in many ways a secularizing process," writes Peter Williams, "and generally results in what we might call the 'desacralization' of the world." Its impact on religion is that "the role of the supernatural as a direct, tangible force is downplayed considerably."[10] A second and related ramification is that a sense of profane time supplants the mythic realm of sacred time so elegantly portrayed by Mircea Eliade as central to millenarianism.[11] John Dwyer has noted that "the subjection of man to [nonmythical] history is the insight which, more than any other, characterizes the modern age."[12] Such subjection, however, is precisely what is absent in the "history-lessness" of primitivism and millenarianism. While the more celebrated clashes between modernism and traditionalism have dealt with conceptions of creation, compared to the social sciences, the challenge presented by the physical and life sciences has been "relatively mild."[13] Notions of doctrinal rather than biological evolution, and of cultural and ethical relativism, have been far more threatening to primitivist millenarians.[14]

Latter-day Saints have responded, and continue to respond, to these influences in much the same way that conservative religionists do generally—by rejecting them for a universe thoroughly grounded in absolutes and the supernatural. As much as any other factor, what makes this possible for Mormons today is their core conviction that they are led by a living prophet and living apostles. Admittedly, their modern Moses may be dressed in a three-piece suit, but he still provides a symbolic connection with the mythic world of the sacred past. Through a living prophet and continuing revelation, Mormonism is prepared to respond to change without succumbing to desacralization. The overarching issue from the LDS perspective is not whether the church is abandoning traditional ways for modern ideas, but whether God's hand is in it.

While current prophets may theoretically supersede their predecessors, ancient or modern, in reality they are restrained by a primitivist respect for an additional primordium—the corpus of modern prophetic pronouncement.

The speeches and writings of apostles and prophets throughout the history of the church provide a large body of material generally regarded as on par with Scripture. Where particular comments stray too far, their noncanonical status can be invoked, but by and large Latter-day Saints, leader and layperson alike, are as loath to contradict what an apostle in the 1800s declared as they are to challenge the writings of Paul.

Thus, the millenarianism of earlier years tends to be preserved by respect for previous prophetic declarations. During the 1980s, the LDS apostle and theologian Bruce R. McConkie published the longest work ever written by a Latter-day Saint on eschatological matters. What is striking is how little McConkie's millennial treatise differs from those written during Mormonism's first generation. The same supernatural biological and geological changes anticipated then are expected today, including the abolishment of infant mortality, the herbivorization of carnivores, the unification of continental landmasses, and the commingling of mortals and resurrected immortals. That such views seemed plausible in the early nineteenth century is perhaps not surprising. That they are still maintained today provides dramatic testimony of the degree to which LDS millenarianism in particular and Mormonism in general have resisted the encroachments of modernity.[15]

The pendulum, however, should not be swung too far in the opposite direction. A study of leaders' discourses at the church's general conferences over the past 150 years reveals that millenarian rhetoric "diminished drastically after 1920." Thus, "even though an apocalyptic scenario of the last days is still a central Mormon doctrine, it is no longer enunciated by modern conference speakers with anything like the emphatic fervor of nineteenth-century leaders."[16] Though Latter-day Saints still talk about the end times, for many Mormons these doctrines have a detached and textbookish quality. The social ramifications of their eschatology are rarely if ever discussed today, and soteriological dualism is disparaged. The term "wicked," for instance, no longer refers to all unbelievers. Today, it is applied only to the morally corrupt, and the good and honorable of all religions are expected to be alive during the millennium. As people make their peace with the world, the apocalyptic dream of the "great reversal" diminishes. In short, the more abrasive features of millenarianism which served LDS needs in an earlier period have been quietly, perhaps unwittingly, laid aside in recent years.

Still, though Mormonism has acquired the institutional accouterments of modernization, its persistent supernaturalism keeps it intellectually insulated from the acids of modernity. It has gone far toward modernizing without becoming secularized. Key has been its conviction of continuing revelation.

Primitivism produced living prophets and, in turn, has been preserved by them. So has millenarianism. But the door is always open to change. Shrouded in the "sacred canopy" of modern revelation, Mormons are free to pick and choose their way into modernity. Inspired guidance from living prophets gives them the confidence to feel that they can truly live "in" the modern world and yet be "of" it only to a degree not harmful to their sacred enterprise. Whichever path they are counseled to pursue, Latter-day Saints continue to expect that it will lead them to an actual thousand years of paradisiacal peace and prosperity which they call the millennium.

Notes

1. Robert G. Clouse, ed., *The Meaning of the Millennium: Four Views* (Downers Grove, Ill.: Intervarsity Press, 1977), 7.

2. Information in this and subsequent paragraphs is drawn from Klaus Koch, "What Is Apocalyptic: An Attempt at a Preliminary Definition," in *Visionaries and Their Apocalypses,* ed. Paul D. Hanson (Philadelphia: Fortress, 1983), 16–36; John J. Collins, ed., *Apocalypse: The Morphology of a Genre,* vol. 14 of Semeia (Missoula, Mont.: Scholars Press, 1979); John J. Collins, "Apocalyptic Literature," in *Early Judaism and Its Modern Interpreters,* ed. R. Kraft and G. W. Nickelsburg (Chico, Calif.: Scholars Press, 1986), 345–70; Paul D. Hanson, "Apocalypticism," *Interpreter's Dictionary of the Bible: Supplementary Volume;* and Paul D. Hanson, "Apocalyptic Literature," in *The Hebrew Bible and Its Modern Interpreters,* ed. Douglas H. Knight and Gene M. Tucker (Chico, Calif.: Scholars Press, 1985), 465–88.

3. Orson Hyde, "A Prophetic Warning," *Latter-day Saints' Messenger and Advocate* 2 (July 1836): 344–45.

4. Signey Rigdon, "Millenium. No. VI.," *The Evening and the Morning Star* 2 (June 1834): 162. That Rigdon is the author of this fourteen-part series is acknowledged in *Latter-day Saints' Messenger and Advocate* 1 (Nov. 1834): 25–26.

Regarding millenarian hermeneutics, see W. H. Oliver, *Prophets and Millennialists: The Uses of Biblical Prophecy in England from the 1790s to the 1840s* (Auckland: Auckland University Press, 1978), 18–21; and Ernest R. Sandeen, "Millennialism," in *The Rise of Adventism: Religion and Society in Mid-Nineteenth-Century America,* ed. Edwin S. Gaustad (New York: Harper and Row, 1974), 104–18.

5. Acts 3:231.

6. Signey Rigdon, "Millenium. No. III.," *The Evening and the Morning Star* 2 (Feb. 1834): 131.

7. This quotation is from the first verse of LDS apostle Parley P. Pratt's 1840 hymn "The Morning Breaks, the Shadows Flee." Its ongoing popularity is recognized by its placement as the first hymn in *Hymns of the Church of Jesus Christ of Latter-day Saints* (Salt Lake City: Church of Jesus Christ of Latter-day Saints, 1985), 1.

8. John F. Wilson, "Modernity," in *Encyclopedia of Religion,* ed. Mircea Eliade (New York: Macmillan, 1988), 20.

9. Thomas G. Alexander, *Mormonism in Transition: A History of the Latter-day Saints, 1890–1930* (Urbana: University of Illinois Press, 1986); Mark P. Leone, *Roots of Modern Mormonism* (Cambridge, Mass.: Harvard University Press, 1979); Gordon Shepherd and Gary Shepherd, *A Kingdom Transformed: Themes in the Development of Mormonism* (Salt Lake City: University of Utah Press, 1984); Richard O. Cowan, *The Church in the Twentieth Century* (Salt Lake City: Bookcraft, 1985); James B. Allen and Glen M. Leonard, *The Story of the Latter-day Saints,* 2d. ed., rev. and enl. (Salt Lake City: Deseret Book, 1992); Leonard J. Arrington and Davis Bitton, *The Mormon Experience: A History of the Latter-day Saints* (New York: Knopf, 1979); Klaus J. Hansen, *Mormonism and the American Experience* (Chicago: University of Chicago Press, 1981); Jan Shipps, *Mormonism: The Story of a New Religious Tradition* (Urbana: University of Illinois Press, 1985); and Armand L. Mauss, *The Angel and the Beehive: The Mormon Struggle with Assimilation* (Urbana: University of Illinois Press, 1994). From another angle, Mario S. De Pillis, in "The Persistence of Mormon Community into the 1990s," *Sunstone* 15 (Sept. 1991): 28–49, looks at how Mormons have managed to maintain their communitarian quality amid modernity.

10. Peter Williams, *Popular Religion in America: Symbolic Change and the Modernization Process in Historical Perspective* (Englewood Cliffs, N.J.: Prentice-Hall, 1980), 12.

11. Mircea Eliade, *Cosmos and History: The Myth of the Eternal Return* (New York: Harper and Row, 1954); Mircea Eliade, *The Sacred and the Profane* (New York: Harper and Row, 1957); and Mircea Eliade, *Myth and Reality* (New York: Harper and Row, 1963). Especially relevant is Robert A. Segal, "Eliade's Theory of Millenarianism," *Religious Studies* 14 (June 1978): 159–73.

12. John C. Dwyer, *Church History: Twenty Centuries of Catholic Christianity* (New York: Paulist Press, 1985), 352.

13. Peter L. Berger, *A Rumor of Angels: Modern Society and the Rediscovery of the Supernatural* (Garden City, N.Y.: Doubleday, 1969), 38–39.

14. Charles E. Garrison, *Two Different Worlds: Christian Absolutes and the Relativism of Social Science* (Newark: University of Delaware Press, 1988).

15. That other groups also retain supernaturalism in their eschatology is demonstrated in Paul Boyer, *When Time Shall Be No More: Prophecy Belief in Modern American Culture* (Cambridge, Mass.: Harvard University Press, 1992).

16. Shepherd and Shepherd, *A Kingdom Transformed,* 196.

11

The Basis of Mormon Success:
A Theoretical Application

Rodney Stark

On 6 April 1830, Joseph Smith, his brothers Hyrum and Samuel, Oliver Cowdery, and Peter and David Whitmer met in the Whitmer home in Fayette, New York—a farming village in the western part of the state. That day these six young men organized the Church of Christ, and afterward Joseph Smith served communion and "confirmed" the world's first Mormons. Of course, they didn't call themselves Mormons then, and it was not for several years that they adopted the name the Church of Jesus Christ of Latter-day Saints.

In the years since these obscure beginnings, the Latter-day Saints have sustained an amazingly rapid rate of growth, having nearly ten million members worldwide in 1996. And if this growth rate continues much longer, Mormonism will become the first new *world* religion to appear since the Prophet Mohammed rode out of the desert. However, the likelihood that this immense future growth will be achieved can be adequately assessed only if we first understand why the LDS Church has been growing. That is my primary purpose in this essay.

This discussion will begin by summarizing the history and extent of LDS growth, noting that in recent decades, despite the Latter-day Saints' continuing rapid growth in the United States, LDS growth rates have been substantially faster in Europe, Latin America, and in parts of Africa and Asia. Indeed, on 25 February 1996, LDS Church officials marked the crossover of worldwide membership from a U.S. to a non-U.S. majority.

Against this background, I present a more refined version of a theoretical model of why religious movements succeed. The initial version of this model (Stark 1987) was stimulated by the observation that the many case studies of new religious movements were in almost every instance a study of a group that had failed or would soon do so. How could the failures be separated from the rare groups that succeed? An integrated set of eight propositions was developed and illustrated with historical materials. More recently, the model was incorporated in a lengthy study of the rise of Christianity (Stark 1996a). Subsequently, the model was extended to apply to all religious movements, having initially excluded sects (Stark 1996b). That is the version utilized here, and I will examine whether (and to what extent) the Latter-day Saints satisfy each element of the theory. Rather than using illustrative and qualitative materials alone, I will test major propositions using quantitative data from a variety of sources.

LDS Growth

As can be seen in table 11.1, originally there were only six Latter-day Saints. But within days they were joined by others—mostly their immediate relatives and closest friends—and by September 1830 there were sixty-two Latter-day Saints. At that point, missionaries were dispatched to carry the Latter-day Saint message to the world. Thus, late that first year, four members who had been assigned as missionaries to the Indians in Missouri, led by Oliver Cowdery, stopped along the way in Kirtland, Ohio. There they succeeded in converting Sidney Rigdon, a Campbellite preacher who had just broken with the Disciples of Christ. Rigdon, in turn, was able to recruit more than a hundred members of his congregation. So, by 31 December 1830 (less than a year after the church was founded) there were 280 Latter-day Saints.

When word came back to New York about the conversion of Rigdon and his congregants, Joseph Smith decided to merge the two groups and lead his followers west to Ohio, making Kirtland the center of the new movement. By the summer of 1835 there were at least two thousand Saints living in and around Kirtland, and work was nearly complete on the first LDS temple, a fifteen-room, sandstone structure. Meanwhile, a second major center of the movement had been established in Missouri, where several thousand more flocked to the new faith (Arrington and Bitton 1979). By 1835 there were 8,835 Latter-day Saints.

It is appropriate to pause here to justify use of such detailed numbers on LDS membership. Because from the very first the church has kept detailed records on every person who ever joined (as well as all their relatives and, eventually, their ancestors), the LDS Church today can provide the name and biographical information for nearly every Latter-day Saint, ever. As for the church's membership statistics, these are updated weekly and are subject to on-the-spot audits. These are extremely accurate data.

Between 1835 and 1840 LDS membership almost doubled to 16,865. But the church's troubles had begun. In Missouri, public officials moved against "her-

Table 11.1. LDS Membership, 1830–1995

Date	Number of Latter-day Saints	Percent Increase
1830 6 April	6	
1830 31 December	280	
1835	8,835	
1840	16,865	91
1845	30,332	80
1850	51,839	71
1855	63,974	23
1860	61,082	-5
1865	76,771	26
1870	90,130	17
1875	107,167	19
1880	133,628	25
1885	164,130	23
1890	188,263	15
1895	231,116	23
1900	283,765	23
1905	332,048	17
1910	398,478	20
1915	466,238	17
1920	525,987	13
1925	613,572	17
1930	670,017	9
1935	746,384	11
1940	862,664	16
1945	979,454	13
1950	1,111,314	13
1955	1,357,274	22
1960	1,693,180	25
1965	2,395,932	50
1970	2,930,810	22
1975	3,572,202	22
1980	4,639,822	30
1985	5,641,054	22
1990	7,761,112	38
1995	9,439,000	22

etics" and jailed Joseph Smith for six months in 1839. Keep in mind that this had nothing to do with polygamy, which had not yet begun, but was motivated entirely by claims by local divines that these people were not Christians. Seeking elbow room to freely construct their own society, about five thousand Latter-day Saints migrated to western Illinois (then a sparsely settled frontier), where in 1839 they founded the city of Nauvoo (Flanders 1965). Upon his release from jail Joseph Smith joined them there, and the city flourished, soon becoming the largest city in the state with a population of more than eleven thousand (Chicago was still a tiny trading village). Many other Saints settled on farms near Nauvoo. By 1845 there were 30,332 Latter-day Saints on earth.

But Joseph and Hyrum Smith were not among them. On 22 June 1844 they were arrested on charges arising from a dispute with the territorial governor of Illinois. Then, on 27 June a lynch mob broke into the jail at Carthage, Illinois, and shot the Smith brothers. A power struggle ensued among Smith's lieutenants. Although Brigham Young was rapidly ratified as Smith's successor, significant numbers defected to follow other leaders, and many also simply drifted away. Sidney Rigdon led one splinter group away from Nauvoo (having been excommunicated for his unwillingness to accept Young's authority). A far larger group (perhaps numbering two thousand) chose to follow James J. Strang to rural Wisconsin and eventually to Beaver Island in northern Lake Michigan. Among Strang's followers were several very prominent members, including William Smith, another brother of Joseph Smith. But the most successful dissident faction united behind Joseph Smith's young son Joseph Smith III and the prophet's widow Emma. Breaking with the Young faction, this group returned to Missouri, where the Reorganized Church of Jesus Christ of Latter Day Saints was established in Independence. As of 1996 this group had about 190,000 members.

In addition to their losses to dissident groups, LDS numbers were reduced as members drifted away or simply stayed behind when the main body began its long and perilous trek west in 1846 (the first major contingent arrived in Utah in 1847). Amazingly, despite all of these losses, the total number of Saints in 1850 was 51,839, an increase of 71 percent. How could this possibly have been achieved?

The British to the Rescue

One of the most astonishing episodes in LDS history, little known outside LDS circles, involves the incredible success of the church's mission to Great Britain. On 4 June 1837 Joseph Smith approached Heber C. Kimball in the temple in Kirtland, Ohio, and told him that the Lord had revealed to him, "Let my servant Heber go to England and proclaim my gospel and open the door to salvation of that nation" (Allen, Esplin, and Whittaker 1992, 23). Thus on 13 June 1837 Kimball and Orson Hyde, both members of the Council of the Twelve Apostles (the LDS governing body), along with Joseph Fielding and Willard Richards, left for Great Britain. Pausing in New York for a week to raise funds to pay their passage on the sailing ship *Garrick,* the LDS missionary party land-ed in Liverpool after eighteen days at sea. The missionaries were immediately struck by the immense class distinctions. Kimball later wrote in his *Journal*, "wealth and luxury, penuary and want abound. I there met the rich attired in the most costly dresses, and the next moment was saluted with the cries of the poor, without covering sufficient to screen them from the weather; such a distinction I never saw before" (16). As soon as their baggage cleared customs (it took three days), the missionaries moved to Preston, a rapidly growing mill town, and began public preaching in Vauxhall Chapel. They met with immediate success, and by the end of the year they had recruited and baptized several hundred followers. The next year all of the missionaries but Joseph Fielding returned to America. Then in January 1840, John Taylor and Wilford Woodruff, both members of the Council of the Twelve, were sent to Great Britain. In April, Brigham Young, Heber Kimball, and Orson and Parley Pratt, also members of the Twelve, accompanied by the young George A. Smith (Joseph's cousin), arrived to help teach the British. And teach they did. With half of the Council of the Twelve traveling the country and preaching, the ranks of British Saints swelled rapidly. By the end of 1840 they numbered 3,626, and by the end of the decade there were 30,747 Latter-day Saints in Britain (see table 11.2).

Table 11.2. The Impact of British Membership and Immigration, 1840–90

Year	Cumulative No. of LDS in Great Britain	Total LDS Immigration to USA	Membership Worldwide	Membership Minus British Saints[a]
1840	3,626	291	16,865	12,948
1841	5,814	1,346	19,856	12,696
1842	8,467	2,960	23,564	12,137
1843	8,848	3,732	25,980	13,400
1844	8,057	4,376	26,146	13,713
1845	10,956	4,787	30,332	14,589
1846	11,573	4,969	33,993	17,427
1847	13,993	4,993	34,694	15,708
1848	20,212	5,747	40,477	14,518
1849	27,912	7,572	48,160	12,676
1850	30,747	9,437	51,839	11,655[b]
1851	32,339	10,797	52,165	9,029
1852	32,339	11,577	52,640	8,724
1853	30,828	14,203	64,154	19,123
1854	29,441	17,377	68,429	21,611
1855	26,001	21,918	63,974	16,055
1856	22,502	25,688	63,881	15,691
1857	15,220	27,682	55,236	12,334
1858	14,186	27,860	55,755	13,709

Table 11.2. Continued

Year	Cumulative No. of LDS in Great Britain	Total LDS Immigration to USA	Membership Worldwide	Membership Minus British Saints[a]
1859	13,027	28,670	57,038	15,341
1860	13,853	30,079	61,082	17,150
1861	14,893	32,038	66,211	19,280
1862	14,327	35,635	68,780	18,818
1863	13,851	39,282	71,770	18,637
1864	13,301	41,969	74,348	19,078
1865	12,403	43,269	76,771	21,099
1866	10,782	46,605	77,884	20,497
1867	10,872	47,265	81,124	22,987
1868	10,719	50,495	84,622	23,408
1869	10,980	52,832	88,432	24,620
1870	8,804	53,749	90,130	27,577
1871	8,246	55,266	95,596	32,084
1872	6,842	56,932	98,152	34,378
1873	6,061	59,469	101,538	36,008
1874	5,423	61,469	103,916	37,024
1875	5,411	62,995	107,167	38,761
1876	5,408	64,281	111,111	41,422
1877	5,188	65,860	115,065	44,017
1878	4,842	67,913	125,046	52,291
1879	5,257	69,430	128,386	53,699
1880	5,112	71,267	133,628	57,249
1881	5,180	73,578	140,733	61,975
1882	4,790	76,341	145,604	63,473
1883	4,402	78,568	151,593	68,623
1884	4,173	80,471	158,242	73,598
1885	3,991	82,161	164,130	77,978
1886	3,588	83,668	166,653	79,397
1887	3,493	85,538	173,029	83,998
1888	3,193	86,932	180,294	90,169
1889	3,142	88,421	183,144	91,581
1890	2,770	89,695	188,263	95,798[c]

a. British Saints = Latter-day Saints in Britain plus cumulative emigration from Britain.
b. U.S. Census of 1850 reported 11,354 white persons living in Utah.
c. Non-British Saints outnumbered British Saints for the first time since 1845.

What makes this total even more remarkable is that, from the very start, large numbers of British converts departed for America. In 1840 immigration to the United States totalled 291 British Saints. The next year 1,346 came over—130 of them sailing from Liverpool on 21 April with Brigham Young as their group leader. As the decade passed, increasingly large numbers of British Saints arrived. Despite these departures, the number of Latter-day Saints in Britain also grew rapidly. Indeed, by 1848 half of all Latter-day Saints lived in Britain, and by 1850 six of ten Saints did so.

It was the British mission that more than accounted for Latter-day Saint growth during the terrible decade of the 1840s. The column at the far right of table 11.2 shows LDS membership with the contributions of the British mission removed. That is, the number of Saints in Britain, plus the number who had already emigrated, have been subtracted from the worldwide total of members. Notice the lack of growth and then the period of decline that occurred among non-British Saints. Put another way, LDS membership would have been greatly reduced and subsequent growth severely slowed had it not been for the astonishing results of the mission to Britain. In fact, in 1890, the first time since 1845 that non-British Saints made up half of the membership, the Latter-day Saints would have numbered only 95,798 without the British contribution. With it, they numbered 188,263.

Why did the Latter-day Saints do so well in Britain? The 1840s were very stressful times there. The enclosure movement had driven millions from rural areas to lead lives of desperate poverty and misery in the polluted industrial cities. The majority of Britain's seventeen million people were extremely poor; they lived in squalid, crowded tenements or were homeless on the streets. Given these conditions and the extraordinary class contrasts reported by Kimball, it is no surprise that there was increasingly bitter class antagonism. A substantial amount of this antagonism was directed toward the conventional churches; nearly all of them, including the "fundamentalist" sects, not only opposed the working class in terms of politics but also charged pew rentals that were well beyond the means of most citizens. Of course, most denominations offered some free seats, but they were clearly set apart, and most people found it degrading to use them. In contrast, all seats in LDS meeting halls were free.

But of even greater importance, Mormonism represented the American dream in very tangible ways. For people who still lacked the vote, had no realistic hope of ever owning property, and whose children would be lucky to attend school for even a year or two, America was a land of incredible plenty. Rich farm and ranch land was there for the taking. The income of the average American family was many times greater than the average income in any European nation, and even in remote wilderness areas, where there were settlers there were schools. It is no surprise that many people joined the LDS Church expecting to immigrate to the United States under church auspices. From the beginning, British Saints crossed the Atlantic on ships chartered by the church. In 1849 the Perpetual Emigration Fund was established, not only to pay travel expenses, but also to advance sufficient funds to help the immigrants get started. Once they were established, the immigrants paid back their advance, thus restoring funds to be used by others to come over.

It is important to recognize that British immigrants did far more than swell the church rolls, for few of them were cynical opportunists. Once in America, surrounded by a Latter-day Saint society, the British Saints were models of devotion whose descendants still make up a significant portion of Utah Latter-day Saints. In 1990 the U.S. Census asked Americans their ancestry. In Utah, 44 percent said they were "English," as compared with 30 percent in Maine, 29 percent in Idaho, 26 percent in Vermont, and 24 percent in New Hampshire (these were the top five). Examination of counties reveals an even more pronounced concentration of people of English ancestry in LDS areas. Of the twenty-five counties with the most English ancestry, nineteen are in Utah, and the other six are in southern Idaho (which is overwhelmingly LDS). In Utah's Beaver County, 66 percent claimed English ancestry, in Juab County 64 percent, in Rich County 62 percent, and in Garfield County 60 percent.

Building a Global Movement

In the twentieth century LDS growth no longer depended on the British mission, but it was impeded by world events. In 1914 World War I broke out in Europe, and soon travel abroad—including that of LDS missionaries—was curtailed. LDS growth slowed to only 13 percent between 1915 and 1920 (see table 11.1). Following the war, growth returned to prewar levels, only to be sharply reduced during the Great Depression. Then came World War II, and once again foreign travel was impossible. LDS men who might have gone on missions were in the armed forces instead. Then, with wars and the depression behind them, the Latter-day Saints entered a period of very rapid growth—never below 22 percent for any five-year period since 1950. In 1995 LDS membership was nearly ten million.

As a result of this rapid growth, Mormonism is no longer an American or British-American movement. As of 1996 more than 50 percent of all Saints lived outside the United States. Indicative of this rapid rate of growth, Brazilian male converts often have been called to be bishops within a year of their baptism, and as of 1994 half of all bishops, branch presidents, and stake presidents in Brazil were under age forty (Martins 1995). In fact, mission presidents in many nations, including most of Latin America, devote effort to *limiting* rates of conversion so as not to overwhelm their wards with uninstructed newcomers. Table 11.3 shows that LDS growth is rapid in all parts of the world, but growth in Europe is slower than in Latin America, Asia, the South Pacific, or

Table 11.3. LDS Growth Rates, 1978–93

	Percent Increase
Worldwide	156
Africa[a]	963
Asia	524
Canada	91
Europe	117
Latin America	501
South Pacific	158
United States	82

a. Nearly all members are in sub-Saharan nations where, except for South Africa, LDS missions began only very recently.

Africa—where LDS missions have only just begun (except for South Africa). Reasons for these regional variations are considered later.

Indicative of the globalization of Latter-day Saint membership, eight nations have higher LDS membership rates than does the United States. In Tonga Latter-day Saints make up 37 percent of the population; in Samoa, 25 percent are LDS. Tahiti, the Cook Islands, the Marshall Islands, Chile, New Zealand, and Uruguay finish out the list of eight, while Guatemala, Fiji, Ecuador, and Peru are close behind.

This long-term pattern of rapid growth can be explained with ten propositions that attempt to specify the necessary and the sufficient conditions for the success of religious movements. I will apply each proposition to the LDS Church in this chapter.

Conservation of Cultural Capital

It is axiomatic in the social sciences that, within the limits of their information and available choices, guided by their preferences and tastes, humans will tend to maximize—to attempt to acquire the most while expending the least. Put another way, humans will seek to conserve their capital. When economists apply this principle they concentrate on efforts to acquire and retain capital of the monetary variety, but the same principles hold when applied to *cultural* capital.

Cultural capital is the result of socialization and education. When we are socialized into a particular culture we also are investing in it—expending time and effort in learning, understanding, and remembering cultural material. For example, persons raised to be Christians have accumulated a substantial store of Christian culture—a store that can be conceived of as cultural capital. When faced with the option of shifting religions, the maximization of cultural capital leads people to prefer to save as much of their cultural capital as they can and to expend as little investment in new capital as possible (Stark and Bainbridge 1996, 220; Iannaccone 1990; Sherkat and Wilson 1995).

Stated as a proposition: *People will be more willing to join a religious group to the degree that doing so minimizes their expenditure of cultural capital.* An example may be helpful. A young person from a Christian background and living in a Christian society is deciding whether to join the Latter-day Saints or the Hare Krishnas. By becoming a Latter-day Saint this person retains his or her entire Christian culture and simply adds to it. The LDS missionaries, noting that the person has copies of the Old Testament and the New Testament, suggest that an *additional* Scripture, the Book of Mormon, is needed to complete the set. In contrast, the Hare Krishna missionaries note that the person has the *wrong* Scriptures and must discard the Bible in exchange for the Bhagavad Gita. The principle of the conservation of cultural capital predicts (and explains) why the overwhelming majority of converts within a Christian context select the Latter-day Saint rather than the Hare Krishna option, with the reverse being the case in a Hindu context.

In the form stated above, the principle of the conservation of cultural capital explains individual behavior vis-à-vis conversion. Since my concern here is with the fate of religious movements, a macro level form of the proposition is needed and becomes the first of the ten propositions comprising the theory: 1. *New religious movements are likely to succeed to the extent that they retain cultural continuity with the conventional faith(s) of the societies in which they seek converts.*

Mormonism is deeply rooted in Christian culture. It is not transplanted Hinduism or a novel amalgam of eastern mysticism or pure novelty. Rather, Mormonism embraces the *entire* Christian-Judaic tradition and adds to it in logical fashion, incorporating a more modern worldview. Latter-day Saints continue to read and study the Old and New Testaments, but they also accept the authority of the Book of Mormon, "Another Testament of Jesus Christ." Here the scriptural narrative of the Bible is continued to include the New World. Indeed it continues the story of Israel, beginning with the settlement of the New World by Hebrews well before the birth of Jesus.

The first two books, 1 and 2 Nephi, explain how Lehi, with his wife Sariah, his four sons—Laman, Lemuel, Sam, and Nephi—and their families and followers left Jerusalem just before the Babylonian captivity, boarded a large ship, built by Nephi and his brothers at God's command, and sailed off to a new land across the sea:

> And it came to pass after we had all gone down to the ship, and had taken with us our provisions and things which had been commanded us, we did put forth into the sea and were driven forth before the wind towards the promised land. (1 Nephi 18:8)

> And it came to pass that after we had sailed for the space of many days we did arrive at the promised land; and we went forth upon the land, and did pitch our tents; and we did call it the promised land. (1 Nephi 18:23)

According to the Book of Mormon, these were the main ancestors of the population of the Western Hemisphere. Eventually they split into two great tribes, the Lamanites (descendants of Lehi's wicked son Laman) and the Nephites (descendants of Lehi's faithful son Nephi). A series of battles between the two is described until 3 Nephi, which recounts Christ's visit to the New World following the Resurrection and the long period of peace subsequent to this visit. But in Mormon we learn that the people turned once again to sin and conflict, leading to a great battle fought at the Hill Cumorah whereupon the Nephites were wiped out. Thus, all persons descended from pre-Columbian inhabitants of the Western Hemisphere are called Lamanites, although because of intermarriage between groups they may also have Nephite and other ancestry.

The Book of Mormon not only extends the geographic scope of the Bible but also clarifies it in many ways. Thomas F. O'Dea (1957, 30) noted the impressive intellectual clarity of the work: "There is nothing obscure or unclear in its doctrine. Even the notion of prophecy and revelation, so central to it, leads to intellectual clarity. The revelation of the *Book of Mormon* is not a glimpse of higher and incomprehensible truths but reveals God's word to men with a democratic comprehensibility. 'Plainness' of doctrine—straightforwardness and an absence of subtle casuistries—was for its rural audience a mark of its genuineness." Joseph Smith's subsequent revelations added to this clarity and provided a much fuller and more comprehensible view of Jehovah and of the fundamental basis of existence. Smith did not add mysteries to Christianity; he dispelled them and offered a more complete cosmology.

In an age such as ours, marked by rapid change and constant technological innovation, there is a widespread predisposition to expect new tidings of all kinds. We expect to know more about everything than once was known. Yet Christianity has, for the most part, argued that the Age of Revelations is past—that two thousand years ago, God said everything there was to be said. In contrast, the Latter-day Saints argue that God has more to say as humans gain in their capacity to understand: "And now, O all ye that have imagined up unto yourselves a god who can do no miracles, I would ask of you, have all these things passed, of which I have spoken? Has the end come yet? Behold I say unto you, Nay; and God has not ceased to be a God of miracles" (Mormon 9:15). Even the most bitter Christian critics of the Book of Mormon have noted its modernity and the immense suitability of the Latter-day Saint message for the contemporary consciousness. Indeed, they have used this as proof that the work is of modern authorship. But for the Latter-day Saints, this is simply proof that it was intended by God for latter-day readers, and they dare Christian theologians to deny that God is capable of foreseeing history.

I shall delay an examination of important LDS additions to Christian theology until the discussion of tension and strictness. Here we may examine several tests of the principle of the conservation of cultural capital.

The first of these is that Jehovah's Witnesses will have an advantage over the Latter-day Saints when both seek converts within Christian societies. This is supported by the fact that Witnesses outnumber Latter-day Saints by 3.4 to 1 in Europe. In contrast, the two movements have achieved quite similar results in Asia, where both lack cultural continuity.

The immense Latter-day Saint preponderance in the South Pacific is easily understood despite the LDS religion's apparent lack of continuity with local religious culture. Polynesians are an unhistorical people in that they do not appear in secular histories until the arrival of European explorers, and very little then. However, a passage in the Book of Mormon (Alma 63:5)[1] has long been interpreted to refer to the settlement of Polynesia, and a considerable amount of Latter-day Saint culture has grown up on this topic. Polynesians have responded very favorably to their LDS history.

At first glance it would seem that the Christian sects such as the Jehovah's Witnesses should have an advantage in Latin America on the basis of cultural continuity. This is not reflected in membership statistics, however, as the Witnesses are outnumbered by Latter-day Saints 2.3 to 1 in Latin America. But upon closer inspection it appears that Latter-day Saints enjoy greater cultural continuity in Latin America than do the Witnesses, despite claims that this is a Catholic continent.

The principle of the conservation of cultural capital favors the Witnesses over the Saints *only if* Latin America has been sufficiently Christianized. But it appears to me that most Latin Americans have such a small investment in traditional Christian cultural capital that the Witnesses have little advantage. Moreover, the cultural continuity between Mormonism and pre-Columbian faiths which have never died out may give the Latter-day Saints a substantial advantage.

Elsewhere I have demonstrated that, despite claims that these are Catholic societies, they are exceedingly unchurched (Stark 1992). Although more than 90 percent of the population in most Latin American nations are claimed as Catholics, levels of practice are extremely low, and for huge numbers of people "religion" is probably little more than an exotic mixture of fragments of Christianity and pre-Columbian religion, plus a great deal of folk magic.

Some evidence of this can be seen in the widespread belief in reincarnation found in Latin American nations. According to the World Values Surveys conducted in 1990 and 1991, 56 percent of Brazilians, 49 percent of Chileans, 43 percent of Mexicans, and 40 percent of Argentinians believe in reincarnation. Furthermore, within these Latin nations belief in reincarnation is concentrated among the Catholics. For "Catholics" who believe in reincarnation (and probably many other notions heretical to mainstream Catholicism), conversion to a Christian sect such as the Jehovah's Witnesses probably would require as large a capital investment as would conversion to the LDS Church.

Furthermore, according to the Book of Mormon, today's descendants of pre-Columbian Americans are, through Lehi, direct descendants of Abraham. To be Latter-day Saints is their birthright, and many Latin American Saints interpret this as a superior claim to membership in comparison with Saints of European ancestry who are, in some sense, Latter-day Saints only by "adoption" (Murphy 1996). Moreover, the Book of Mormon is accepted by Latin American converts, especially in Central America, as the authentic history of pre-Columbian times. Thomas Murphy (1996) found that Guatemalan Latter-day Saints referred to many ancient Mayan ruins by names found in the Book of Mormon. Of equal significance are the many parallels Guatemalan Saints identify between the Book of Mormon and a pre-Columbian Mayan epic known as the *Popol Vuh*. According to Thomas W. Murphy (1996, 182–83): "The *Popol Vuh* . . . is required reading in public schools. . . . Guatemalan members told me that although the names of the people and places were different, both books spoke of the visit of Jesus to the Americas, gods, wars, the tower of Babel, creation, trinity, and Satan. . . . Jesus was explicitly identified by Guatemalan Mormons with the Sovereign Plumed Serpent in the *Popol Vuh*."

Not only does the focus of Mormonism on the Western Hemisphere and on pre-Columbian times provide substantial cultural continuity with indigenous religious culture but it also has had a major impact on LDS missionary approaches to that culture. Recall that only a few months after the founding of the church in 1830, four missionaries were sent to the Indians in Missouri. This reflected the immense concern Latter-day Saints have about all of the peoples native to the New World. Consequently, the Saints have directed a very substantial proportion of their missionary effort to Latin America. This extra effort may also help explain why they have out-performed the Jehovah's Witnesses there.

Finally, Mormonism is very closely associated with Americanism—if for no other reason than the presence of large numbers of young American missionaries. Given the alienation of most American intellectuals (and especially social scientists) from American culture, it would be easy to overlook the immense admiration for this culture that exists in many other parts of the world. Just as British converts to Mormonism might have found it hard to distinguish the attractions of the religion from the attractions of emigration, so too many Latin American converts would find it very difficult to separate Mormonism from the modern American lifestyle. Indeed, many Latin American leftists cannot separate the two (Young 1994). Thus in 1989 leftist terrorists in Bolivia murdered two young LDS missionaries on grounds that they were violating Bolivia's sovereignty on behalf of Yankee interests. The same rationale was expressed by the Shining Path terrorists in Peru following their murders of Latter-day Saint missionaries. In fact, there have been hundreds of bombings, arsons, and acts of vandalism against LDS Church buildings in Latin America, reflecting attacks on "whatever smells Yankee," according to a U.S. State Department spokesperson (Young 1994, 51). Indeed, rapid LDS growth arouses the political Right as well as the Left in many Latin nations, because the Saints proselytize the Indians, which antagonizes the wealthy landowners (Young 1994).

Lawrence A. Young (1994, 52) has written of the "challenges encountered by the Mormon church as it seeks to enter Latin America, where the church . . . carries a heavy load of cultural baggage related to its being marked an American church." He also suggests the need for the church to "develop indigenous religious expressions." These points are probably well taken, especially in an analysis of causes of conflict between the Latter-day Saints and various host societies, but it seems important not to overlook the attractions of Americanism in the overall conversion process. Nor should we minimize the impressions made on locals by the mere fact that all these attractive, lively, young, *American* missionaries are self-supporting volunteers—that people who could be in college or otherwise enjoying the fruits of North American prosperity have instead chosen to share their faith with Latin Americans, regardless of their social status.

If Prophecy Fails

Other things being equal, failed prophecies are harmful for religious movements. Although prophecies may arouse a great deal of excitement and attract many new followers beforehand, the subsequent disappointment usually offsets these benefits. Contrary to textbook summaries, cognitive dissonance theory does not propose that failed prophecies typically strengthen a religious group. Nor is it established that religious groups respond initially to a failed prophecy with increased levels of proselytizing. A careful reading of the famous example (Festinger, Riecken, and Schachter 1956) reveals no such group effect actually occurred, nor have any subsequent studies found it (Bainbridge 1996).

This discussion leads to the second proposition in the theory: *2. New religious movements are likely to succeed to the extent that their doctrines are nonempirical.* That is, religions are less vulnerable to the extent that their doctrines are focused on a nonempirical reality and are not subject to empirical tests.

Latter-day Saint liberals often concern themselves with conflicts between the Book of Mormon and archaeological research. Claims that Lehi and his followers found wild cows and horses do not seem to square with the fossil record. Of course, Christian liberals have long been expressing similar concerns about the biblical account of the Creation and the flood. But if these things worry liberals, it must be noticed that tens of millions of evangelical Christians are not troubled about the flood, nor are millions of Latter-day Saints worried about Lehi's horses.

The basic problem for both Christian and Latter-day Saint liberals is that they inevitably project their inability to believe on everyone else. Latter-day Saint liberals worry about disconfirmations of the Book of Mormon because they don't really believe this is an ancient and inspired Scripture, but something composed, consciously or otherwise, by Joseph Smith. Orthodox Saints, believing the book to be the word of God, are not only able to accommodate some discrepancies but also fully expect archaeologists to find evidence in support of Scripture, which is why the LDS Church has supported a considerable amount of New World archaeology.

Interestingly enough, the orthodox have had some substantial successes. For example, John L. Sorenson (1985) devoted many years to constructing a map of the Book of Mormon. Working entirely with textual references, he located places in relation to one another (how long did it take to walk from Nephi to Zarahemla and in what direction?) and to the topography as described therein. This map turned out to be a remarkable fit for the area surrounding the

Isthmus of Tehuantepec in southern Mexico and northern Guatemala. In any event, fundamental assertions about geography and culture found in the Book of Mormon are not very susceptible to disproof by archaeologists or anyone else, and LDS doctrines are not at risk of being too empirical. Of perhaps even greater importance, the LDS Church is not given to empirically vulnerable prophesying, unlike various Protestant sects that engage in dating the end of time. It is these short-term and dramatic prophecies that cause so much damage when they fail, as shown by studies of the impact of the failure of the end to come in 1975 upon commitment among Jehovah's Witnesses (Singelenberg 1989).

Medium Tension (Strictness)

In order to grow, a religious movement must offer religious culture that sets it apart from the general, secular culture. That is, movements must be distinctive and impose relatively strict moral standards. *3. New religious movements are likely to succeed to the extent that they maintain a medium level of tension with their surrounding environment—are strict, but not too strict.*

In its initial form (Stark 1987), the proposition made no mention of strictness. However, the implications of the proposition are more fully revealed if the theoretical work on "strictness" is made an explicit part (Kelley 1972; Iannaccone 1992, 1994; Stark and Iannaccone 1993). Strictness refers to the degree that a religious group maintains "a separate and distinctive life style or morality in personal and family life, in such areas as dress, diet, drinking, entertainment, uses of time, sex, child rearing, and the like." Or, a group is not strict to the degree that it affirms "the current . . . mainline life style in these respects" (Iannaccone 1994, 1190).

To anticipate the argument, strictness makes religious groups strong by screening out free riders and thereby increasing the average level of commitment in the group. This, in turn, greatly increases the credibility of the religious culture (especially promises concerning future benefits, since credibility is the result of high levels of consensus) as well as generating a high degree of resource mobilization.

Free rider problems are the Achilles' heel of collective activities. Other things being equal, people will not contribute to a collective enterprise when they can fully share in the benefits without contributing. This is called free-riding, and the collective consequence of free-riding is that insufficient collective goods are created because too few contribute. Everyone suffers—but those who give most generously suffer the most. Because religion involves collective action, and all collective action is potentially subject to exploitation by free riders, religious groups must confront free-riding.

One need not look far to find examples of anemic congregations plagued by free rider problems—a visit to the nearest liberal Protestant church will usually suffice to discover "members" who draw upon the group for weddings, funerals, holiday celebrations, daycare, and even counseling, but who provide little or nothing in return. Even if they do make substantial financial contributions, they weaken the group's ability to create collective religious goods because their inactivity devalues the religious capital and reduces the "average" level of commitment. However, strictness in the form of costly demands offers a solution to this problem.

At first glance it would seem that costly demands must always make a religion less attractive. And, indeed, the economists' law of demand predicts just that, *other things remaining equal.* But it turns out that other things do not remain equal when religions impose these kinds of costs on their members. To the contrary, costly demands strengthen a religious group in two ways. First, they create a barrier to group entry. No longer is it possible merely to drop in and reap the benefits of membership. To take part at all you must qualify by accepting the sacrifices demanded from everyone. Thus high costs tend to *screen out* free riders—those potential members whose commitment and participation would otherwise be low. The costs act as nonrefundable "registration fees" which, as in secular markets, measure seriousness of interest in the product. Only those willing to pay the price qualify.

Secondly, high costs tend to *increase* participation among those who do join by increasing the rewards derived from participation. It may seem paradoxical that when the cost of membership increases that the net gains of membership increase, too. But this is necessarily the case with collectively produced goods. For example, an individual's positive experience of a worship service increases to the degree that the church is full, the members participate enthusiastically (everyone joins in the songs and prayers), and others express very positive evaluations of what is taking place. Thus, as each member *pays* the costs of membership, each *gains* from higher levels of production of collective goods.

From the start, Latter-day Saints have maintained a relatively high, but usually manageable level of tension with their surrounding society. When anti-Mormon antagonism in Illinois resulted in the murder of Joseph and Hyrum Smith, and mobs demanded that Latter-day Saints leave the state at once, their initial response was to withdraw into their own isolated society in Utah. But as non-Mormons began to populate the West, persecution resumed, focused on plural marriage, which was by then openly practiced, especially by the most prominent Saints. During the 1880s, the federal government launched an all-out effort to prosecute polygamists under a new statute. Some polygamous families fled to Canada, others to Mexico; many church leaders went into hiding. Faced with these dangers, the church reduced its tension with the external society in 1890 by prohibiting new plural marriages. This drew a favorable response from President Benjamin Harrison, who in 1893 issued a proclamation of amnesty to all polygamists who had entered into that relationship prior to 1 November 1890.

Subsequently, the church periodically has moved to prevent its tension with non–Latter-day Saint society from becoming excessive, most dramatically in 1978 when the revelation was announced that henceforth men of all races would be eligible for the LDS priesthood. This is not to suggest that the church changed its position in response to external pressures (which actually seem to have been lower in 1978 than during the 1960s). Indeed, it appears to this outsider that the pressures were largely internal as many members, including the president of the church, did a lot of praying about the matter. In any event, the effect of this and other modifications has been not so much to decrease tension with the outside world as to keep it within tolerable limits. Put another way, the Latter-day Saints have softened many of their original positions on a variety of issues, and they have modified many practices, but the net result has been to maintain a relatively similar degree of tension over time (Mauss 1994).

Today, Latter-day Saint tension with the outside world takes two primary forms. First, the Saints are stricter in terms of the moral rules governing their lifestyles and the levels of commitment expected of the individual member. Second, they embrace a significantly different theology.

Latter-day Saints abstain from most forms of caffeine and therefore do not drink coffee or tea. Many also avoid caffeinated soft drinks. They also reject tobacco and alcohol. It is worth noting that these are *norms*, not rules, in that no one is expelled for drinking caffeine or liquor or for smoking. All that happens to people who do these things is that their LDS friends and relatives will indicate strong disapproval. Latter-day Saints also condemn pre- and extra-marital sex, and the latter can draw official church sanctions. In addition, Mormons are expected to devote a great deal of time and energy to church activities and to tithe their incomes.

Table 11.4 demonstrates the positive effects of strictness by comparing active and nominal Mormons and then merging the two groups to show what Mormon congregations would look like if the free riders were included. The data are based on the merged 1972 through 1994 General Social Surveys, which in-

Table 11.4. Active and Nominal Latter-day Saints, General Social Surveys 1972–94

	Active	Nominal	Combined	U.S. (GSS)
	(239)[a]	(191)	(430)	(31,945)
"Strong" identification with denomination	91%	25%	62%	39%
Pray daily	92	46	71	56
Spouse is LDS[b]	99	92	97	
	(167)	(72)	(239)	
Who smoke	0%	33%	13%	35%
Who drink	6	59	27	71
Who go to a bar at least once a year	5	50	26	49

a. Number of cases is slightly smaller for items not asked every year.
b. Married persons only.

cluded 430 persons who identified themselves as Latter-day Saints (excluding Reorganized Mormons). Active Saints are defined as those who attend church at least once a week. Nominal Saints attend less often—two-thirds said they attended less than once a month. Of course, all church congregations have some very active and some very inactive members. What strict congregations lack is an excess of lukewarm members who do participate some, but not very enthusiastically. That is, Latter-day Saints who don't go every week tend not to show up often enough to reduce the religious rewards of the active members.

More than 90 percent of active Mormons strongly identify with their faith. But this would fall to less than two-thirds if the nominal Mormons were counted. Prayer activity would fall drastically in a congregation in which the nominals took some part, but intermarriage would not be affected at all—mixed marriages being almost unknown even among nominal Latter-day Saints. No active member in the sample smokes, but nominal Mormons smoke at the national average. Hardly any (6 percent) of active Mormons drink alcohol, but the majority of nominal Mormons do. The same contrast shows up on going to bars and taverns. Thus strictness creates highly committed, distinctive LDS congregations by weeding out the potential free riders.

Distinctiveness also characterizes Latter-day Saint theology, for it is as much a departure from traditional Christianity as that faith was, in turn, from Judaism. LDS theology deals with many questions left unanswered by Christianity, including the origins of God, the creation of new souls, and the ultimate aim of the individual human biography. LDS theology postulates an infinite number of universes, each created and ruled over by an omnipotent God *and his wife*—the couple is the basic unit in Latter-day Saint thought. We live in one of these universes. Where did God and his wife come from? Once they were mere humans just as we are. They rose to divinity and hence to create and rule their own universe after a long period of spiritual development. Individual humans on earth possess immortal souls infused in each at the moment of birth. These souls, in turn, are the offspring of the divine couple, produced through their union. Each human thus begins not merely in the image of God, but as the literal child of the gods, possessed of the divine substance. Therefore each human can aspire to godhood, and each Latter-day Saint couple can hope one day to create and rule their own universe, which is why eternal, celestial marriages, sealed in LDS temples, are of such great significance. Latter-day Saints do not mean merely to worship God, nor do they contemplate only spending eternity with God. They mean to become divine.

These novel aspects of LDS theology are more than sufficient to generate several shelves of angry anti-Mormon books in every evangelical Christian bookstore. And this ad ran for years in *Christianity Today:* "MORMONISM IS A FALSE RELIGION. For a FREE one-year subscription that offers a revealing look at Mormonism from a Christian perspective, call . . ."

Legitimate Authority

While it is convenient to speak of organizations doing this or that, we must always keep in mind that, in fact, organizations never do anything. Only people can act, and individual actions can be interpreted as on behalf of an organization only to the extent that they are coordinated and directed. That is, all successful social movements require effective leaders, and this, in turn, requires that their authority be seen as legitimate. Stated as a complex proposition: *4. Religious movements will succeed to the extent they have legitimate leaders with adequate authority to be effective.*

This, in turn, will depend upon two factors:

4a. Adequate authority requires clear doctrinal justifications for an effective and legitimate leadership.

4b. Authority is regarded as more legitimate and gains in effectiveness to the degree that members perceive themselves as participants in the system of authority.

There are many bases for legitimate authority within organizations, depending on factors such as whether members are paid to participate and/or whether special skills and experience are recognized as vital qualifications to lead. However, when organizations stress doctrines, as all religious movements do, these doctrines must define the basis for leadership. Who may lead and how is leadership obtained? What powers are granted to leaders? What sanctions may leaders impose? These are vital matters, brought into clear relief by the many examples of groups that failed (or are failing) for lack of doctrines defining a legitimate basis for effective leadership.

That doctrines can directly cause ineffective leadership is widely evident in contemporary New Age and "metaphysical" groups. If everyone is a "student," and everyone's ideas and insights are equally valid, then no one can say what must be done or who is to do what, when. The result is the existence of virtual nonorganizations—mere affinity or discussion groups incapable of action (Wagner 1983). In similar fashion the early Christian gnostics could not sustain effective organizations because their fundamental doctrines prevented them from ever being anything more than a loose network of individual adepts, each pursuing secret knowledge through private, personal means (Pagels 1979). In contrast, from the start Christianity had doctrines appropriate for an effective structure of authority since Christ himself was believed to have selected his successors as head of the church.

LDS doctrine speaks with a clear, powerful voice on the matter of leadership. The president of the church is acknowledged to be "prophet, seer, and revelator." That is, since Joseph Smith was granted revelations by God, his successors to the presidency gain similar powers—what Max Weber described as a replacement of the charisma of the prophet by the charisma of office. The president gains office simply by being the senior member of the Council of the Twelve, which serves as the ruling body of the church. The council selects its own new members to replace those who die and those who join the First Presidency. This presidency comprises the president and two counselors he chooses through inspiration and with the approval of the rest of the council.

The First Presidency and the Council of the Twelve oversee both the temporal and the spiritual affairs of the church. They frequently promulgate new policies and affirm old ones, often doing so in a letter to general and local church officers. This example, as reported in the 1995–96 *Deseret News Church Almanac,* is instructive: The First Presidency and Council of the Twelve reaffirmed the church's policy on discipline 2 November 1993, saying, "We have the responsibility to preserve the doctrinal purity of the Church." The letter explained that apostasy refers to church members who "repeatedly act in clear, open and deliberate public opposition to the Church or its leaders; or persist in teaching as Church doctrine information that is not Church doctrine after being corrected by their bishops or higher authority; or continue to follow the teachings of apostate cults (such as those that advocate plural marriage) after being corrected by their bishops or higher authority."

The references to offenders being corrected by bishops affirm local LDS authority. Each ward (congregation) is led by a bishop and his counselors. They may inspect the lives of the rank-and-file and impose a number of sanctions upon miscreants. They can withdraw a member's temple "recommend," without which no one may enter an LDS temple. Members may also be disfellowshipped for a period during which they may not perform various ward functions such as teaching Sunday school or giving prayers at meetings. Excommunication is the most severe sanction and is very rarely used.

The LDS Church enjoys a vigorous leadership whose legitimacy is clearly and firmly based on doctrines. But it would be wrong to stress only the hierarchical nature of LDS authority and its authoritarian aspects, for the Latter-day Saints display an amazing degree of amateur participation at all levels of their formal structure. Moreover, this highly authoritarian body also displays extraordinary levels of participatory democracy—to a considerable extent the rank-and-file Saints are the church. A central aspect of this is that among the Latter-day Saints, to be a priest is an unpaid, part-time role that all committed males are expected to fulfill.

First of all, Latter-day Saint men serve as priests[2] within their own families. The family home evening is conducted by the father and is partly devotional, partly focused on family activities together, and partly given to exploring any problems within the family. Secondly, LDS men serve as priests to one another's families through their role as monthly visitors. Every Latter-day Saint household (including single people living alone) is visited each month by two LDS men from the ward within which the household is located. The visitors are assigned on a regular basis, and the visit is devoted to religious and personal counseling. Questions concerning a teenager's new friends could easily come up during a home visit, as could family financial problems, marital difficulties, or absences from religious services. Indeed, Latter-day Saints who have not attended for years are still visited monthly. Visitors are required to call unless a person requests formal excommunication—a step many members do not take even if they are quite disaffected. Hence, should their outlook ever change, the church is still in touch with them and positioned to welcome them back.

While the impact of the visitor system must be great on Latter-day Saints generally, consider the impact on the visitors themselves. They routinely perform pastoral duties of great importance—they are being real, not nominal, priests. Indeed, all LDS priests are unpaid "amateurs"—each ward is led by a bishop who must earn his own living in a secular occupation, all stake presidents are self-supporting, and on up through the church. Although the president of the church and the Council of the Twelve do devote full time to their church duties and receive living expenses, they rose to those lofty ranks without payment from the church. This is also true for the thousands of young Latter-day Saint missionaries around the world. The church provides a ticket to and from their mission post. All other expenses during their two-year tour are paid by their families or by funds they saved prior to going on their mission—no missionary is permitted to work a regular job during a mission.

An unpaid, lay priesthood has several very important consequences. First, the Latter-day Saints attract no clergy motivated by a secure living, for the job of bishop usually involves financial sacrifices. Second, they do not suffer from having their affairs directed by persons of very little practical experience, something which tends to be true for groups having a professional clergy. Latter-day Saint leaders typically have had very successful secular careers. The late Ezra Taft Benson (1899–1994), thirteenth president of the church, served as secretary of agriculture from 1953 to 1961 during the administration of Dwight Eisenhower. His successor, the late Howard W. Hunter (1907–95), fourteenth president of the church, was a prominent corporate lawyer before being named to the council. One member of the council served as president of the Society for Vascular Surgery, another was a nuclear engineer, and former corporate executives abound.

To more fully appreciate the diffusion of authority within the LDS Church, consider the composition of the average congregation gathered in any ward hall on Sunday. Unpaid amateurs conduct the services. Many of those sitting in the audience have conducted the services in the past and could again on a moment's notice. Many present are former bishops or assistants. Many others will become bishops. A substantial number in attendance (male and female) have gone on two-year missions. Everyone, male and female, devotes a substantial number of hours each month to volunteer work for the church. How could they not feel that they participate in the system of authority?

Moreover, for an "authoritarian" body, the LDS Church is amazingly unspecific and nondirective on many important issues. Consider the tithe. What could be more important to an organization than funding? Yet, the LDS Church steadfastly refuses to define the tithe. Is it 10 percent of gross income or of after-tax income? Both views are widely held. If a family has someone on a mission, can their expenses be deducted from the tithe? Some say yes, some say no. The church won't say. How is it determined who has tithed? Each year the bishop asks the head of each household whether the family tithed in the past year. Those who say yes, did. And what if a Latter-day Saint responds that he or she gave less than a tithe? Seldom will the bishop express disapproval.

The LDS Labor Force

In order to grow, religious movements need missionaries. Other things being equal, the more missionaries seeking converts, and the harder these missionaries work, the faster a religious movement will grow. In addition to doing missionary work, a large, volunteer religious labor force contributes to the strength of religious movements in other important ways (Iannaccone, Olson, and Stark 1995). For example, labor can often be substituted for capital. Thus, while many religious groups not only must pay their clergy but also must pay for all their clerical, cleaning, and maintenance services, other groups are able to rely on volunteer labor to provide all these things. This leads to the following proposition: 5. *Religious movements will grow to the extent that they can generate a highly motivated, volunteer religious labor force, including many willing to proselytize.*

The Latter-day Saints rely entirely on volunteers to perform all activities in the local congregation. This is facilitated by the fact that Saints are expected to contribute time to church work. In fact, this generates so much local labor that bishops and others in the ward devote substantial effort to finding things for volunteers to do, and it often turns out that a lot of the time is spent performing social services for other members.

But the most visible part of the LDS labor force is made up of those young men and women who knock on your door and offer to tell you about their religion. In 1994, there were 48,567 Latter-day Saints serving as missionaries. Most of them were under twenty-one, although an increasing number of LDS couples go on missions when they retire.

It must be recognized, however, that missionaries are not the primary agents of conversion. Data based on church records show that only one out of every thousand "cold calls" by missionaries leads to a conversion. In contrast, when missionaries encounter a person by prearrangement in the home of a Latter-day Saint friend or relative, a conversion occurs 50 percent of the time (Stark and Bainbridge 1985). But if missionaries are not the primary source of converts, they do serve as the primary means for bringing a conversion to fruition as they take primary responsibility for religious instruction both before and after the person is baptized into the church. That is, missionaries often enter the picture when a person has already been brought to a serious level of interest by LDS friends and/or relatives. The latter also are a major part of the LDS labor force.

It is possible that going on a mission has more impact on Latter-day Saint commitment than it does on LDS conversion. Preparing to go on a mission motivates years of preparation by LDS teenagers who attend seminary sessions each morning before school. Then the missionary experience not only reflects commitment, it builds it. It is one thing to be raised in a religion; it is quite something else to go out in young adulthood and witness full time for your religion—not only to teach your religion to others but also to participate in their conversion. The missionary experience ensures a deep level of understanding of LDS doctrines in intellectual terms, and also at the gut level of how they inspire the individual. Moreover, to have gained converts serves to validate the truth of the religion to the missionary (Festinger 1957). In fact, to gain converts greatly increases the missionary's obligation to remain faithful—to then lapse from the church is, in a deeply emotional way, to break faith with those converts.

The immense importance of the missionary experience for Latter-day Saints is underscored by the frequency with which reunions are held to draw together members of all ages who served in a particular mission area. Just prior to the semiannual general conference of the LDS Church, the Salt Lake City press carries hundreds of reunion notices. Much as their common experience once bound together Americans who had served in the armed forces (an experience that cuts across age differences and cuts out nonveterans), so does the mission experience provide a common cultural currency for Latter-day Saints.

But it is not faith alone that sustains LDS commitment to the mission. Latter-day Saints fully recognize its remarkable socializing effects on those who go. This is evident on a visit to Brigham Young University, where large numbers of students (especially men) are returned missionaries. Not only are they two years older than the average undergraduate elsewhere but they are also far more self-assured, polished, mature, and, above all, confident. A Latter-day Saint colleague who sent five sons on missions told me: "A boy who has spent two years going door to door in a strange place, where they may speak a strange language, trying to get people to join a strange religion, never lacks for confidence again in his life. Whatever else happens to him, he knows in his heart that he can handle tough assignments and that earning a living is not going to be a problem." Moreover, people who have been on missions are extremely well prepared for the life-long sharing of faith that really gets results—forming attachments to non–Latter-day Saints and building their interest in the church. Latter-day Saints are also good recruiters because they are unusually successful people. That is, when non–Latter-day Saints encounter the LDS subculture they meet a closely knit community with an exemplary family life and a community of high achievers.

The LDS Ethic

In my judgment, Latter-day Saint success is rooted in theology. Christian theology enjoins people not to sin, but acknowledges that no human is capable of sinlessness. LDS theology maintains that each person is expected to achieve sinlessness. The process may take several million years of posthumous effort, but there is no reason not to get started on the job now. If Christians feel guilt when they sin, Latter-day Saints often seem to feel disappointment and impatience. This seems to be the psychological basis for the very optimistic, "can-do" spirit so many have noticed among Latter-day Saints. A person who aspires to divinity is not likely to flinch from challenges in a business or professional career.

LDS theology also stimulates achievement in very direct ways, for it places a premium on rationality and intellectual growth. As Thomas O'Dea (1957, 147–48) pointed out, the expectation that Latter-day Saints can achieve divinity rests not only on spiritual development but also on knowledge. God is not merely pure in spirit, but he fully comprehends the whole universe—indeed, he is its creator. Thus: "The Mormon definition of life makes the earthly sojourn basically an educative process. Knowledge is necessary to mastery, and the way to deification is through mastery, for not only does education aid man in fulfilling present tasks, it advances him in his eternal progress."

Joseph Smith wrote in the Doctrine and Covenants that the knowledge "we attain unto in this life will rise with us in the resurrection," and therefore the more we learn now, the more our "advantage in the world to come." Elsewhere in the same work Smith urged, "Seek ye out of the best books words of wisdom; seek learning, even by study and also by faith" (see O'Dea 1957, 147–48).

These were not pious platitudes. Mormon emphasis on education, both for children and for adults, was manifested in schools and in formal educational programs almost from the initial founding of the church. Considering the virtual nonexistence of higher education in America in the 1840s, it is astonishing that the Latter-day Saints established a municipal university in Nauvoo, where it is believed that modern and ancient languages, history, literature, and mathematics were taught (O'Dea 1957). Then, in 1850, when the Latter-day Saints had only begun their immense struggle to create a new society in Utah, Brigham Young set aside funds to support a public university—the University of Deseret, now the University of Utah. The university opened briefly in the 1850s, but then was put on hold as other matters became too pressing. It was reopened for good in 1868 with 223 pupils, 103 of them women. Sixteen of the women belonged to Brigham Young's family, and his daughter Susa edited the college paper (Arrington 1985, 337). This was entirely in keeping with Young's views that "we have sisters here who, if they had the privilege of studying, would make just as good mathematicians or accountants as any man" (Arrington and Bitten 1979, 227). It should be noted too that one of the conditions imposed by the federal government in extending statehood to Utah in 1896 was the *repeal* of woman's suffrage. Until then, women voted in Utah.

Not content with a state university, the LDS Church opened in 1875 what would become Brigham Young University in Provo, Utah. Today it is the largest private or church-supported university in the nation, enrolling more than thirty thousand students.

The Latter-day Saint emphasis on education has been translated into achievement. Thus, data collected by the American National Survey of Religious Identification (Kosmin and Lachman 1993) show that 26 percent of adult Latter-day Saints are college graduates, and another 31 percent have attended college. Conversely, only 9 percent of Latter-day Saints did not complete high school. Not surprisingly, these exceptional educational achievements translate into high incomes—the ANSRI data show that 41 percent of LDS households had annual incomes above thirty thousand dollars in 1990, well above the national median for that year.

Adequate Fertility

In order to succeed, *6. Religious movements must maintain a level of fertility sufficient to at least offset member mortality.* If a religious movement's appeal is too narrow this may result in a demographic composition incapable of sustaining its ranks. If a group is unable to replace itself through fertility, when the initial generation of converts begins to die its rising rate of mortality may cancel a substantial rate of conversion. In contrast, a religious movement can sustain substantial growth through fertility alone. For example, the Amish have not attracted converts for several centuries, and in each generation there is substantial defection. Yet, at the end of each year the number of Amish is greater than before due to their normal demographic composition and a high fertility rate.

Religious movements typically overrecruit women (Stark and Bainbridge 1985; Cornwall 1988; Thompson 1991; Miller and Hoffman 1995; Stark 1996a). But, this seems not to matter unless it reduces fertility. Thus, the early Christian communities had a substantial excess of females, but Christian women probably had higher rates of fertility than did pagan women (Stark 1996a). However, when movements greatly overrecruit women who are beyond their childbearing years, that is quite another matter. For example, by greatly over-recruiting older women, Christian Science soon faced the need for very high rates of conversion merely to offset high rates of mortality (Stark and Bainbridge 1985). Thus, what had been a very rapidly growing movement suddenly ceased to grow and soon entered a period of accelerating decline.

Latter-day Saints have larger families than do non–Latter-day Saints. This has been carefully documented many times.

Ecological Factors

To the extent that a religious economy is crowded with effective and successful firms, it will be harder for new firms to make headway (Stark 1985; Stark and Bainbridge 1985, 1996, 1997; Stark and Iannaccone 1993, 1994). Stated as a proposition: *7. Other things being equal, new and unconventional religious organizations will prosper to the extent that they compete against weak, local conventional religious organizations within a relatively unregulated religious economy.* Put another way, new religious organizations will do best where conventional religious mobilization is low—at least to the degree that the state gives such groups a chance to exist. Thus, we ought to find that where conventional church membership and church attendance rates are low, the incidence of unconventional religious movements will be high.

The individual level form of this proposition is that *converts to religious groups will come primarily from the ranks of the religiously inactive,* people already involved in a religious body will be relatively unlikely to switch. There has been a considerable amount of research sustaining both the macro and the micro level versions of the proposition (Stark and Bainbridge 1985, 1996).

Applied to the Latter-day Saints this suggests that their growth will be more rapid where there is a relatively larger population of the unchurched and inactive. Table 11.5 shows tests of this hypothesis in Canada and in the United States. The data based on the twenty-five Canadian metropolitan areas show a strong correlation between LDS membership and the percent who gave their religious affiliation as "none" in the 1991 census. As predicted, the Saints thrive where there is a lower overall level of religious affiliation.

To test the hypothesis in the United States requires recognition that the extremely high LDS membership rates for Utah and Idaho are more the result of migration and fertility than of conversion. For the rest of the nation, however, conversion overrides migration as the source of local Latter-day Saints. Thus, with Utah and Idaho omitted from the calculations, the predicted correlations show up strongly. Latter-day Saints are relatively more numerous

Table 11.5. Religious Ecology and LDS Growth

	25 Canadian Metropolitan Areas (1991) Correlations (r) with percent giving their religious affiliation as none
LDS membership	.60**

	American States (1993) Correlations (r) with:	
	Percent giving their religious affiliation as none[a]	Church membership rate per 1,000
LDS membership[b]	.65**	−.52

Note: *p < .05; **p < .01
a. Based on the ANSRI data. Alaska and Hawaii not included in the survey.
b. 2. Utah and Idaho omitted as extreme outliers.

where local churches are weak, as measured both by membership rates and the percent giving their religious affiliation as "none."

Network Ties

Religious commitment is sustained by interpersonal attachments. People value their religion more highly to the extent that a high value is communicated to them by those around them. Moreover, social relations are part of the tangible rewards of participating in a religious movement—affection, respect, sociability, and companionship being vital exchange commodities. Therefore, religious movements lacking strong internal networks of social relationships—being made up of casual acquaintances—will be notably lacking in commitment as they will also be lacking in the capacity to reward members.

Weak internal networks have doomed many religious movements. I have already noted how doctrines and practices leading to singularity have impeded authority; they also undercut network ties within groups such as the gnostics or various New Age movements. Moreover, I suspect that all movements lacking in strictness will also be lacking in network ties, for there is nothing about their religion that sets them apart from the general public. Liberal Protestant denominations illustrate this principle. Their congregations are more like theater audiences than groups, for only small minorities of liberal Protestants report having close personal friends among members of their local congregation. In contrast, large majorities of members of conservative Protestant sects report that most or all of their best friends are members of their congregation (Stark and Glock 1968).

On the other hand, many religious movements are also doomed because of internal networks that are too all-embracing, thus making it difficult and often impossible for members to maintain or form attachments with outsiders. When that is the case, conversion is impossible. People do not usually join religious groups because they suddenly find the doctrines appealing. They convert when their ties to members outweigh their ties to nonmembers—for most people, conversion consists of aligning their religious behavior with that of their friends (Lofland and Stark 1965; Stark and Bainbridge 1980c, 1985, 1996; Kox, Meeus, and Hart 1991). When members do not have outside friends, such realignments do not occur. Hence, this proposition: *8. New religious movements will succeed to the extent that they sustain strong internal attachments, while remaining an open social network, able to maintain and form ties to outsiders.*

The need for strong internal social networks is particularly great to the extent that the group is in tension with its sociocultural environment. Thus, Latter-day Saints in Utah and southern Idaho are reinforced in their commitment not only in church, or within an LDS subculture, but daily from a Latter-day Saint–dominated environment. Elsewhere, however, strong LDS networks are needed to sustain Saints within a "Gentile" society. Such networks are established and sustained in a number of ways. First, the ward hall is not simply a church. It is a community and social center providing scouting, sports teams, teen social activities including dances,[3] activities for singles, for young marrieds, for widows, and so on. An array of volunteer social services also are organized through the ward, such as hospital and nursing home visitation, taking meals to the ill and elderly, baby-sitting cooperatives, daycare, and more.

The seminary system also plays a crucial role in forming and sustaining teenage network ties. Rather than sending their children to parochial schools, Latter-day Saints send their teenagers to religious instruction classes (seminary) before the regular school day begins. In consequence, LDS teenagers go off to school with their seminary classmates, the shared before-school activity serving to form them into LDS cliques at school. Given that LDS prohibitions on premarital sex, coffee, colas, alcohol, cigarettes, and drugs are at variance with current secular teenage norms, these cliques play a very important role in effective adolescent socialization. Of course, the system sometimes fails, but there is much truth to the joke that rebellious LDS teenagers show off to their friends by sneaking a Pepsi.

It would be quite wrong, however, to describe Latter-day Saints in non-LDS communities as an isolated subculture. Most LDS children and teens have non-LDS friends. Most LDS adults have a great deal of contact with non–Latter-day Saints and have non-LDS friends. Indeed, their church urges them to cultivate such friendships since this is the primary source of converts. Church publications offer many suggestions about how to make friends with neighbors, especially newcomers to the neighborhood, and how to include them in ward social activities. They also are advised to avoid premature discussions of religion, letting that wait until potential converts have built ties to LDS social networks (Stark and Bainbridge 1980a, 1985).

Staying Strict

If strictness is the key to high morale and rapid growth, then: *9. Religious movements will continue to grow only to the extent that they maintain sufficient tension with their environment—remain sufficiently strict.*

Earlier in the chapter I noted that over the years the Latter-day Saints have modified their position on a number of issues, thus keeping their tension with the outside world within tolerable limits. When federal officers searched for church leaders intending to have them sent to prison on bigamy charges, the level of tension began to exceed the level compatible with continued growth. The church met the crisis by rejecting polygamy. It must also be noted, however, that plural marriage was not only an *external* source of tension. The fact is that most Mormon families were not polygamous—natural sex ratios and inadequate wealth inevitably limited polygamy to social elites. This resulted in some resentment on the part of the nonpolygamous majority. In similar fashion, when the church extended the qualifications for the priesthood to include nonwhite males, it not only reduced outside attacks on the church as racist but also defused growing internal dissatisfaction and resolved confusions and inconsistencies in foreign missions where many nonwhite males already had been admitted to the priesthood.

However, as mentioned before, the major aspect of the modification of LDS doctrines and practices is that most respond to general social changes in a way that sustains a *constant degree* of tension over time. A fine study by Laurence R. Iannaccone and Carrie A. Miles (1991) shows that the church has responded to changes in women's roles in the general society, but at a rate that has kept the gap between Latter-day Saint and secular sex role norms at a relatively similar level over time. For example, although the LDS priesthood is still restricted to males, it has now become common for young women, rather than only men, to go on missions, and the scope of female responsibilities has generally been expanded. However, the emphasis on distinctive gender roles, and particularly on the father as head of the household, continues to draw feminist antagonism, indicative of tension.

The tendency for Saints to maintain a sort of moving equilibrium vis-à-vis their differences from non–Latter-day Saints can be seen in fertility trends. Latter-day Saint fertility has paralleled changes in the general American fertility throughout the twentieth century. Just like non-LDS fertility, Latter-day Saint fertility declined sharply during the Great Depression, rose rapidly during the baby boom, and subsequently has been declining. But throughout, LDS fertility has exceeded that of non-LDS Americans at a relatively constant rate of about 50 percent (Heaton and Calkins 1983).

Despite their higher fertility, however, the Latter-day Saints currently grow far more rapidly through conversion than fertility. In 1993, for example, 76,312 children of LDS parents were baptized, compared with 304,808 adult converts. Thus, the church benefits from the well-known fact that converts are far less willing than those born into a faith to accommodate doctrines to reduce strictness.

Effective Socialization

To succeed, *10. Religious movements must socialize the young sufficiently well as to minimize both defection and the appeal of reduced strictness.* As mentioned, many groups have perished for lack of fertility. A sufficiently high rate of defection by those born into the faith produces the same effect as low fertility. That is, much conversion is needed simply to offset mortality if fertility is canceled by defection. Furthermore, religious movements must socialize the young sufficiently well not only in order to minimize defections but also to minimize pressures to reduce strictness.

An important mechanism in this regard is to involve people in the movement while they are young. As noted earlier in the chapter, the mission plays a vital role in this task. Teenagers who anticipate going on missions will invest greater time and effort in really learning LDS history and doctrines, and this will have very significant socializing effects even on many of those who end up not going.

Finally, because strictness generates strong congregational life wherein the enthusiasm of each member communicates a high value of the religion, Latter-day Saint children grow up in an atmosphere which strongly reinforces their commitment. Moreover, the most attractive role models within the LDS subculture are notable for their religious enthusiasm. Latter-day Saint religious life is not directed by a bookish, professional clergy, many of whom lack any obvious worldly abilities, let alone accomplishments. LDS leadership (male and female) involves the most prominent and successful members. Hence, the message to ambitious young Latter-day Saints: successful people are religious people.

Conclusion

Some years ago I was invited to contribute an article to a special issue of the *Review of Religious Research* devoted to research on the Latter-day Saints. The result was "The Rise of a New World Faith" (1984), the heart of which is a set of projections of LDS growth spanning the century from 1980 through 2080. When I learned that this essay was to be collected in the present volume, I updated it to take account of the additional fifteen years of growth. What the updating shows is that even though I projected as many as 260 million Latter-day Saints in 2080, during the first fifteen years of the projections, actual LDS growth has surpassed my highest projections by almost a million members. Consequently, I am convinced that by late in the twenty-first century the Church of Jesus Christ of Latter-day Saints will be a major world religion. Hopefully, the theory outlined in this chapter provides valid insights into *why* this will happen.

Notes

Through the years many members of the church have patiently tutored me in LDS doctrines and culture, and it is appropriate to thank them all: Marie Cornwall, James T. Duke, Tim B. Heaton, Armand Mauss, Darwin Thomas, Stan Weed, and Lawrence A. Young.

1. "And it came to pass that Hagoth, he being an exceedingly curious man, therefore he went forth and built him an exceedingly large ship, on the borders of the land Bountiful, by the land Desolation, and launched it forth onto the west sea, by the narrow neck which led to the land northward." This is interpreted as a voyage of settlement to Polynesia from somewhere along the Pacific coast of central Latin America. Thor Heyerdahl's *Kon Tiki* voyage in 1947 from Peru to Polynesia was regarded by many as confirmation of the story of Hagoth.

2. I use the word *priest* in the generic sense, knowing that there are various levels of the LDS priesthood.

3. Church headquarters issues periodic "play lists" to guide the selections of disk jockeys at church-sponsored dances. Because these events are carefully supervised, many non-LDS parents prefer that their teenagers go to these parties.

References

Allen, James B., Ronald K. Esplin, and David J. Whittaker. 1992. *Men with a Mission, 1837–1841: The Quorum of the Twelve Apostles in the British Isles.* Salt Lake City: Deseret Book.

Arrington, Leonard J. 1985. *Brigham Young: American Moses.* New York: Knopf.

Arrington, Leonard J., and Davis Bitton. 1979. *The Mormon Experience: A History of the Latter-day Saints.* New York: Knopf.

Bainbridge, William Sims. 1978. *Satan's Power.* Berkeley: University of California Press.

———. 1996. *The Sociology of Religious Movements.* New York: Routledge.

Bradley, Martin B., Norman M. Green Jr., Dale E. Jones, Mac Lynn, and Lou McNeil. 1992. *Churches and Church Membership in the United States, 1990.* Atlanta: Glenmary Research Center.

Cornwall, Marie. 1988. "The Influence of Three Agents of Religious Socialization: Family, Church, and Peers." In *The Religion and Family Connection: Social Science Perspectives,* ed. Darwin L. Thomas. Provo: Religious Studies Center, Brigham Young University. 207–31.

Cornwall, Marie, Tim B. Heaton, and Lawrence A. Young, eds. 1994. *Contemporary Mormonism: Social Science Perspectives.* Urbana: University of Illinois Press.

Desert News 1995–96 Church Almanac. 1994. Salt Lake City: Deseret News.

Festinger, Leon. 1957. *A Theory of Cognitive Dissonance.* Stanford: Stanford University Press.

Festinger, Leon, Henry W. Riecken, and Stanley Schachter. 1956. *When Prophecy Fails.* Minneapolis: University of Minnesota Press.

Flanders, Robert Bruce. 1965. *Nauvoo: Kingdom on the Mississippi.* Urbana: University of Illinois Press.

Heaton, Tim B., and Sandra Calkins. 1983. "Family Size and Contraceptive Use among Mormons: 1965–75." *Review of Religious Research* 25:102–13.

Iannaccone, Laurence R. 1990. "Religious Practice: A Human Capital Approach." *Journal for the Scientific Study of Religion* 29:297–314.

———. 1992. "Sacrifice and Stigma: Reducing Free-Riding in Cults, Communes, and Other Collectives." *Journal of Political Economy* 100:271–91.

———. 1994. "Why Strict Churches Are Strong." *American Journal of Sociology* 99:1180–211.

Iannaccone, Laurence R., and Carrie A. Miles. 1991. "Dealing with Social Change: The Mormon Church's Response to Change in Women's Roles." *Social Forces* 64:1231–50.

Iannaccone, Laurence R., Daniel Olson, and Rodney Stark. 1995. "Religious Resources and Church Growth." *Social Forces* 74:705–31.

Kelley, Dean M. 1972. *Why Conservative Churches Are Growing.* New York: Harper and Row.

Kosmin, Barry A., and Seymour P. Lachman. 1993. *One Nation under God: Religion in Contemporary American Society.* New York: Crown.

Kox, Willem, Wim Meeus, and Harm't Hart. 1991. "Religious Conversion of Adolescents: Festing the Lofland and Stark Model of Religious Conversion." *Sociological Analysis* 52:227–40.

Lofland, John, and Rodney Stark. 1965. "Becoming a World-Saver: A Theory of Conversion to a Deviant Perspective." *American Sociological Review* 30:862–75.

Martins, Marcus Helvécio T. A. 1995. "The LDS Church in Brazil: Past, Present, and Future." Paper presented at the annual meeting of the Society for the Scientific Study of Religion, St. Louis.

Mauss, Armand L. 1994. *The Angel and the Beehive: The Mormon Struggle with Assimilation.* Urbana: University of Illinois Press.

Miller, Alan S., and John P. Hoffman. 1995. "Risk and Religion: An Explanation of Gender Differences in Religiosity." *Journal for the Scientific Study of Religion* 34:63–75.

Murphy, Thomas W. 1996. "Re-Inventing Mormonism." *Sunstone* 29:177–92.

O'Dea, Thomas F. 1957. *The Mormons.* Chicago: University of Chicago Press.

Pagels, Elaine. 1979. *The Gnostic Gospels.* New York: Random House.

Sherkat, Darren E., and John Wilson. 1995. "Preferences, Constraints, and Choices in Religious Markets: An Examination of Religious Switching and Apostasy." *Social Forces* 73:993–1026.

Singelenberg, Richard. 1989. "'It Separated the Wheat from the Chaff': The 1975 Prophecy and Its Impact on Dutch Jehovah's Witnesses." *Sociological Analysis* 50:23–40.

Sorenson, John L. 1985. *An Ancient American Setting for the Book of Mormon.* Salt Lake City: Deseret Book.

Stark, Rodney. 1985. "Europe's Receptivity to Religious Movements." In *New Religious Movements: Genesis, Exodus, and Numbers,* ed. Rodney Stark. New York: Paragon. 301–43.

———. 1987. "How New Religions Succeed: A Theoretical Model." In *The Future of New Religious Movements,* ed. David G. Bromley and Phillip E. Hammond. Macon, Ga.: Mercer University Press. 11–29.

———. 1992. "Do Catholic Societies Really Exist?" *Rationality and Society* 4:261–71.

———. 1995. "Reconstructing the Rise of Christianity: The Role of Women." *Sociology of Religion* 56:229–44.

———. 1996a. *The Rise of Christianity: A Sociologist Reconsiders History.* Princeton: Princeton University Press.

———. 1996b. "Why Religious Movements Succeed or Fail: A Revised General Model." *Journal of Contemporary Religion* 11:133–46.

Stark, Rodney, and William Sims Bainbridge. 1980a. "Networks of Faith: Interpersonal Bonds and Recruitment to Cults and Sects." *American Journal of Sociology* 85:1376–95.

————. 1980b. "Secularization, Revival, and Cult Formation." *Annual Review of the Social Sciences of Religion* 4:85–119.

————. 1980c. "Towards a Theory of Religion: Religious Commitment." *Journal for the Scientific Study of Religion* 19:114–18.

————. 1985. *The Future of Religion: Secularization, Revival, and Cult Formation.* Berkeley: University of California Press.

————. 1996. *A Theory of Religion.* New Brunswick, N.J.: Rutgers University Press.

————. 1997. *Religion, Deviance, and Social Control.* New York: Routledge.

Stark, Rodney, and Charles Y. Glock. 1968. *American Piety: The Nature of Religious Commitment.* Berkeley: University of California Press.

Stark, Rodney, and Laurence R. Iannaccone. 1993. "Rational Choice Propositions and Religious Movements." In *Religion and the Social Order: Handbook on Cults and Sects in America,* ed. David G. Bromley and Jeffrey K. Hadden. Greenwich, Conn.: JAI Press. 109–25.

————. 1994. "A Supply-Side Reinterpretation of the 'Secularization' of Europe." *Journal for the Scientific Study of Religion* 33:230–52.

Statistics Canada. 1993. *Religions in Canada: The Nation.* Ottawa: Statistics Canada.

Thompson, Edward H. 1991. "Beneath the Status Characteristic: Gender Variations in Religiousness." *Journal for the Scientific Study of Religion* 30:381–94.

Wagner, Melinda Bollar. 1983. "Spiritual Frontiers Fellowship." In *Alternatives to American Mainline Churches,* ed. Joseph H. Fichter. New York: Rose of Sharon Press.

Young, Lawrence A. 1994. "Confronting Turbulent Environments: Issues in the Organizational Growth and Globalization of Mormonism." In *Contemporary Mormonism: Social Science Perspectives,* ed. Marie Cornwall, Tim B. Heaton, and Lawrence A. Young. Urbana: University of Illinois Press. 43–63.

————, ed. 1995. *Assessing Rational Choice Theories of Religion.* New York: Routledge.

Contributors

ERIC A. ELIASON is an assistant professor of English at Brigham Young University, where he teaches courses on folklore and Mormon literature. He has published articles on Mormon, Western, and folklore topics in scholarly and popular publications.

TERRYL L. GIVENS is an associate professor of English at the University of Richmond. He has published numerous articles on Mormon studies, aesthetics, and literary criticism. He is currently finishing work on a history of the Book of Mormon.

NATHAN O. HATCH is a professor of history and vice president for graduate studies and research at the University of Notre Dame. His book *The Democratization of American Christianity* won the American Studies Association's John Hope Franklin Publication Prize in 1990.

MICHAEL HICKS is a professor of music at Brigham Young University. He has published books and articles on Mormonism, American experimental music, European avant-garde music, and rock music of the 1960s.

RICHARD T. HUGHES is Distinguished Professor of Religion, Pepperdine University. A leading scholar of primitivist religious impulses in America, he has published extensively on this subject.

BERNHARD LANG is professor of religion and Old Testament studies at the University of Paderbon in Germany. Recently he added *Sacred Games: A History of Christian Worship* to his published works.

DEAN L. MAY, former editor of *Journal of Mormon History,* is a professor of history at the University of Utah in Salt Lake City. His most recent book is *Three Frontiers: Family, Land, and Society in the American West, 1850–1990.*

COLLEEN MCDANNELL is a professor of history and the Sterling McMurrin Chair of Religious Studies at the University of Utah. Among other publications, she is the author of *Material Christianity: Religion and Popular Culture in America.*

RICHARD D. POLL was professor of history and vice president of administration at Western Illinois University. He previously taught American and Mormon history for over twenty years at Brigham Young University. He passed away in 1994.

JAN SHIPPS is a professor of history and religious studies at Indiana University–Purdue University at Indianapolis. Author of the highly acclaimed *Mormonism: The Story of a New Religious Tradition,* she is the coeditor of *Religion and American Culture: A Journal of Interpretation.* She is a past president of the Mormon History Association and the first non-Mormon to hold that position.

RODNEY STARK is a professor of sociology and comparative religion at the University of Washington. He is the author of twenty-two books, including *The Rise of Christianity* and *Acts of Faith: Explaining the Human Side of Religion.*

GRANT UNDERWOOD is professor at the Joseph Fielding Institute for LDS History at Brigham Young University in Utah. He has served on the executive council of the Mormon History Association and on the board of editors of the *Journal of Mormon History.* He has published a prize-winning book and a number of articles in various historical journals.

Index

Typeset in 10.5/13 Minion
with Folio Extra Bold display
Designed by Dennis Roberts
Composed by Jim Proefrock
at the University of Illinois Press
Manufactured by Thomson-Shore, Inc.

University of Illinois Press
1325 South Oak Street
Champaign, IL 61820-6903
www.press.uillinois.edu